Nathan Leamon has a decade of experience working in elite sport. He is currently the Lead Analyst with the England One-Day and T20 teams, and Strategy Consultant for the Kolkata Knight Riders. His first book *The Test* was long-listed for the William Hill Sports Book of the Year. When not on the road he lives in Berkshire with his wife and two daughters.

Ben Jones is an analyst at CricViz, the world's leading cricket analytics provider. He read English Literature at Cambridge and now lives in Oxford. He has written for, amongst others, *Wisden Cricket Monthly*, *Hindustan Times* and *Daily Telegraph*.

Praise for *Hitting Against the Spin*

'"He held degrees in both English and Economics, and the ability to to articulate the world of one, with the words of the other." The writer here is Nathan Leamon and the subject is baseball pioneer Bill James. But Leamon (both a novelist and a data analyst) could just as easily be writing about himself. Leamon has a rare kind of high intelligence: he is open to all kinds of knowledge, not just scientific knowledge, and he understands which method is appropriate in which circumstance. Put differently, he is not only clever and original, but also wise' Ed Smith, National Selector for England cricket & author of *What Sport Tells Us About Life*

'Fascinating and insightful . . . lifts the curtain to reveal the inner workings of international cricket. A must-read for any cricketer, coach or fan' Eoin Morgan

'Sport has been revolutionized by data. In their path-breaking book, Nathan Leamon and Ben Jones use data to show that many of our preconceptions are false and reveal astonishing new insights into international cricket. Compulsory reading for fans, commentators, captains and players' Mervyn King

'Deeply thoughtful, clever and open-minded . . . One way of viewing this book is as cricket's *A Brief History of Time*, a layman's guide to deep complexity, an act of communication as much as one of science. On that level it works beautifully well, engaging with concepts in attention-grabbing ways' *Wisden Cricket Monthly*

'Fascinating' *The Times*

Hitting Against the Spin

Nathan Leamon and Ben Jones

....

How Cricket Really Works

CONSTABLE

CONSTABLE

First published in Great Britain in 2021 by Constable
This paperback edition published in 2022 by Constable

7 9 10 8 6

Diagrams by David Andrassy/Andrassy Media

The moral right of the authors has been asserted.

A CIP catalogue record for this book
is available from the British Library.

ISBN: 978-1-47213-126-3

Typeset in Sentinel Light by Hewer Text UK Ltd, Edinburgh
Printed and bound in Great Britain by Clays Ltd, Elcograf, S.p.A.

Papers used by Constable are from well-managed
forests and other responsible sources.

Constable
An imprint of
Little, Brown Book Group
Carmelite House
50 Victoria Embankment
London EC4Y 0DZ

An Hachette UK Company

www.hachette.co.uk

www.littlebrown.co.uk

For Mum and Dad – N. L.
For Dah – B. J.

Contents

Foreword

As has long been recognised, cricket is a team game where the path to victory involves overcoming a series of individual encounters. One thing I have come to realise is that the first encounter to overcome, the first battle to win, usually takes place within. These first battles manifest themselves in a variety of forms: struggles with technique, with self-doubt, with form, with injury, or in coping with the vagaries of selection. Talk about a corridor of uncertainty!

These internal conflicts mean that a professional cricketer is often in search of information: to improve his game, to inform his choices, to bolster his confidence, or to help him find his way back to his own best self. But in modern professional sport, where information is never in short supply but quality is, finding the right information is rarely straightforward.

Historically, as now, cricketers in search of that information could reflect on their own experience, listen to trusted coaches and other players, or fall back on the game's received wisdom. Now though, in addition to those sources, they have another resource. One that has increased and enhanced our understanding of the game as never before.

Since the release of the seminal book and motion picture *Moneyball*, the role of data in sport has grown exponentially. In doing so it has not only increased the knowledge and tools available to coaches and players, but it has also created a new market for tech-savvy, sports-loving number-crunchers. Sports that I enjoy, such as American football, golf, rugby, horse racing as well as cricket, have led the way in presenting an alternative approach to analysis.

This method of 360-degree assessment has helped open the sport to a new audience and provided a market for more data-driven coverage and insights. And consequently, as a player, there are even fewer corners in which to hide!

When Nathan Leamon joined the ECB back in 2009, it was at a time when the landscape of data, the crunching of numbers and deciphering of cricket's code was still in its infancy. My generation of players – and the one above – were probably quite stubborn, a bit more rigid in our ways when it came to the technological advances that the game was evolving towards.

If you cast your mind back to that golden era, England had regained the Ashes and were on the cusp of an ICC World T20 title in the Caribbean the next year. The team was winning; we had a squad packed with international talent and the seeds of identifying specialists across the three various formats were being sown.

Nathan would have known the talent that was in the England changing room and the personalities involved, spread right the way across the career spectrum. Don't underestimate how big a challenge it must have been, coming from a school environment into an international dressing room full of high-end, professional athletes largely set in their ways, where he had to build trust and implement his ideas.

In the years since, the demand for more insights and greater understanding of each nuance of the game has intensified. The analyst – in all his or her various roles – has become integral to the success of a team.

Be it as a quasi-coach, mentor, organiser, nurturer, sounding board or even therapist, the role of the analyst has evolved in recent years to such an extent that they have as significant an input as more hands-on, on-field coaches.

The modern cricketer has access to so much footage and data that it is becoming increasingly challenging to find new ways to overcome opponents. Unlocking data, embracing change and being resourceful and open-minded about the advances of the game has helped me enormously. And I am sure it will help me further over the coming years as I transition from my playing career to a coaching one.

I am indebted to people like Nathan who, throughout my career, have helped me fulfil my potential, both as a batsman and as a captain, and in doing so helped to unlock the unknown. As a man he is empathetic, pragmatic and resourceful, someone who understands the game and the psychology of dealing with players.

The analyst is often a key buffer for players and their respective coaches. There can be uncomfortable truths, but the level of trust is such that the players can have full faith that the analyst, in our case Nathan, knows their game and is able to bring clarity and insight to enable them to deliver.

During a typical international series, we are in constant contact, either in person, by phone or e-mail, sharing thoughts and insights or simulating games. In and around match days it is invaluable for me to have a pragmatic sounding board like Nathan: emphasising key points, discussing potential match-ups, reiterating our game plan, providing a fresh, alternative captain's perspective, or just there to bounce ideas off.

In this book, Nathan and Ben Jones lift the curtain and give you a tour of the ideas and understanding that modern analytical techniques make possible. They show you patterns and mechanisms within international cricket that you have probably never noticed.

This book also gives a fascinating and insightful account of the role that analysis played, alongside our medical, coaching and other support staff, to help drive the England team towards new standards over recent years. Success is a journey rather than a destination, but by embracing change and being open-minded about new methods, I believe that it helped England deliver that inaugural ICC Cricket World Cup title in the summer of 2019.

The beauty of cricket is that it tests you emotionally, physically, tactically and technically. You have to think fast, and you rely heavily on the information you have about your opponent, the pitch, weather conditions etc. to try to gain a competitive edge. It is one thing to have the information; it is another to implement it.

We spend so long charting courses, analysing strengths and identifying weaknesses, strategising and using best practice methods to engage and inspire. We are all chasing that nth degree. The extra 1 per cent. There is a time to analyse and a time to go with your gut. And, at all times, it is a balancing act between keeping one eye on the present and another on the future.

Cricket, like much of life, is ever-evolving. The moment one problem is resolved, another emerges.

But that is the thrill of the chase, the reason why we keep coming back for more. That appetite for learning and continuous improvement shapes our identity. Hopefully it will continue to inspire us in the future, for the rest of our careers and beyond.

Eoin Morgan, December 2020

Introduction:
Counting Matters

It is 2004, and a young boy is watching Ashley Giles bowling for England. There is no obvious reason why it is Giles who becomes an inspirational figure for him, but something clicks. Perhaps it is the rhythm of the approach or the whir of the arms that's appealing; perhaps it's just the sunglasses.

When the boy learns to bowl, it is Giles's action he copies. Mirrors, because the boy is right-handed. He wanders up to the crease, raises his non-bowling arm and pulls it right across his body, looking to the left of the forearm. He bends his left wrist right back, so the palm faces the sky, just like his hero. As the action unfurls, the bowling arm is high, and brushes his ear, just like you are always told it should.

Then in 2005, Shane Warne comes to England along with the rest of the Australian team. It is cricket's Golden Summer. The year the nation falls back in love with the game, when cafés hum with the sound of *Test Match Special*, 'Jones . . . Bowden' and 'That. Is. Very. Good' fills the air. But for the boy all the pageantry and redemption is irrelevant – the summer is about Warne.

He watches the way Warne bowls with confusion. The amount of spin he gets on the ball is absurd; the way no English batsman is able to predict what will happen feels almost unfair, like it should be against the rules.

The way Warne approaches the crease, level, slow and precise, is the opposite of Giles's vertical hop, skip and swivel.

Watching wicket after wicket fall to Warne, the boy thinks he might be on to something. Perhaps – but only perhaps – this is a better model for a young leg-spin bowler than Ashley Giles.

So he goes out into the garden, with a notebook and a pen, a ball and some stumps. He bowls delivery after delivery at the stumps with the old action, Giles's action, noting down whenever he hits the stumps. Then, after he's bowled 100 deliveries with that action, he switches (the distance between the two sets of stumps is 20 metres).

Now he bowls 100 deliveries with the new action, Warne's action. This low, slow, round-armed approach, twisting the wrist. Every time he hits the stumps, he marks it down.

Wandering back up the garden path, the notebook is telling a clear story. The rain may have made the ink run, but the results are obvious. The new changed action is more effective.

Armed with the new Warne-inspired action, Ben turns out for his cricket club Under-11s in the next match . . . and takes a hat-trick. (From memory, the third and final victim, having never played the game before, was out stumped having wandered down the pitch unaware of the rules.)

It's a vindication for science! And somewhere in Ben's head cogs have started to turn. Counting can make you a better cricketer! Collecting evidence can tell you things you didn't know.

The same summer that Ben is counting leg-breaks, Nathan is counting too. Counting steps, dropped passes, missed tackles, down in Tonbridge, Kent.

In September he starts his second season coaching the school's Rugby First XV. He spends the holidays pulling apart every training drill, every practice, reorganising, redesigning. Every footstep is counted, every metre run.

Distances and running lines are adjusted to get the maximum possible impact from the minimum possible distance covered and energy expended. Timings and number of players per station are tweaked to optimise recovery.

Videos of old practices are dissected so that the number of dropped passes, successful and failed attempts can be adjusted, tuned into the magic sweet spot that will maximally accelerate skill acquisition.

Every stray stride is cut, every ounce of unnecessary effort carved away, until the whole training programme is as lean and efficient as he knows how to make it.

Again, there is a vindication of sorts. The team goes on to win every match they play for the next three years. Indirectly, it leads to him being recruited into Andy Flower's England cricket set-up.

And at the same time that we were both counting in our different ways, other people had started to count too. That counting and the things they started to count are ultimately where this book began. Because it is around that time that the collection of serious data on international cricket started in earnest.

For the first time, there was a concerted effort to record the details of every ball that was bowled in any high-level cricket match anywhere in the world. At the same time, ball-tracking technology in the form of Hawk-Eye started to provide hitherto undreamed of levels of accurate data about the raw mechanics of Test match and white-ball cricket.

This book is the story of that data, and what it can tell us about how cricket really works.

IT TOOK THE WHOLE HISTORY OF
CRICKET TO PRODUCE VIRAT KOHLI

There is an old Buddhist fable that we have used in the past to explain how many aspects of cricket work and why. That is, in ways that don't always seem to make sense. It goes like this.

High, high in the Chinese hills there was once a monastery where a distinguished Taoist guru lived with his disciples.

In the evenings the monks would gather in the Great Hall to listen to their leader's teachings and to meditate. But there was a stray cat that had adopted the monastery, and each evening it would follow the monks into the hall. It would mewl, scratch and generally be annoying throughout their silent meditation.

It did this every night until the great teacher became so irritated by it that he told his followers to put a collar on the cat and tether it on the far side of the monastery each evening.

This worked well, and for a while, teacher, cat and monks all went through their nightly routine.

One day, the learned teacher died. But the monks continued to tie up the cat each evening.

More years passed.

And eventually the cat died.

So the monks went down to the nearest village, found a replacement cat, and tied it up each evening instead.

Two centuries later, religious scholars write learned essays on the importance of tying up a cat prior to evening meditation.

This is how cricket works.

There are many Tethered Cats in cricket, habitual actions that have outlived the conditions that created them. It is the case in most sports, but cricket seems to be particularly well-resourced in that regard.

More recently we discovered a second story, that we see as a counterpoint to the story of 'The Tethered Cat' – well, if not quite a counterpoint, then certainly a companion piece – and that story concerns 'Chesterton's Fence'.

G. K. Chesterton was a writer, lay theologian and arch-conservative thinker. He used the story to illustrate the importance of 'small c' conservative thinking.

There was once a man who had a long way to walk to work, and every day he had to go well out of his way because a large hedge blocked the most direct route. Every day he walked over a mile further in the morning, and again on his way home in the evening because the hedge was in his way.

Day after day, he looked at the hedge and thought, *If that hedge wasn't there, I could save myself an hour of walking every day*.

Eventually he had had enough and decided to make a hole in the hedge so that he could walk the shorter route and save himself time. And that was the day that the bull who lived on the other side of the hedge killed him.

Chesterton used the story to illustrate his principle that you should not be allowed to remove a rule or a tradition unless and until you fully understand the reasons why it was first put in place, and all the effects that its presence has.

Modern cricket is a nest of Tethered Cats and Chesterton Fences. Every aspect of the game from technique and tactics to selection strategy is guided by traditions and received wisdom, some of which goes back decades. Some of those tenets, while universally accepted, turn out to be wrong. Others that are not accorded the same reverence are more important than most people realise.

The game has evolved over hundreds of years, sometimes at random, sometimes by design. And the beautiful, maddening, fascinating game that we love in turn shapes with unseen hands the cricketers and teams that play it. It pushes here, it pulls there. With one hand it allows some things to work, with another it stops other things from being effective at all.

A hawk is shaped by the environment it lives in, every muscle and ligament perfectly tuned by the forces of evolution to survive and succeed in the world it is designed for.

'It took the whole of Creation / To produce my foot, my each feather' as Ted Hughes puts it in 'Hawk Roosting'.

In the same way, every player and team evolves under the forces created by cricket itself. Technique, tactics, selection, everything is shaped by what works and what doesn't work. We do some things because they work, we don't do other things because they don't. And just as 'It took the whole of Creation' to create a hawk, it took the whole history of cricket to produce Virat Kohli. If you had changed the laws of the game 30 years ago then Kohli would not now bat the way Virat Kohli bats.

There are other unseen hands at work. As human beings, brilliant but endearingly fallible, we share a set of strong subconscious biases – the unconscious mistakes that we all tend to make in predictable ways. We all suffer from confirmation bias, for example. We are all loss averse.

We also share certain physiological limitations. There are things none of us can do. No matter how hard we train, none of us can react to something in less than a tenth of a second.

And just as cricket shapes cricketers, cricket itself is shaped by the inbuilt biases that all cricketers have. That all of us have. Closely examine the decisions coaches and players make at the highest level and you can detect the unseen hands that guide our behaviour, for good or ill.

For example, if human beings were not loss averse then the game of cricket would look different; bowlers would bowl different lengths, captains would make different choices at the toss.

If our reaction speed as a species was slightly faster, then the optimum length to bowl in Test cricket would have to be fuller, and it would change the comparative advantage that left-arm seamers have over their right-handed brethren in T20 cricket.

Every cricketer at every level of the game is shaped by the unseen hands, influenced by their own physiology, psychology and by the underlying structure of the game. But as you climb upward through the levels from club cricket, to First Class, to internationals, those forces grow stronger and stronger.

As the air becomes more rarefied and the margin between success and failure becomes smaller and smaller, the more important those small advantages become and the harder it becomes to work against the unseen hands.

So, while 20 per cent of club batsmen bat left-handed, in county cricket this figure is over 35 per cent, and in Tests nearly 50 per cent. The size of the relative advantage doesn't change, but the importance of that slight edge increases.

That is what we will explore in this book. We will lift the lid on international cricket and explain its hidden workings and dynamics. We will look at the forces that shape cricket and, in turn, the cricketers who play it. We will uncover the unseen hands that determine which players succeed and which fail, which tactics work and which don't, which teams win and which lose.

Fifteen years ago, no one could have written this book. Although the theories, the ideas, the questions and the debates have been around forever, there simply wasn't a way of answering those questions, of settling those debates definitively.

But then the counting started, and with it came an explosion of new information. The advent of modern sports analysis techniques means that now data is collected on every detail of every ball in every First Class or List A cricket match in the world. For many of those matches and for all internationals and major T20 leagues we also have Hawk-Eye (or Hawk-Eye-style) ball-tracking data.

And ball-tracking data transforms everything. Every ball is tracked to within millimetres, its release point, speed and bounce point are measured, as are how much the ball swings, how much it deviates off the pitch, the exact height and line that it passes the stumps, and multiple other variables.

The effect of this in terms of our ability to understand the game is profound. Every ball bowled becomes an independent experiment into how cricket works. After 15 years, we now have the results of millions of such experiments, which contain within them everything you could want to know about international cricket. To discover what we wish to know, all we need do is ask the right questions.

This book will take you on a whistlestop tour of modern cricket and sports analytics. We will uncover the unseen hands that have shaped the game and those who play it. Hopefully, we will solve some puzzles you have pondered for years and introduce some others you have never considered. It will be a little complicated in places, and it will be as geeky as you choose to make it. But it will be fun, and you won't look at cricket in the same way afterwards.

We will answer questions that have been asked for 100 years – 'Why is a good length a good length?' – and questions that have never been asked before – 'Why don't Indians bat left-handed?'

We will ask and answer the perennial commentators' bugbear, 'Why don't they pitch it up?'

We will look at left-handedness and talk about its advantages and disadvantages. Should you turn your young, right-handed child round and turn them into a leftie? Well, it turns out that that depends on where you live.

We will discover why the ball swings, swerves and dips in the air, how bowlers use it to their advantage, and how batsmen counter it.

We will look at how the stadium bands of Sri Lanka differ from England's Barmy Army and discover what that tells us about those two countries' cricketers, but we will first examine how the same ideas help professional poker players manage risk.

We will explore the new world of franchise cricket where Billy Beane wannabes try to 'Moneyball' their way to success.

And we will get you fully up to speed on T20 cricket, its techniques, tactics and strategies. We will take you to the cutting edge of the format that has evolved so rapidly it has left coaches and commentators in its wake.

Lastly, we will look in detail at the stats behind some success stories: how England won the World Cup; how the Multan Sultans are breaking new ground in innovation, recruitment and tactics; and how England became the only Test team to win a series in India in the last 15 years.

And along the way, we will make the invisible visible. We will show you the unseen hands that shape cricket and help make it the greatest game in the world.

Part One

Mechanics of the Game

Strong Back, Soft Front, Wild Heart – How to Win a World Cup

....

Recognising quickly that the single wasn't on, the batsman turned and dived full-length back into his crease.

It was a typically athletic movement from one of the best athletes in world cricket, and he regained his ground easily. Even given the tense position of the run chase, and the vital importance of the match, there was only a subdued appeal from the Bangladesh fielders.

The appeal went upstairs to the third umpire, and the players went back to their positions as they waited for the replay to confirm what they all knew.

It took only one replay to confirm that Chris Jordan's bat had been grounded over the line comfortably before the ball hit the stumps. And yet the replays kept coming. From multiple angles. Freeze frame after freeze frame of the moment the bails were broken.

There was some puzzlement and dismay in an already fraught England dugout.

'What's he looking at now?'

'Why are they showing it over and over?'

It seemed that the third umpire was fixating over the fact that as the bat continued to slide over the line, part of it had been levered back up off the turf as Jordan continued to slide. Even though the entirety of the blade was over the line as the bails were removed the moment was being examined in excruciating detail.

Given the way England's World Cup campaign had gone, there was an inevitability about the fact that when the decision eventually flashed up on the big screen, the third umpire had managed to conclude from a series of ambiguous images that no part of the bat was in contact with the ground when the bails were dislodged and gave Jordan 'Out'. (It was exactly the sort of farcical decision that led to a long-overdue law change shortly afterwards, but that was of no consolation to Jordan or England.)

In a sense it was immaterial; England had been the architects of their own downfall having made a hash of a chase they were winning at a canter halfway through, and Bangladesh were clear favourites to go on and win the match even before the run out. But it was the moment when reasonable hope finally died for England, the last nail in the coffin of their mishap-strewn World Cup campaign, as they slipped to a 15-run defeat, and were unceremoniously ejected from the tournament before they had even finished playing their group matches.

Their failure was made more abject by the fact that the draw had dealt them such a favourable hand. The structure of the tournament meant that even after heavy defeats to Australia, New Zealand and Sri Lanka, they were still assured of a place in the knockout rounds if they could beat Afghanistan, Bangladesh and Scotland. But even that was beyond them.

In the aftermath a visibly shellshocked Peter Moores, England's head coach at the time, gave a BBC interview during which he was asked to explain his team's poor performance. His reply was reported as the infamous 'we'll need to take a look at the data'. Moores has always asserted that what he actually said was 'we'll need to look at it later', but the misquote had flashed around the world before the correction had a chance to lace its shoes.

The Twitter-verse exploded with derision; the sports pages were equally savage. That Moores and his England regime had made less use of data than the coaches who came before and after him did not get in the way of a good story. The newspapers were as disgusted as you might expect:

'Peter Moores risked piling embarrassment on to humiliation today when the England coach said that he would "look at the data" to find an explanation for his team's shambolic early exit from the World Cup' (Sam Munnery, *The Times*); 'much worse than anybody could possibly have imagined in their most horrific nightmare' (Stephen Brenkley, the *Independent*); 'England were a laughing-stock ... trying to offer some excuse for the poor beleaguered Poms, the presenters in both cases called England spineless' (Brenkley); 'We seem to be light years behind other teams in the way we think about one-day cricket' (Geoffrey Boycott, BBC Sport); 'one of the biggest humiliations in the national team's history' (Jonathan Agnew).

Another World Cup, another England humiliation. They seemed further from the top of the One Day game than they had ever been.

For the demoralised England squad and staff there remained the ignominy of a final, pointless group match against Afghanistan. While England warmed up, the DJ at the Sydney Cricket Ground entertained them by belting out a series of his favourite songs over the sound system: 'Going Home', 'Leaving on a Jet Plane', 'Homeward Bound', 'Take Me Home, Country Roads', 'On the Road Again', 'Good Riddance' ... the list went on.

Winning that match, which England at least went on to do, provided nothing other than the avoidance of further self-harm. The fallout from the debacle was almost as brutal and far-reaching as that which had followed the Ashes loss in Australia 12 months earlier. Moores was sacked shortly afterwards. Five of the squad never played ODI cricket for England again, and three others only played a handful more games.

STRAUSS GOES TO WORK

Two months after the England squad flew home after the World Cup, the England and Wales Cricket Board (ECB) appointed Andrew Strauss as their new Director of Cricket. It

13

quickly became clear that he was determined to take a very different approach to white-ball cricket than England had in the past.

One Day cricket had always been the poor relation to Test cricket in English eyes – T20 cricket even more so once it started to gain a foothold in the international game. When players needed to be rested, it was done during the white-ball series, never the Tests. ODI series, even World Cup campaigns, never got the same level of advance planning and attention to detail that an Ashes series, or a Test series against India, were routinely given.

Two of Strauss's first actions were to remove Peter Moores and to confirm Eoin Morgan as England's captain for the foreseeable future. (Morgan had been appointed captain on the eve of the World Cup, replacing Alastair Cook.)

Trevor Bayliss was appointed as the new England team coach. Another distinctly white-ball focused decision. Although Bayliss (and his second-in-command Paul Farbrace) had enjoyed success with the Sri Lankan Test team, it was in white-ball cricket that he had made his name and reputation as a coach, first at New South Wales and then with Kolkata Knight Riders. Farbrace, who was head coach of Sri Lanka when England recruited him, had just won the T20 World Cup with them. This was a coaching unit with formidable white-ball pedigree.

The next step was a restructuring of the England players' central contracts to give white-ball performances increased value, and the introduction of a North v. South season curtain-raiser including the best One Day players in county cricket.

At the same time Strauss launched a comprehensive review into ODI cricket. This took a twin-pronged approach. There was a full statistical analysis undertaken of past World Cups focusing on the traits and methods that differentiated past winners from the other teams involved. At the same time, senior ex-players, both from England and from overseas, were mined for their thoughts on success in white-ball cricket. The conclusions of those research projects shaped how England sought to transform themselves as an ODI team.

A HISTORY OF FAILURE

So what did the analysis show? Were England as bad at World Cups as everyone seemed to think?

Well, the short answer to the question was 'Yes.' (The slightly longer answer was 'Yes, they were really bad.')

In the five World Cups between 1999 and 2015, England progressed to the knockout stages only once, in 2011, when they promptly lost a quarter-final to Sri Lanka by ten wickets. In those five World Cups England played 22 matches against other Test-playing nations. They won only 7 of those matches. Going out in the group stages had felt like a shock in 2015 but, historically, it was just par for the course.

So why were England so poor at World Cups? And, more importantly, what were the main features of World Cup-winning teams?

In terms of the second question, it turned out that there were some clear traits that World Cup finalists and winners shared. And while most were obvious and none of them was a surprise, it was interesting that a long list of other things you would think were equally important turned out to have little impact.

At this stage, the analysis was general and broad brush. In white-ball cricket the rules have a strong influence over successful tactics and style of play, and they had been different at each of the previous World Cups, often quite significantly different. So a retrospective study such as this could only deal in generalities. Even so, it gave a very useful template for success.

BATTING STRENGTH

The best predictor of success at World Cups that we found was batting strength. Average scoring rates for a team in the two years prior to a World Cup were a better indicator than any other as to how they would perform.

Batting Records in 2 years prior to each World Cup

1999	Avg	S/R	2003	Avg	S/R	2007	Avg	S/R	2011	Avg	S/R	2015	Avg	S/R
Pak	30	79	Aus	35	81	Aus	36	83	SA	37	91	NZ	33	91
Aus	31	78	SA	34	77	SA	35	81	Ind	35	88	Aus	34	90
SA	30	77	Ind	29	77	NZ	28	81	SL	33	84	Ind	36	88
SL	28	77	WI	32	76	Ind	31	80	Aus	36	83	SA	34	87
WI	27	75	Pak	29	76	SL	29	78	ENG	29	81	SL	30	84
Ind	31	74	ENG	26	74	Pak	28	77	NZ	25	80	ENG	28	83
Zim	28	74	SL	28	73	ENG	27	76	Pak	25	79	WI	28	82
ENG	27	71	Zim	25	70	WI	27	73	WI	24	78	Ban	27	80
NZ	26	70	NZ	24	68	Ban	24	66	Ban	28	77	Pak	27	79
Ban	17	58	Ban	17	57	Zim	20	60	Zim	23	72	Zim	21	69
			Kenya											

■ Winner   ■ Finalist   ■ Semi-Finalist

It was no surprise that teams with stronger batting line-ups perform better, but it was surprising how strong that correlation was. Particularly when you look at the correlation between bowling strength and success, which was negligible. It wasn't entirely clear why there was such a discrepancy between batting and bowling strength, but while the sample size was small, it was compelling.

WINNING RECORD

Unsurprisingly, another thing that correlated very strongly with success at World Cups was a team's playing record in the two years leading up to the competition. The top two ranked teams going into the tournament had won four of the last five World Cups – the only exception being India in 2011, and they had a healthy 60 per cent win record going into the tournament, a figure that would often have placed them in the top two.

Win Percentage in 2 years prior to each World Cup

1999			2003			2007			2011			2015	
SA	79%		Aus	73%		SA	71%		Aus	70%	H	Aus	67%
Aus	58%	H	SA	63%		Aus	65%		SA	65%		Ind	63%
Ind	52%		Pak	62%		Pak	54%	H	SL	63%		SA	61%
SL	52%		SL	55%		Ind	53%	H	Ind	60%	H	NZ	57%
Pak	48%		Ind	53%		NZ	52%	H	Ban	50%		SL	53%
ENG	47%		WI	49%		SL	51%		ENG	50%		WI	47%
WI	45%		NZ	43%	H	WI	43%		Pak	38%		Ban	42%
NZ	39%		ENG	40%		Ban	41%		NZ	36%		Pak	40%
Zim	34%	H	Zim	24%		ENG	39%		Zim	24%		ENG	39%
Ban	0%		Ban	0%		Zim	14%		WI	22%		Zim	15%

■ Winner   ■ Finalist   ■ Semi-Finalist   H = Host

EXPERIENCE

A third good predictor of success at World Cups was the level of ODI experience in the squad, as measured by the average number of ODI caps in the squad. In fact, in the last 20 years only one of the ten teams that made the final didn't come in the top half in average number of caps.

Average Caps per Squad at World Cups

1999		2003		2007		2011		2015	
SL	128	Pak	145	Ind	172	Ind	128	SL	125
Pak	123	SL	129	SL	127	SL	116	Ind	86
Ind	114	Ind	126	Pak	118	Aus	110	NZ	84
Aus	82	RSA	99	RSA	111	Pak	99	WI	82
RSA	76	Aus	85	Aus	94	NZ	79	Pak	78
WI	74	NZ	82	NZ	88	WI	66	Aus	72
NZ	54	WI	72	WI	84	ENG	64	ENG	67
Zim	48	Zim	71	Ban	48	Ban	64	RSA	66
ENG	46	ENG	51	ENG	41	RSA	64	Zim	64
Ban	13	Ban	19	Zim	34	Zim	58	Ban	59

■ Winner   ■ Finalist   ■ Semi-Finalist

It's easy to look at those three metrics and say, 'Well, that's pretty obvious! Strong batting, winning record, lots of experience, that's exactly what I'd expect to win World Cups.' So it is also worth noting the many things that had no correlation with success at World Cups. Bowling strength is one surprising one that we've already mentioned. Consistency of selection is another. There was no correlation between the number of players a team had used in the previous year and how they then fared at the World Cup.

Now crucially, look at England historically, measured against these criteria. Not once in five World Cups had they been ranked in the top four in any of those three metrics, and their average ranking was eighth.

It was clear that whatever hopes they had when they went into those five previous World Cups, England had no right to expect any sort of success. Far from underperforming, they had performed exactly as expected given the squads they took to those tournaments.

THE BLACKBOARD OF THE OBVIOUS

You can put analytical methods into four categories, ranked in descending order of sexiness:

- Generate new ideas.
- Find counterintuitive truths.
- Rank the obvious.
- Measure and improve.

I want to spend a little time talking about the middle two.

Whenever anyone reads *Moneyball*, or some other funky version of analytics in sport, the thing they then want to look for is the counterintuitive truth. They want to unearth the stat or piece of data that turns conventional wisdom on its head. It's the question journalists always ask you, it's what the coaches and players who buy into these methods want you to come up with (whether they then believe you when you do is another matter, as counterintuitive is counterintuitive for a reason).

Now those little gems do often exist – we've covered a few of them in this book. But to fixate on that method of using analysis is to miss out on a simpler and often more useful means of gaining a competitive advantage from data, which can be summed up as 'the ranking of the obvious'.

I often explain this idea using a thought experiment I call 'The Obvious Blackboard'.

Let's say you are a coach and you want to make your team better. You decide to start by taking a blackboard and scribbling down everything you can think of that helps teams win.

'Catch our chances in the field', 'Score highly in the PowerPlay when batting', 'Take wickets in the middle overs with the ball', 'Boundary hitting', 'Running singles', etc.

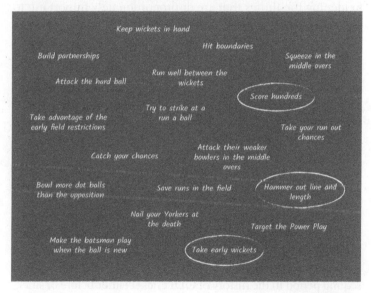

You could fill that blackboard with ideas within a few minutes; with longer to think and a few colleagues to help generate ideas, you could easily fill multiple blackboards. And here's the thing, pretty much *all* of those ideas will work. If you run the numbers, almost everything that sounds like it will help a team win, does.

Taking more chances in the field correlates with winning.

Scoring more runs in the PowerPlay correlates with winning.

Taking more wickets in the middle overs correlates with winning.

(Occasionally one of the obvious things doesn't correlate with winning, so that's your counterintuitive truth, and if you're really lucky it will be something that you can use to your advantage as a tactic, game plan or selection strategy.)

But that doesn't mean that all the other items on your blackboard are equally valid, and it certainly doesn't mean that you can do them all. You can't set up a side to do everything you've written on your board. You've got to choose which two, three or four ideas to focus on. So then the value of good analysis is to identify the things that are disproportionately important; to put a circle round the things on the board that are relatively easy for you to achieve but make a significant difference to your chances of winning.

It's worth noting that this may not be the same for every team. Some teams will have resources available that allow them to pursue a certain strategy, whereas for other teams that same strategy is a non-starter because they simply don't have the players to pursue it. *There isn't one correct solution to how to play winning cricket.*

A NEW SET OF RULES

In 2015 England had been caught out by a rapidly changing game. Scoring patterns that had stayed relatively constant over the previous five years or so, even up to 2013 and early 2014, had suddenly shifted, and the totals that teams were setting and chasing down had soared. The first half of 2015 was the highest scoring period in the history of ODI cricket either before or since.

At the 2011 World Cup, played largely on fast-scoring Indian grounds, the average first innings score by the top ten nations was 235. At the 2015 World Cup it was 268. In 2011, only 3 of the 27 matches between major nations saw scores of over 300. In 2015 there were 14. It was an explosion of scoring, from roughly one match in ten seeing a 300+ total to over half.

There has been a steady rise in scoring rates throughout the history of One Day Internationals.

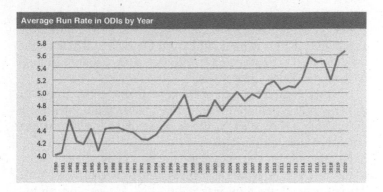

Average Run Rate in ODIs by Year

You will hear many explanations for this steady rise that are focused on improvements in batting: the influence of T20 cricket, 'bigger' bats, etc. Some of those have had an influence. But there have been parallel improvements in bowling technique and tactics: slower balls, yorkers, better fields and tactics for run saving. There has also been a huge increase in the quality of fielding and the importance placed upon it.

You would expect those two areas of improvement, batting and bowling/fielding, to roughly cancel each other out, not result in a 40-year unbroken trend of higher and higher scores.

Generally, in most sports, there is a balanced arms race between attack and defence. Whenever attacking methods take a step forward, defensive tactics evolve to counter them. And when defensive systems improve, attackers are forced to innovate so as to find ways through or around them. This homeostatic equilibrium can hold steady for long periods and does so in many two-sided sports. Scoring rates in baseball, for example, have remained remarkably constant for nearly a hundred years. But that is not entirely by chance.

There is a third force maintaining this homeostasis, and that's the rule book. In most sports, the rules are the biggest single determining factor in scoring rates. One of the reasons for that remarkably flat average scoring in baseball is that whenever attack or defence has looked like gaining control, the governing body has tweaked the rules to redress the balance – they started replacing the ball regularly so as to counter the advantage pitchers were getting from the wear and tear on the ball, and later they adjusted the height of the pitcher's mound to again rebalance the contest.

Lawmakers are generally seeking to do one of two things by this type of legal engineering: either maintain the integrity of the sporting records set in the past, or make the sport more enjoyable to watch (and play).

For example, in February 2008 the new LZR range of swimming suits was unveiled at a press conference in New York. Their greater buoyancy was a huge advantage and almost every swimming world record was broken within the next few months. The governing body FINA (Fédération internationale de natation/International Swimming Federation) promptly banned the new suits and reinstated the old-world records.

A similar motivation drives changes to the rules in baseball (and indeed in Test cricket): those in charge don't want Babe Ruth's records to disappear under an avalanche of new higher scoring by lesser players, they want the balance between bat and ball to stay the same as it has always been.

In rugby, on the other hand, where individual records have never been anywhere near as important, scores have increased steadily for decades, as the rule makers have tried to make the game more exciting to watch and play. One Day cricket has followed a similar path.

In the early days of One Day cricket, 220 was an excellent score and gave you a very good chance of winning the match. In the first 50 One Day matches between major nations there were only 15 first innings scores over 200, even though most of these games were 55 or 60 overs long.

But those matches were played with a red ball, no fielding restrictions, no height or legside wides rule, no restrictions on bouncers, and boundaries as big as the playing area at the ground would allow. If we played a One Day match under those rules now, with modern players, then 220 would still be a good score.

For the most part it is rule changes that have driven scoring rates higher and higher in One Day cricket and the 2015 World Cup was no different.

TWO NEW BALLS AND ONLY FOUR MEN OUT

The proximate cause of the surge in scoring at the 2015 World Cup was the rule changes that had been introduced two years earlier at the start of 2013.

At the time, they seemed quite significant changes, and indeed they were to have a marked if slightly delayed impact on scoring rates. In 2013 the new ICC rules for 50-over cricket introduced the idea of two new balls per innings (one to be used from each end), reduced the number of fielders outside the ring from five to four, and mandated that the Batting PowerPlay occur in overs 36 to 40. The effect of all these changes was to give batsmen the upper hand at the end of the innings. The interesting thing is how long it took for teams to learn how to take advantage of this edge.

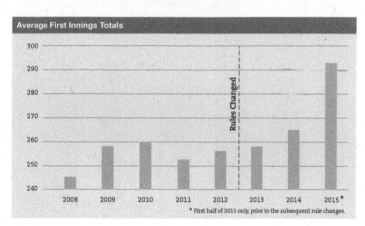

*First half of 2015 only, prior to the subsequent rule changes.

For the five years preceding the change, scoring in ODI cricket had remained relatively stable. The average first innings total for each of those years was between 250 and 260. And for almost two years after the rule changes, that is where it stayed. I don't know if it quite qualifies as a Tethered Cat, but it is a good illustration of the power of inertia and expectation that teams continued to score what they expected to score for over a year-and-a-half after the rule changes had made higher scores far more possible. It was only towards the end of 2014 that scoring started to explode, and only in the first half of 2015 that it reached its fullest extent.

For our tale of England's World Cup triumph, it is important that we understand not just why scoring suddenly spiked, but also how: the mechanism by which those rule changes produced higher totals. Because it was by understanding this, and more importantly the subsequent set of rules that followed (introduced in July 2015), that England were able to reinvent ODI batting.

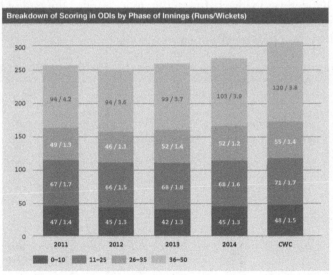

Scoring rates in fact changed very little in the first 35 overs of the innings. Boundaries contributed a higher proportion of runs under the new rules, as you would expect, but overall, the changes were relatively small.

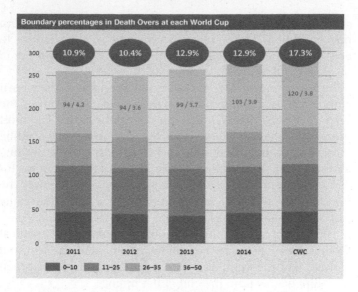

It was in the last 15 overs that there was a sudden spike in scoring rates. And the whole of that increase came in more boundaries. The rule changes had two main effects:

- Two new balls meant that the ball at the end of the innings was newer, harder and whiter. It was easier to see and hit, and came off the bat faster, making boundary hitting easier. It was also far less likely to allow reverse swing, removing one of the main weapons of death bowlers in the previous era.
- Fewer fielders outside the ring for the last 15 overs opened up large gaps and made it significantly easier for batsmen to find the boundary. And here the effect of T20-driven innovations in batting, particularly the skill to hit boundaries in the full 360-degree range, exacerbated this increased opportunity.

The rule changes had created an explosion of opportunity for scoring at the death, during a period when death batting and death bowling were probably the England team's biggest weaknesses. The game had shifted decisively against them in the year leading up to the World Cup and their humiliation should not have been unexpected. Their 2011 post-mortem had identified this as a key component of their failure to compete at the World Cup, and they were determined not to be caught out again.

In the summer of 2015 (after the World Cup had been completed), partly in response to this explosion of scoring, the ICC once again tweaked the rules of ODI cricket. The most important changes were that they removed the batting PowerPlay entirely, and allowed five fielders outside the ring for the last ten overs of the innings. As part of their planning for 2019, England immediately set to work to understand the ramifications of these changes and build a team and game plan to take advantage of them.

Having spent some time building complex, mathematical models of matches played under the new regulations, England realised that the optimum scoring opportunities for batsmen had shifted away from the end of the innings.

The simplest analogy is of a runner or cyclist doing a time trial over a set distance. Let's say that you are running 10,000 metres on a flat course and want to run your best possible time. The optimum approach would be to run at roughly the same speed throughout (runners actually often front-load these efforts for physiological reasons, but it is a difference of 1 to 2 per cent). Each runner has a 'cruising speed', which he can maintain for a long period of time without significant impairment to his performance. The further he goes above this speed, however, the more quickly he fatigues, and the more his performance for the remainder of the race is impacted. On the other hand, racing at below his optimal speed fails fully to utilise his resources.

He will maintain the highest possible average speed by bleeding out his effort evenly over the whole course.

Now imagine the course he is running is not flat. The first 2000 metres of the course are downhill, the middle 6000 are flat and the last 2000 are uphill. In other words the course gets progressively harder as you progress along it. It no longer makes sense for him to try to maintain a constant speed for the whole race. If he only runs down the hill at the start at the speed at which he can run uphill at the end, he will be going much too slowly for the terrain at the start and in the middle of the race.

It would make more sense and be much more efficient to keep his level of effort constant, so go faster at the start, and slower up the hill at the end.

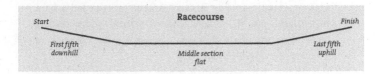

Racecourse

Start | First fifth downhill | Middle section flat | Last fifth uphill | Finish

The same is true of pacing a limited overs innings in cricket. In this analogy, the excess effort the runner puts in above his cruising speed equates to excess risk for the batsman. The risk of getting out does not rise smoothly for a batsman. Like a runner he has a natural cruising speed; below this rate, the risk he has to take stays fairly flat, but above it, the risk rises rapidly. As the key to the runner achieving his optimum score is keeping the rate at which he accumulates lactate fairly constant, so the key to optimising scoring is to keep the level of risk taking fairly level through a team's innings.

As it turned out, the new ODI regulations were akin to the course described above. The easiest time to score quickly was at the start of the innings when only two fielders were allowed outside the ring, the second easiest time was in the middle overs when four boundary fielders were allowed, and the time when the bowlers had the most protection was the last ten overs.

So, for a team to balance the distribution of risk evenly through their innings they had to show much greater attacking intent at the beginning of the 50 overs, and then look to maintain that high level of scoring through the middle overs. The rules perfectly delineated the ideal batting line-up, which consisted of:

A) Aggressive Openers (batsmen 1 to 3) who could take down the PowerPlay. The first 60 balls of the innings are by far the easiest time to hit boundaries. But you also have the best opposition bowlers bowling with two hard new balls and looking to take wickets. Attacking effectively under those conditions takes great skill, not just intent.

B) Middle-over Cruisers (batsmen 3 to 5) who would spend most of their innings in the middle 30 overs. As such they needed to have a high cruising rate, that is be able to score quickly without taking undue risks, particularly against spin as spinners bowl the bulk of the middle overs in ODI cricket.

C) Death Hitters (batsmen 5 to 7). Once you are into the last ten overs your capacity for scoring quickly, with five fielders on the boundary, comes down to your ability to clear the ropes. Power and the ability to score through 360 degrees become the key attributes needed.

The key to using the scope of the new rules to their fullest was to front-load the innings, and maintain a hitherto unseen level of aggression throughout.

This was a stroke of luck for England. Not only did they have a captain who had already openly committed to the aggressive game plan that best suited the new regulations, but he was also, as a player, the embodiment of that optimal approach.

In addition to that, the ECB had by happy coincidence just engineered a generation of players perfectly suited to the way Morgan and Bayliss wanted to play.

'STRONG BACK, SOFT FRONT, WILD HEART'

Buddhists speak of needing three things to survive and be happy in life. A 'strong back', to stand tall in the face of adversity, to labour long and hard without flagging. A 'soft front', the ability to remain open and friendly to the world and to others, to not hide behind a brittle, defensive shell. And a 'wild heart', to dream and dream again of things undreamed.

The England team has been fortunate of late in its captains. From Strauss to Cook to Root there has for over a decade been consistent leadership characterised by decency, fortitude and work ethic, fine cricketers, good captains and admirable men. But well though England had been served by its Roundhead generals, what its One-Day team needed in 2015 was a Cavalier.

Eoin Morgan is not your typical English cricketer. Born and raised in the housing estates of Dublin, he first represented Ireland in ODI cricket before making his England debut in 2009. By the 2015 World Cup he had represented England across all three formats. Calm, charismatic and unflappable, he was universally liked and respected by his fellow players and had always looked like a future leader of England's white-ball teams.

One of the first of England's cricketers to embrace the brave, new T20 world, he had gained a wide experience of cricket and cricketers from every corner of the globe. This, married with a deep understanding and feel for white-ball cricket, and an unwavering determination to build a team that could and would truly express itself, made him the perfect leader for England's reinvented ODI team.

Unfortunately for him, his opportunity came when the previous captain Alastair Cook was dropped on the eve of the 2015 World Cup. And so, having been thrown one of the bigger hospital passes in cricket history, his first experience of captaincy was seeing his England team out-thought, outplayed and embarrassed on the biggest possible stage.

In another era, that might have been the end of it, and England might have missed out on one of its finest captains. Luckily, that wasn't the case. Morgan was the man Strauss wanted.

England had found its Cavalier general.

'He could have easily pushed me to one side,' says Morgan, 'and decided [he wanted a] completely new voice, completely new captain, but he didn't.'

'It was unbelievable. The only thing I can relate it to is when you're a kid, and you're in trouble, or you're not sure if you've done something wrong. And your dad comes in, defends you and backs you up.

'I remember Paul Farbrace describing it in a similar way.

'Having that clarity, right from Straussy all the way down to us, gave us huge confidence . . . and allowed us to implement that with the team.'

Having been confirmed as England's captain for the foreseeable future, Morgan lost no time in remaking the team in his own image. Jason Roy, Alex Hales, Ben Stokes, Jonny Bairstow were all given debuts or recalled from the wilderness. Suddenly, Morgan was surrounded by batsmen who, like him, were capable of terrifying opposition bowlers and captains.

'He [Strauss] sat in on selection meetings,' says Morgan, 'and after each name was mentioned . . . he would say "Hold on! Is this guy gonna be around in four years? Is he going to play the right way? If not, we don't want him anywhere near [the squad]."'

More importantly, Morgan, with the backing of Strauss, explicitly gave the new team the freedom to fail. The message was clear. We are going to do something new. We are going to do something different. We are not necessarily going to succeed straight away. That's fine. You will be given the time and the opportunity to make mistakes and learn.

The first chance to put this new mentality into action came against the New Zealand team that the new England had in part taken as inspiration, in terms of both conduct and style. Under the temporary stewardship of Paul Farbrace, England played a five-match series against New Zealand in the spring of 2015, the last series to be played under the old ODI rules. It was an opportunity to place a marker down, and they did so with relish. In their first ever outing the new batting line-up smashed 408, passing 400 for the first time in England's history. There followed a riotous series full of mammoth totals and freakish hitting.

But in the deciding match of the rubber New Zealand were bowled out for the smallest total of the series. In the previous match, England had chased down 350 with six overs to spare and seven wickets in hand. They looked heavy favourites to get the requisite runs once Duckworth–Lewis had adjusted the target. True to their new colours, rather than throttle back, England came out to smash the smallish total as emphatically as possible. Wickets tumbled in a flurry of expansive shots and after eight overs the score was 45 for 5.

Of course, if you had thought that the England batting line-up's barnstorming series up to that point would have won them some leeway then you would have been wrong. Immediately, there were the same old voices talking about England's 'naivety', 'stupidity' and less kind terms. And those voices would never completely go away for the next four years. (Never really until an evening in July 2019, at Lord's, in a match also against New Zealand.)

On this occasion it was left to Jonny Bairstow to drag his team over the line with a brilliant 83 not out and secure the series victory. The tone for the next four years had been set.

Morgan was clear on England's priorities. 'During that first period the biggest thing was not focusing on winning the match, or the series. It was focusing on change. Change for the right reason.

'And the right reason . . . is the final product in four years' time, when we play in the World Cup.

'So, having accountability in questioning our mistakes . . . that's where TB [Trevor Bayliss] was very good. When we came up against a challenge, or got bowled out, [he would ask] "All right, do we need to change it? Or do we need to get better at it?"

'And then the players would answer with: what they would do, and how that looked moving forward.

'I thought that was huge. Because there wasn't just one or two voices in the changing room, me and TB, there were actually four or five who felt empowered to make that change.'

Although Morgan's batsmen were pushing the envelope of the possible, his bowling attack was less settled, less certain and often under huge pressure at the hands of opposition batsmen. So over the next few years we were given ample opportunity to observe him under pressure in one of the hardest situations with which a captain has to deal. A bowling attack on the rack, and a match being pulled from his grasp by the opposition batsmen's onslaught. Morgan never gave any hint of that pressure and the bowlers, for their part, were universal in their praise of his rock-like support.

Somehow England's limitations with the ball were easier for people to understand. They were the traditional travails associated with supporting our One Day team. Their occasional batting failures seemed harder for people to reckon.

Still the questioning, silent during the periods of success, never entirely went away. And for all their mercurial brilliance, England's batsmen still supplied enough grist for the critics' mills. There were collapses from winning positions, generally when 'over-attacking', and misfires on pitches that offered the new ball some assistance. Each time, the voices of 'Old England' both inside and outside the set-up would start to chunter. And each time, Morgan and his senior players would calmly but forcefully refuse to compromise.

Morgan was more than ready to accept the negative metric, and in fact felt that the questioning was a good sign. 'That's always a good indication that it's the right thing to do. The fact is it's been like that for so long. And the results that [England] have not achieved for decades are there to see.

'And the results that we've been getting now wouldn't exist if we had continued to play the way [they want us to] . . . everyone would say, "Oh well done, this is lovely, scored another hundred, I know you lost the game, but you know, you win some you lose some."

'If people are complaining about us being bowled out, or giving us stick for playing too aggressively, then it's a bloody good sign.

'Part of the journey is you have to lose. You have to lose games of cricket. You have to have bumps and scars. So that you can say, "We've lost that game, why did we lose it?" Was it because we didn't bat the overs? Or was it because we didn't play aggressively well enough? Why?

'You ask the fella in the street he'll say, "Bat the overs." You ask the guy who belongs [in this team] and he'll say, "Get better at playing aggressively."'

This, then, was the crux and crucial heart of Morgan and Bayliss's approach. It was a growth strategy, a recognition that they were not yet as good as they could be. They were still in possession of their Licence to Fail, and they would keep using it as a waiver to do so, but only to fail in the *right* way. That licence gave the team the freedom to push the boundaries of what they could do. It was in essence a four-year-long bet, that if they kept hitting gamble they would force themselves to grow the skills they needed, to become the team they needed to be, to win the only game that mattered to them, at Lord's on 14 July 2019.

Morgan and his senior players had set their course. Like its estimable captain, this England team would have a strong back, a soft front and a wild, wild heart.

A HAPPY ACCIDENT

In 2010, the England and Wales Cricket Board opted to slim down their domestic List A calendar, reducing it from two competitions (one 50 overs-a-side, one 40 overs-a-side) down to a single 40-over tournament. It was a fan-oriented decision. Counties found it far easier to sell tickets for 40-over matches, crowds were better, and one can imagine that the improved product this offered to television was in no small part a consideration.

It wasn't universally popular, however, with those more closely affected by the change. As CricInfo writers Andrew McGlashan and Andrew Miller noted at the time:

> England's players, however, seem less convinced ... 'Ideally, you
> want county cricket to mirror international cricket,' said Paul

Collingwood, England's captain for their ODI against Ireland in the absence of Andrew Strauss. 'If you're not playing the 50-over form domestically, it's a bit of a hindrance ... Hopefully, it won't be a massive jump ... but we'll have to wait and see next time players come into the international game.'

There was clearly a concern that the difference between the rule changes at international and domestic level would make player development more challenging. How could a young batsman playing his formative List A cricket across 40 overs adapt to the challenges of longer cricket when promoted to the ODI set-up?

Certainly, the difference in scoring rate between the two formats was clear. In every year where the 40-over league was played concurrently with a 50-over league, the 40-over scoring rate was much higher, as you would expect.

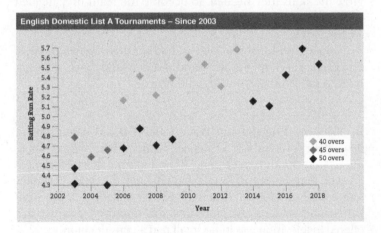

Yet when the format returned to being 50 overs, the high run rates remained and batsmen's averages went up. The players in the competition had adapted to the 40-over format, and were playing their newly natural game in the 50-over format in terms of the accelerated scoring rate, and were doing so while not getting out anywhere near as frequently.

Four years of playing solely 40-over cricket had had a profound effect on England's generation of young cricketers. As many had predicted, it significantly impacted the development of that crop of players born in the late 1980s and early 1990s. What few had predicted, however, was that it would help to produce unarguably the finest collection of white-ball batsmen that England has ever produced.

Jos Buttler made his debut in September 2009. So did Joe Root. Ben Stokes made his debut three months earlier, Jonny Bairstow a month later. Alex Hales and Jason Roy had debuted the previous year. Within a little over 12 months, six of the batsmen who would power England to two world-record totals inside two years came to prominence. And the List A cricket they played, for the majority of their white-ball apprenticeships, was 40 overs long.

When the ECB brought in these changes, they had an England ODI side filled with a particular profile of player. Of their established performers, only Owais Shah managed to both score more quickly and lose his wicket more rarely than the average ODI top-order batsman. Plenty managed the latter, but only Flintoff, Pietersen and Shah himself could match the rate of scoring that others were setting. England's talent pool was solid, but slow.

England's Leading ODI Batsmen 2007				
Player	Run Rate	RR – global average RR	Dismissal Rate	DR – global average DR
A. Flintoff	4.81	0.1	28.3	-14.4
O.A. Shah	4.75	0.0	51.5	8.8
K.P. Pietersen	4.71	0.0	53.9	11.2
P.D. Collingwood	4.66	-0.1	57	14.3
M.J. Prior	4.5	-0.2	30.5	-12.2
I.R. Bell	4.36	-0.4	53.4	10.7
R.S. Bopara	4.21	-0.5	33.7	-9.0
M.P. Vaughan	4.1	-0.6	30.4	-12.3
E.C. Joyce	4.01	-0.7	50.6	7.9
A.N. Cook	3.98	-0.7	43.3	0.6
A.J. Strauss	3.94	-0.8	30	-12.7

The difference by 2018 was staggering. England not only had three players (Root, Morgan and Buttler) who managed to outperform both the average scoring rate and dismissal rate, but they were also far more skewed towards rapid scoring than they had been. Their personal records resemble those from 40-over cricket, far more than they do typical 50-over stats.

The ECB had, by happy chance, force-grown a generation of cricketers who could do exactly what was required to play the style of cricket that Morgan and his analysts felt gave them the best chance of winning the World Cup.

England's Leading ODI Batsmen 2018				
Player	Run Rate	RR – global average RR	Dismissal Rate	DR – global average DR
J. M. Bairstow	7.09	2.1	39.4	-0.9
J. C. Buttler	6.81	1.8	49.2	8.9
J. J. Roy	6.3	1.3	38.6	-1.7
E. J. G. Morgan	5.62	0.6	44.7	4.4
A. D. Hales	5.5	0.5	38.3	-2.0
M. M. Ali	5.39	0.4	22	-18.3
J. E. Root	5.03	0.0	70.4	30.1
B. A. Stokes	4.61	-0.4	58.1	17.8

KEY INDICATORS REVISITED

When England took the field against South Africa on 30 May 2019 in the first match of the Cricket World Cup they were ranked number one in the world, and were the bookies' favourites. More than that, they were the first team in recent history to top the table in each of the three success indicators that had been identified almost exactly four years before.

Through the chaos of a four-year cycle of the international fixtures calendar, Bayliss, Morgan and the England selectors, overseen by first Strauss and then subsequently by Ashley Giles, had managed to hit their marks perfectly. Batting power, win rate and squad experience had been nailed down one after the other exactly as planned. They had won 78 per cent of their matches against other senior teams in the previous 24 months.

Win Rate in 2 Years Prior to CWC	
	Win %
England	78%
India	73%
South Africa	65%
New Zealand	61%
Afghanistan	60%
Bangladesh	55%
Pakistan	45%
Australia	38%
West Indies	29%
Sri Lanka	22%

They were well clear at the top of the batting strike-rate table, the clearest predictor of World Cup success.

Batting in 2 Years Prior to CWC	
	RR
England	6.25
India	5.69
New Zealand	5.65
Australia	5.61
South Africa	5.54
Pakistan	5.47
West Indies	5.39
Sri Lanka	5.21
Bangladesh	5.20

And they were the most experienced team at the World Cup. While the hugely experienced Indian and Bangladesh squads had more caps in total, those caps were largely contributed by a smaller group of immensely experienced players. England's experience was spread much more evenly through the squad, and they had no fewer than nine players with 75 caps or more.

Squad Experience at CWC	75+ caps
England	9
India	7
Bangladesh	6
New Zealand	6
Sri Lanka	6
South Africa	6
Australia	6
Afghanistan	5
Pakistan	4
West Indies	4

And what about the roles and skillsets in the batting order that England had identified, that would make best use of the current rules in ODIs: openers who could attack the PowerPlay while the fielding restrictions were in place; top-order batsmen with a high cruising speed against spin in the middle overs; and finishers who could consistently clear the ropes at the end of the innings?

In the two years leading up to the World Cup, England led the way in PowerPlay batting. In Roy and Bairstow they had two of the most destructive batsmen in the world at the top of the order.

Top 3 Batsmen in PP, 2017–19			
Player	Team	RR	Ave
J. M. Bairstow	Eng	114	67.2
C. Munro	NZ	112	27.0
J. J. Roy	Eng	103	53.1
D. P. D. N. Dickwella	SL	98	32.3
S. Dhawan	India	93	41.3
Q. de Kock	SAf	88	95.3
Fakhar Zaman	Pak	87	44.3
W. U. Tharanga	SL	84	29.5
M. J. Guptill	NZ	83	41.3
P. R. Stirling	Ire	81	45.5
V. Kohli	India	79	76.7
S. F. Mire	Zimb	79	21.9
A. J. Finch	Aust	75	48.6
R. G. Sharma	India	71	34.6
H. Masakadza	Zimb	68	27.4
S. D. Hope	WI	68	44.9
Babar Azam	Pak	64	37.0
Imam-ul-Haq	Pak	62	42.1

Team Batting in PowerPlay		
Team	RR	Ave
England	6.0	49.6
South Africa	5.0	42.5
Australia	4.9	43.3
New Zealand	4.9	35.1
Sri Lanka	4.8	28.9
India	4.7	42.7
West Indies	4.7	35.4
Pakistan	4.3	32.9
Bangladesh	4.2	27.4
Afghanistan	3.9	29.5

In the middle overs, their record against spin was the best in the world. A remarkable transformation in an area of traditional weakness.

England v. Spin, Overs 11–36		
Player	RR	Ave
J. E. Root	92	88.6
E. J. G. Morgan	99	132.8
B. A. Stokes	87	143.0
J. C. Buttler	108	155.0

Batting v. Spin, Overs 11–35		
Team	S/R	Ave
England	97	70.2
India	88	63.0
South Africa	87	40.4
Australia	87	40.7
Pakistan	82	57.3
New Zealand	82	47.1
Bangladesh	77	43.9
Sri Lanka	74	30.7
West Indies	73	35.1
Afghanistan	72	34.0

And after the field went back in the forty-first over, England, led by the incomparable Buttler, were the most powerful strikers of the ball in world cricket, with the highest strike rate and boundary percentage.

Batting in Death Overs (41–50)			Batting in Death Overs (41–50)		
Team	RR	Bnd%	Player	S/R	Bnd%
England	7.7	15.1	J.C.Buttler	171	24.1
New Zealand	7.5	13.5	E.J.G.Morgan	155	18.8
Pakistan	7.3	13.0	M.M.Ali	137	16.4
India	7.1	13.4			
South Africa	7.0	13.8			
Australia	6.9	12.0			
Afghanistan	6.9	12.8			
West Indies	6.8	11.8			
Bangladesh	6.3	12.0			
Sri Lanka	6.0	10.2			

None of that ensured success, but one thing was clear. England would probably never have a better chance of winning the World Cup.

THE NEXT LEVEL UP

Another part of England's planning was addressing the physical and emotional toil of a home World Cup campaign played as favourites.

You will often hear about the 'jump' up from domestic to international cricket, or the gulf between the two. You can argue about how big the difference in quality actually is, but the two levels are definitely quite different in many measurable ways. Take bowling speeds for pace bowlers, for example.

In county cricket, 81 per cent of balls are bowled at slower than 82 mph, and almost no deliveries are above 88 mph.

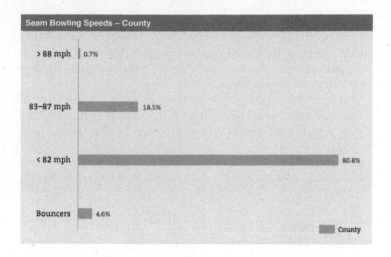

Compare that to Test cricket, where over 60 per cent of the balls bowled are over 82 mph and 17 per cent are over 88 mph. We also move from bouncers making up 4 per cent of balls bowled in county cricket, to nearly three times that many in Test cricket (11 per cent).

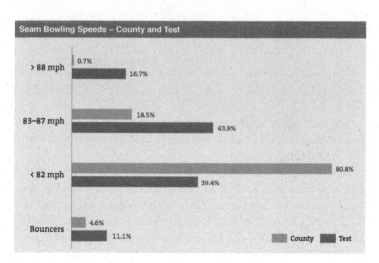

What England had come to realise was that, as well as the step up from county to international cricket, there was another jump from day-to-day internationals up to the level at which marquee series and tournaments were played, things such as the Ashes and World Cups.

For example, during the 2019 Ashes, only 19 per cent of deliveries were under 82 mph and over 20 per cent were 88+ mph, with bouncers now accounting for 14 per cent of balls bowled.

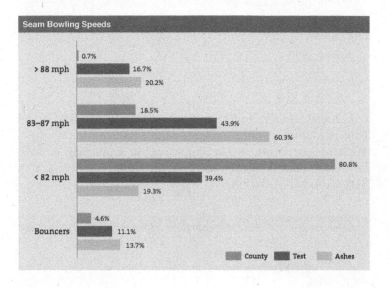

You see a similar progression if you look at bowling speeds in List A and ODI cricket and then compare them to those at the World Cup.

Another way of measuring the intensity of the cricket being played is to look at the physical requirements on players. (There are confidentiality issues with using real GPS data from players, so the figures presented here are illustrative.) At the World Cup, the average distance per match that players sprinted at high-intensity speeds (>20 kph) was

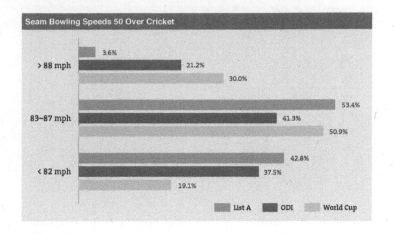

double the average distance covered at those speeds in a typical ODI.

And the distances covered at the very highest intensities were five times higher. In the two years prior to the World Cup, England's players, guided by Phil Scott, their strength and conditioning coach, worked tirelessly to make sure that they had the extra gear physically to be able to cope with that greater intensity.

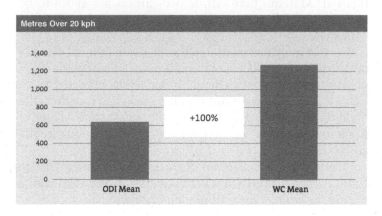

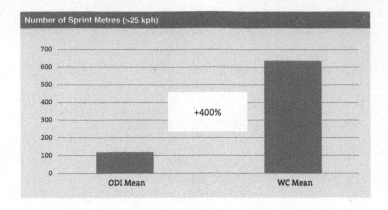

The other feature of World Cup cricket is the increased pressure players are under mentally and emotionally. You would be surprised, I think, to wander into an England dressing room on the morning of a normal match to find there is a relaxed, almost casual feel to preparations. It varies from player to player, but most don't look like they are about to perform in front of a huge, worldwide audience (when you play India, for example, the TV audience is around half a billion people).

That is very different during a World Cup campaign. The atmosphere is noticeably more pressurised and focused. Matches that will define careers are about to be played, with all the nerves and expectation that comes with that.

And that increased mental, physical and emotional demand has a cumulative effect over the campaign. (Particularly when playing at home, and particularly for teams expected to do well.) It accumulates steadily over the weeks and months of the build-up, and in the group stages. One way to see evidence of this is to look at the effect pressure has on teams batting second and chasing a total.

In regular, bilateral series there is a small advantage to batting second in ODI cricket. Since 2011, the side batting second has won 53 per cent of such matches.

STRONG BACK, SOFT FRONT, WILD HEART

But in ODIs played during World Cups in that period the chasing team has won only 40 per cent. Extreme pressure affects both batting and fielding sides, but it seems to have a disproportionately negative effect on batsmen in a run chase.

Sport is not, in any sane final analysis, real life. No one dies, no lives are saved or lost, nothing genuinely momentous occurs. Even those of us who make our living from it know that in the grander scheme of things it doesn't quite matter. But the times when it *does* feel like it genuinely matters not only change the feel of the game, but change the dynamics of the game itself as well.

CAVEAT

As in the rest of this book we seek to tell the story of cricket using numbers and data (that's kind of what the book's about). In chapters such as this where data actually played a part in the story, because we are focusing on the data it can look like we are exaggerating the importance that data played. So, to be clear, England's success in the summer of 2019 was entirely down to the hard work and brilliance of dozens of people working towards a collective goal: players, coaches, selectors, medics and other support staff. Some of this work was data led, much of it was not. But we use data to tell the story. The whole story of how England won the World Cup.

In this chapter, we have explained, using analysis, why that collective effort was successful, and how it differed to previous efforts that were not. Some of this is analysis that helped inform England's planning at the time. Some has been added retrospectively to flesh out our understanding of why the venture was successful.

FOR GOD'S SAKE DON'T LOOK DOWN

The tournament started well for England with a convincing win against South Africa in the curtain-raiser at The Oval. They then managed to catch Pakistan on one of those days when the divine wind is with them and they are near unbeatable, but otherwise they progressed through their group matches much as expected.

Then they suddenly stumbled in a regulation chase of a low total against Sri Lanka at Headingley. There followed a loss to Australia at Lord's where they looked decidedly out of sorts. Tense, hesitant, irritable, they suddenly seemed all the things they never normally were. The horror show at Headingley had turned serene progress into a 'don't look down' panic attack.

They now needed to beat the top two sides in the table, India and New Zealand, to qualify for the semi-final. The unimaginable horror of another group-stage exit was not only a possibility but a likelihood. Four years of planning was unravelling before the cricketing world's eyes.

NOT THE WORLD CUP WE EXPECTED
In the 12 months before the World Cup, England were playing a different game to everyone else in the world'.

Batting in the 12 Months Prior to CWC 10			
Team	RR	Ave	Bnd%
England	6.43	43.7	12.8
New Zealand	5.75	37.1	9.9
West Indies	5.71	35.0	10.0
Pakistan	5.65	39.9	9.0
Australia	5.63	34.6	9.5
Sri Lanka	5.57	26.2	10.0
South Africa	5.56	37.7	10.9
India	5.55	41.3	10.1
Bangladesh	5.28	36.0	8.7
Afghanistan	4.78	30.2	8.4

The next seven strongest batting line-ups in world cricket scored at rates between 5.55 and 5.75 runs per over, while England scored at 6.43. The average number of runs scored in an ODI match during that period was 548. In matches involving England, it was 632.

England had turned 50-over cricket into something that looked at times like a very long T20 match. And that seemed perfect for the conditions expected in a World Cup played in England, where pitches would be flat and true, and outfields fast. In the high-scoring runfest that seemed likely, England would be the one team playing the type of cricket they were used to at home, and to which they were perfectly suited.

But it didn't work out quite like that.

For reasons that are still unclear, many of the pitches the World Cup was played on were not typical early-season English ODI wickets. There had been anxiety going into the tournament about the number of early starts, so perhaps the ICC who took over the management and preparation of the pitches overcompensated. Or perhaps there was a desire to avoid seeing Asian teams blown away on green tops. Or perhaps it was just the added difficulty of preparing multiple surfaces on the same square for matches played in a short period of time. In any case, many of the pitches were dry and inconsistent. Chasing in particular seemed harder than usual, even more so than was usually the case in World Cups.

One of the earliest non-traditional metrics to take hold in One Day cricket was the score-ball percentage (the percentage of balls scored off during an innings). The great Australian side of the late 1990s and early 2000s built their method around winning that particular aspect of the contest. It was a twin-pronged method, better shot-making and more aggressive running between the wickets raising their   batting score-ball percentage, tighter bowling and more alert, athletic fielding lowering that of the opposition's. Win the battle of the score-ball percentage and you usually won the match. In almost every instance this equates to scoring more singles than the opposition. For many years the battle to win white-ball cricket matches was decided by the contest to score most singles.

The arrival of T20 cricket turned that concept on its head. Early in its evolution teams noticed that not only did scoring singles not contribute very much to winning the match, but it actually seemed to be a hindrance. An early piece of statistical analysis showed that in 90 per cent of matches, the team scoring the most singles lost the match.

The reason was fairly straightforward. A single scores you one run off one ball. Do that for a whole T20 match and you get 120. This will lose you almost every match you play. Likewise, if you are the bowling team, restricting the opposition to 120 will almost guarantee victory. So in T20 cricket, every single is a small win for the bowler, and a small loss for the batsman.

The important corollary to this idea is that the batsmen can only win by hitting boundaries (twos and threes contribute a tiny percentage of runs scored in T20 cricket, particularly after the PowerPlay).

For the years running up to the World Cup, the value of a single in England's 50-over matches was similar to one in T20 cricket. For most of the decisive periods in those games the required scoring rate was seven an over or more. It was a boundary-hitting contest, where singles were of negligible importance. This had affected England's approach to setting and chasing totals, both consciously and subconsciously. They had adopted almost a hybrid ODI/T20 style when both batting and in the field. It was what should have made them perfectly suited to the runfest most people expected the World Cup to be. Faced with lower-scoring contests on trickier pitches, it worked against them.

As scoring rates rise, bowlers resort to yorkers, slower balls and other variations more frequently. Bowled well these are harder to hit for boundaries, but easier to knock for a single. Likewise, when boundaries are the primary focus, fielders sit back on the inner ring, giving up the space in front of them in exchange for making it harder to get the ball past or over them.

In the World Cup, England's bowlers were going to their variations too early rather than holding their orthodox heavy lengths; their fielders were hanging back on the ring and leaking singles in front of them. Batsmen chasing low totals on awkward pitches were still targeting boundaries rather than staying busy and industrious at the crease in pursuit of ones and twos.

TIME TO HIT 'RESET'

England's medical team were working like Trojans (Dr Mark Wotherspoon, physiotherapist Craig de Weymarn and veteran Mark Saxby, nominally the massage therapist but actually something more akin to cricketer-whisperer). But the squad and the bowling attack in particular was starting, collectively, to creak. None was entirely injury free, many were on the verge of breaking down physically.

On top of that, the mental and emotional strain of playing a home tournament as favourites, favourites with the weight of 50 years of baggage on their shoulders, was starting to tell.

As one wag put it, England had effectively managed to qualify for the last 16 of a 10-team tournament. They had arrived at a point where, to win the World Cup, they needed to win four matches in a row against the other three best teams in the tournament – against India and New Zealand in the group stage and Australia in the semi-final, and one of those teams again in the final. Without a reset that seemed unlikely to happen.

In a cricketing era of meetings, Morgan and Bayliss's England were almost defined by having very few, and those surprisingly informal. But uniquely for that team, the practice day ahead of the crucial India match started with a very lengthy meeting of staff and players.

Led by Morgan and team psychologist David Young, the players had a frank discussion of where they were. They identified and accepted the areas where they needed to adjust their approach, then drew a line under everything that had happened so far, and returned to the principles of courage and unity that had served them so well in the previous years.

Morgan says, 'There was a build-up in performance-related pressure [as opposed to external pressure] after the Sri Lanka game. And then I think, after we lost at Lord's to Australia – and got hammered – that's when the external pressure started seeping its way in.

'I remember the next day speaking to David Young, having just got off the phone with Jos. Jos had said, "I think we need to do something; I've spoken with a couple of the guys, they're not accepting where we are, and things aren't registering [with them] in the present."

'So I spoke to Youngy about it, I spoke to Wizz [Chris Woakes] and with Mo [Ali], and they said, "One hundred per cent, we just need to have a chat and get everything out."

'David said, "To start with we need to get guys right back to the present." That meant asking them what their level of expectations were coming into the World Cup. Where did they think they would be? Talking about that and then asking them the next question. Where are we right now?

'That should help you accept what's gone before, and then bring you back to the present. And then hopefully start to map out the road of what the next few games look like.

'As the meeting went on, and we talked about where we were, I think a lot of guys got quite a lot out of offloading exactly how they were feeling. They were feeling as if . . . individually each player was losing the game for the team; they were putting themselves under *that* much pressure. So just getting rid of that was quite a weight off their shoulders.

'And then when we talked about moving forward, all they talked about was "How WE Play". If we played the way we had been playing up to that point, we were not going to go anywhere.

'We need to get back to how we usually play, and if we do, we'll win.

'So actually, the mapping out part of the meeting went way

better than I ever thought it would. Because it didn't need to be motivational, we didn't have to pick the guys up. They were just so frustrated in the way that we played. Just accepting that was massively helpful. Accepting where we were, and everyone talking about what they were carrying. For example, Mark Wood talking about the catch he dropped. We won the game, but he dropped Gayle at the Ageas Bowl, and that was something he was still carrying.

'That meeting was the turnaround moment. Straight away afterwards I had guys coming up to me saying, "That was brilliant, I feel great!"

'I was like, are you kidding me? That is exactly right, before the biggest game we'll ever play?'

From the first over of the India match, it seemed like the cloud had lifted. Jason Roy returned to the side; only on one leg but fit enough to bring his usual explosive brilliance to the top of the order. He and Bairstow set the tone, and the rest of the match was a return of the England team that had arrived at the tournament as favourites.

There followed a comfortable win against New Zealand in the last group match. That secured qualification for the semi-final, where they dominated Australia from first ball to last.

And so the project that had started four years earlier against New Zealand finally arced its way back to where it had all begun. New Zealand at home. One match left, to end 50 years of hurt and make 11 England players immortal.

THE HOME OF CRICKET

Three years out from the World Cup, England conducted a deep statistical analysis of all their international venues. It wasn't clear at the time how much say they would have in where they played their World Cup matches, or where they would play specific opponents, but if it was a possibility they wanted to know the optimal choices they could make as to which opponents to play where.

The research was largely inconclusive: there tended to be

more individual variation between different pitches at the same venue than there was between different venues. And as it turned out, there was no opportunity for England to influence the ICC's choice of venues or opponents. It came down to the luck of the draw.

The research did, however, turn up one clear finding. And it was not good news. Of all their home grounds, Lord's, the venue for the World Cup final, did not suit England. It was in fact the worst venue possible for them, both in terms of its characteristics and their playing record there. From 2015 to 2019 England had a winning record at every other home venue; the only exception was Lord's, where they were at 50 per cent. Given that during this period their record away from home was 61 per cent wins, Lord's wasn't just poor for a home venue, it was worse than playing away!

Why was this the case?

The most likely explanation is that, thanks to the famous slope, Lord's is never flat. And England prospered on flat pitches. Lord's has more sideways movement than any other

England's Record by Ground 2015–19	
Ground	Eng Win %
Edgbaston, Birmingham	100%
Riverside Ground, Chester-le-Street	100%
County Ground, Bristol	100%
Kennington Oval, Kennington	83%
Headingley, Leeds	83%
Old Trafford, Manchester	80%
The Rose Bowl, Southampton	71%
Trent Bridge, Nottingham	67%
Sophia Gardens, Cardiff	67%
Lord's Cricket Ground, St John's Wood	*50%*

venue. However good the pitch is there, it slopes. So a surface that at any other venue would be entirely true with little seam movement will still produce sideways deviation at Lord's because the ball will tend to move down the slope on pitching.

Average Sideways Movement – Pace on Deliveries	
Ground	Average sideways movement
Lord's Cricket Ground, St John's Wood	*1.25*
Sophia Gardens, Cardiff	1.21
Old Trafford, Manchester	1.20
County Ground, Bristol	1.20
Edgbaston, Birmingham	1.19
The Rose Bowl, Southampton	1.18
Kennington Oval, Kennington	1.15
Trent Bridge, Nottingham	1.14
Headingley, Leeds	1.13
Riverside Ground, Chester-le-Street	1.0

Scoring by Ground 2015–19		
Ground	RR	Ave
Trent Bridge, Nottingham	6.80	42.5
County Ground, Bristol	6.21	33.3
Kennington Oval, Kennington	6.07	40.7
Riverside Ground, Chester-le-Street	5.87	36.8
Edgbaston, Birmingham	5.78	40.4
The Rose Bowl, Southampton	5.72	40.9
Sophia Gardens, Cardiff	5.64	31.3
Headingley, Leeds	5.61	36.6
Old Trafford, Manchester	5.55	31.8
Lord's Cricket Ground, St John's Wood	*5.37*	*29.7*

England's Batting by Ground 2015–19		
Ground	RR	Ave
County Ground, Bristol	7.32	51.2
Trent Bridge, Nottingham	7.30	54.9
Edgbaston, Birmingham	7.09	66.7
Riverside Ground, Chester-le-Street	6.77	42.7
Kennington Oval, Kennington	6.73	50.5
The Rose Bowl, Southampton	6.58	55.8
Sophia Gardens, Cardiff	6.26	37.5
Headingley, Leeds	5.96	43.0
Old Trafford, Manchester	5.90	35.8
Lord's Cricket Ground, St John's Wood	*5.58*	*29.9*

Partly as a result of this, Lord's is the least batsman-friendly ODI venue in England, with both the lowest run rate and average. England in particular find it a harder place to bat than anywhere else. Their average strike rate at many home venues is over seven runs an over. At Lord's it is just 5.6.

And England definitely fared better in high-scoring contests. In high-scoring matches where at least one of the teams scored at over six an over, England won 78 per cent. In matches where both teams scored at under six an over, England won only 59 per cent.

Indeed, when it came to the World Cup, England won seven of the eight high-scoring matches in which they were involved. Of the three low-scoring matches, they lost two, and the third was the final!

THE WORLD CUP FINAL
We don't know how many words have been written about *that* final, but we think it is enough. And if it isn't, we don't think we have anything further to add that could possibly do it justice. Except to say this.

If you want to make the case that New Zealand were unlucky to lose the final, then you will find few people to argue against you. But we think it is far harder to make the case that England didn't deserve to win the World Cup. They were the bookies' favourites going into the tournament, and they had the best recent record of any team in the world. They hadn't lost a bilateral series in over two years. They had to cope with the favourite's tag, the weight of 50 years of expectation. They coped with pitches unlike any they usually found at home, and to get to the final they had to win three successive must-win matches against the three other best teams in the tournament, and did so with relative ease.

ECHOES

The batsman turns, sprints the length of the pitch, and hurls himself towards the line. It is a fittingly athletic effort from one of the best athletes in world cricket. He makes his ground comfortably, but as the throw arrives it ricochets off his outstretched bat and flies away for four overthrows.

There are two balls left. Instead of needing seven to win, Ben Stokes and England now need just three.

The long, long wait is nearly over.

ADDENDUM

We know that pressure seems to change the balance between chasing and defending, that it increases the demands on the players in any number of ways. But does it also make the game fairer? Does it also mean that the best team wins more often?

The anecdotal evidence seems to suggest it does. It seems strange that of the last six tournaments, four have been won by the best team going into the tournament. That would not be improbable in a league competition. But in a knockout competition, with at least a semi-final and final, the best team should rarely have much better than a 25 per cent chance (indeed at the start of the tournament both our modelling and the markets gave England about a 30 per cent chance of winning the tournament), better than anyone else, but far less than half.

Four winners out of six, each with apparently a 25 to 30 per cent chance of winning, suggests some force we don't understand is putting its finger on the scale. It is not impossible that it is pure chance (there is about a 3 to 4 per cent chance that it would happen through random chance) but it seems unlikely.

Playing Your Natural Game
....

TWO DIFFERENT BANDS

When England tour Sri Lanka, the stadiums are the scene of two battles – one on the pitch between the teams, the other in the stands between two very different styles of music.

The local bands are a jubilant riot of noise and energy. Particularly in places such as Dambulla and Hambantota they can keep up an explosively raucous carnival of dancing, singing and playing for the whole duration of a One Day International.

Set against them are the massed choirs of the Barmy Army led by trumpeter Billy Cooper. Billy is a classically trained professional musician who has played with the London Philharmonic Orchestra. The Sri Lankan musicians on the other hand are, according to the drummer we chatted to on England's last tour, entirely self-taught. Few if any of them have ever had a lesson.

If the difference in the bands' musical education seemed stark, then it was no more so than the parallel contrast that existed on the field of play. There were a number of unorthodox players on display, some of them pretty much unique in top-level cricket. There was a fast bowler with a delivery style all to himself, his arm nearly horizontal as he releases the ball. There was a spinner who bowls both left- and right-handed, often in the same over. There was a left-arm wrist-spinner, and there was an off-spinner who bowls leg-breaks and googlies as part of his standard repertoire.

The striking thing, though, was that all of these players were on the same team. Whereas Sri Lanka had a number of extraordinary and unusual players, England had none. And this was not a single chance instance but part of a well-established pattern (on England's previous tour for example, Sri Lanka had Muralitharan, Lasith Malinga and Ajantha Mendis in the side, along with Tillakaratne Dilshan, the inventor of the Dilscoop). In fact, it is the case whenever England play against Sri Lanka, and is the result of deliberate policies.

Early in their development as an international team, Sri Lanka were confronted with the difficulty of trying to compete effectively against countries with far more experience of international cricket, much bigger playing populations and/or far greater financial resources. They reasoned that they were unlikely to succeed if they took the same approach as everyone else. 'God is on the side of the big battalions,' said Napoleon. And fighting the bigger, richer countries at their own game was more likely to end in failure than triumph.

So they chose to go decisively their own way. Since that decision, Sri Lanka have pursued a deliberate policy of eschewing orthodoxy. They have innovated and improvised whenever possible. In particular, they value and select players with unusual and individual techniques preferentially over those who conform more closely to the game's orthodoxies.

The first time the world saw the impact of this approach was at the 1996 Cricket World Cup, where Sri Lanka were the first side to deploy attacking opening batsmen to take advantage of the fielding restrictions at the start of the innings. At the time 50 or 60 runs in the first 15 overs of a One Day International were considered adequate. Sri Lanka scored 117 runs in their first 15 overs against India, 123 against Kenya and 121 against England. In doing so, the Player of the Tournament Sanath Jayasuriya and his partner Romesh Kaluwitharana changed the nature of One Day cricket and transformed perceptions of what type of scoring was possible. Against Kenya, Sri Lanka went on to make 398 for 5 from their 50 overs, a record highest team score that wasn't beaten until 2006.

Then in the final against Australia they won the toss. All five World Cup finals up to that point had been won by the team batting first. But true to their new principles, Sri Lanka chose to bowl first. Then, having put Australia in to bat, they easily chased down their total of 241 in the forty-seventh over to secure the biggest prize in the game. It was a triumph that changed the world's view of One Day cricket and how to play it.

Since then, the Sri Lankan effort to embrace unorthodoxy, seeing it as a strength rather than a weakness, and something to be promoted rather than discouraged or changed, has produced a steady flow of unique cricketers, totally unlike anything you would normally see in international cricket. The ultimate example is Muttiah Muralitharan, the single most successful bowler in the history of the game and a player who, at times almost single-handedly, carried the Sri Lankan team to some of their most outstanding achievements.

Although Sri Lanka take a different approach to most countries, it is probably England whose coaching and playing culture stands furthest away at the other end of the scale. If Sri Lanka covets the unusual, England seeks out and aims for the apotheosis of the normal.

It is fairly easy to think of genuinely unorthodox players from other Test nations – Steve Smith, Graeme Smith, Ravi Ashwin and Jasprit Bumrah, Brendon McCullum, Saeed Ajmal and Sunil Narine to name a few. With England, it is more difficult. There are some fantastic improvisers, in the style of Joe Root or Jos Buttler, but they tend to improvise from a typically orthodox base technique.

And let's be clear, there is nothing wrong with orthodoxy and technical excellence. Orthodox technique is the refined essence of past success; the empirically tested distillation of the whole of cricketing history's trial-and-error experimentation. In any sport, giving young players proven models for success in performing complex and difficult actions is a valid and valuable part of coaching. 'Technique is freedom', as the great Vaslav Nijinsky put it.

How then do we square that with the success of Sri Lanka's approach?

WHAT CRICKET CAN LEARN FROM POKER

Caspar Berry is a man who thinks differently to everybody else. The fact that it is his job to think differently makes this a good thing, but I suspect he has always thought differently to most people. Perhaps as a result of this he has had a pretty unusual life. The arc from child TV star, through professional poker player, to risk-taking guru for the likes of Google and IBM is not the sort of well-trodden path that a careers adviser might map out for you at school.

In 1989, as a teenager growing up in Newcastle, Caspar was chosen to play a lead role in a new TV show called *Byker Grove*. The show was a huge hit and launched the careers of Anthony McPartlin and Declan Donnelly (Ant and Dec). But for Caspar, this moment of early success didn't spark aspirations to an acting career: 'It really happened like this . . . it was like an epiphany . . . the finger of God came down and pointed at the director . . . and it was like the Universe said, "that is what you want to do!"'

'And so the next ten years of my life were just driven towards that . . . there is no school you can go to, to become a director, but [I was told] that Oxbridge is good – you'll get a load of money, you'll meet lots of talented people and when you screw up no one will care.'

So Caspar went to Cambridge to read Economics and direct plays. 'I was a *way* better director for my age than anything I've ever done since – and I knew exactly what I wanted to do with my life.' He directed a play in his first term and put Robert Webb and David Mitchell together, then he cast the pair of them alongside his good friend Olivia Colman in another production, and quickly established himself at the forefront of a hugely talented generation in the Cambridge drama scene. In the holidays he directed TV commercials, and in his second year wrote a screenplay that was produced by Film4.

'There was a period of my life, a five- or six-year period, when everything I touched turned to gold. I got every part I auditioned for, my scripts were bought and made into films.'

Around 1997, when he was still only 24, the first cracks started to appear in the dream. One of his films was panned by the critics – rightly in Caspar's opinion; he felt his script had been ruined by the director – and he became demotivated by the film industry. A period of depression followed.

It was in these depths that he took a trip to Las Vegas with a friend, and found himself sitting at a poker table. There followed what he described as a 'near religious experience'. He played for 42 hours non-stop and nearly missed his flight home.

'On the plane home I turned to my friend and I said, "That's what I'm going to do." He said, "What do you mean?" and I said, "I'm going to do that professionally."

'Because I'd had a conversation with a guy [at the poker table] who changed my life, I don't know his name, will never meet him again, but he explained the game in the terms that I now teach it, the concept of the calculated risk. I got it immediately, because in many ways it is just an aspect of economics made flesh.

'So that's what I did. I never got a visa, so I flew back and forth, going out to Vegas for three-month periods, and for the next few years I made my living playing poker.'

When several years later the James Bond producers were filming *Casino Royale*, Caspar was the perfect person to hire as on-set poker consultant. But this was not enough to lure him back to the film industry. Instead, he decided to apply what he had learned at the poker table to help companies understand risk and investment.

Since then he has worked with Google, IBM, Coca-Cola, McDonald's, Shell, Walmart and Nestlé, as well as a long list of financial institutions, and he is an outstanding keynote speaker with a comprehensive grasp of his area of expertise: risk. He believes that many companies and organisations are run by people who fundamentally don't understand risk.

Playing poker is, at its core, an exercise in risk-management. The aim is not to win every hand, or even to only bet on winning hands; it is to play each hand in such a way as to make sure that you are maximising your long-term returns.

Let's consider two different bets. The first has a 50 per cent chance of success, and pays you out at evens. If you win, you gain £1, if you lose then you lose £1. Clearly, over time you will break even. If you keep making this bet for long enough then you will not on average make or lose any money. To put it another way, your expected return on this bet is exactly £0.

The second bet also has a 50 per cent chance of success, and if you lose it costs you £1. But this bet pays out £10 if you win. If you make this second bet enough times, you will definitely make money. So even though you are still losing 50 per cent of these bets you will in fact make a profit of, on average, £4.50 per bet. Your success rate is the same, but your expected returns, and your long-term profits if you keep making this bet, are very different to the first bet. On any given toss of the coin, you might win with Bet 1 and lose with Bet 2, but over time Bet 2 will make money and Bet 1 won't.

In his work with financial companies, Caspar uses the strategies of poker to allow companies to examine how they handle and respond to risk and uncertainty. 'Most people, most companies, aren't willing to fail often enough. The second bet is an incredibly good bet. But how many companies are willing to commit to projects that have a fifty per cent chance of failing?

'All decisions are investment decisions. Even if you are only deciding what to do with your time, you are making a decision about how to invest your finite resources so as to produce the best outcome, and generally doing that in an environment of uncertainty and insufficient information.'

In cricket, for example, even if you are an international team and so don't operate in a marketplace, when you are selecting players you are trying to allocate the limited number of caps at your disposal in such a way as to develop the strongest pool of players for your team.

*   *   *

Let's look at three different betting options.

Bet A has a 90 per cent chance of success. If you win you make 10p, if you lose it costs you 90p.

Bet B has a 25 per cent chance of success. If you win you make £4, if you lose it costs you £1.

Bet C has a 5 per cent chance of success. If you win you make £15, if you lose it costs you £1.

Bet A has a high chance of success and breaks even. Bet C is a long shot; it pays off handsomely if it comes off, but is actually a pretty poor gamble that will lose money in the long run.

Caspar says that these two, Bet A and Bet C, typify how most of us live most of our lives. We tend to stick to ventures that have a high probability of success, even if the rewards are not particularly exciting. Then every now and again we flick into gamble mode and take on a low-odds long shot at a big prize that has very little chance of success.

We put our savings away safely in the bank, and periodically buy a lottery ticket.

In cricketing terms, it is like blocking back two overs from the opposition spinner and then trying to hoick one into the stands for six to relieve the pressure.

The only value bet here is Bet B. It fails more often than it succeeds, and the potential rewards aren't large enough to excite us into a gamble, so it is the type of option that we tend to overlook or shy away from. But, partly because of this, it is exactly the type of option that will succeed in the long run.

We can represent this pay-off between risk and reward and the impact that it has on your expected profits by plotting them on a chart. Across the bottom on the horizontal axis we can see the probability of success rising from left to right. On the vertical axis we can see the potential returns on your investment rising higher and higher as you go up the chart. We can plot the break-even threshold as a curve on this graph.

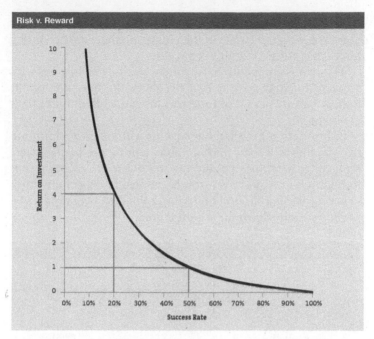

Risk v. Reward

Looking at the risk–reward curve, you can see that every point on the line represents a bet that will in the long run break even. Any point above the line represents a venture that will on average make money. The further above the line, the more money it will make. You might win on this particular occasion, or you might lose, but on average you will expect to make money.

Every point below the line will expect to lose money. Again, you might get lucky on this occasion and win, but if you make this bet often enough you will lose money eventually.

This then, is what you need for a successful strategy, be it in poker, or business, or sport: you need the probability of success and the rewards of success to place you above the curve.

Clearly, the best place to be on the chart is in the top-right corner, where a high probability of success combines with large profits. But any of the areas well above the line will do. There must be reasons why, with most strategies, it is difficult to get into and stay in those areas of the chart. In fact, most common strategies in business and sport are located in the bottom right-hand corner of the chart, and there are two strong forces that ensure that this is the case.

The first is competition. Anyone who finds themselves with a successful strategy (one that sits above the line) and profits from it for any period of time will draw the attention of their competitors.

In business, a firm that has success with a new and innovative product will soon find imitators joining the marketplace, replicating what they do and driving down prices and profits through competition. As a result, we would expect any business venture that sits profitably above the line, over time, to be pushed steadily downwards on the graph.

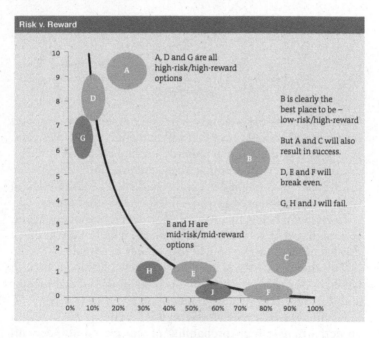

Or, let's say you are a rugby team and have developed a successful strategy at the lineout. It is different to what most teams do, and you are very successful with it for a few matches.

After that, though, teams you play will be aware of your new approach and will start to think of ways to counter it. As the match approaches they will spend time practising how to counter it. Then once one team has been effective in shutting down your new strategy they will be used as the model and their counter-strategies will be copied. As the season goes on, the rewards that you get from your innovation will decrease.

If it is a particularly brilliant innovation, you will find other teams adopting it too, and it will become the norm. At which point the rewards for you will decline further, as teams get used to applying and defending against this strategy week in, week out.

So, the further above the line you are, and the higher the rewards you are getting from your product or strategy, then the stronger the forces will be that drive those profits and rewards down.

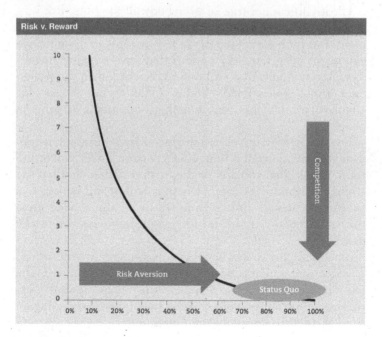

The other force that affects strategies on the graph is loss aversion. Most of us prefer projects or strategies that have a higher chance of success. It has been shown innumerable times, both in experiments and using real-life data, that we are genetically programmed to be risk averse. We will even tend to choose options that are less profitable because they are more likely to succeed.

If you offer people a choice between £900 or a 90 per cent chance of winning £1000, the vast majority of people will choose the first option. Even though the two offers have exactly the same value, people will prefer the slightly smaller sure thing to the larger prize with an element of risk to it.

Indeed, it is stronger than that. When offered £3000 or an 80 per cent chance of £4000, most people will again opt for the sure thing, even though the value of the slightly riskier option (£3200) is higher.

Clearly this is not true of everybody all the time. If it was, then casinos and bookmakers would go out of business overnight. But for the majority of us, the majority of the time, we will adopt safer, less risky options that have a higher success rate. (Interestingly, when all options are bad, then our preferences flip. People offered a certain £900 loss or a 90 per cent chance of a £1000 loss overwhelmingly opt for the 90 per cent chance.)

So competition drives you downwards on the graph whenever you are above the line. Risk aversion drives you to the right. The higher you are, or the further to the left, then the stronger these forces are. This means that the majority of sporting strategies and techniques lie in the shaded area, the 'status quo', at the bottom right-hand corner of the graph.

This being the case, whenever you innovate, whenever you produce a new approach, you are likely to have to move to the left (and hopefully, if it is a successful strategy, upwards), i.e. most genuine innovations almost inevitably carry a higher level of risk than the established methods.

'And here is the duality,' explains Caspar. 'Of course we all want our ventures to succeed, we want to turn the handle . . . and for the client to get the right advice, for the ball to hit the target, for the burger to be served without anyone getting food poisoning. But the effect of that perfectly natural instinct towards success is that we all operate in this pretty small area, which in sport you would call received wisdom, which I would call the comfort zone . . . and the visual impact of the graph is to see this enormous empty space, which is unexploited opportunity.

'ROI [Return on Investment] is measured by your distance above the curve, and so there are enormous areas of potential ROI that go unexploited.'

THE INNOVATION TRIANGLE

Caspar explains the process of breaking out of this status quo using what he calls the innovation triangle. 'If standard technique, or your comfort zone, are in the bottom right-hand corner, most successful innovations will necessitate a move up and left. This is the adoption of a new strategy (which is riskier but brings greater rewards). Then there is a movement to the right, which is honing and perfection (the success rate of the new method rises with practice and refinement) . . . and then the irony is that it is only when it has been refined that it is stolen. While it exists in a volatile state, it looks like the guy who won the poker tournament, it looks like they're just getting lucky.'

But as soon as it starts to look like a reliable, profitable venture the forces of competition are brought fully to bear on it and it starts to move downwards.

THE REVERSE SWEEP

Let's take the example of the reverse sweep. When it was first introduced, the reverse sweep was akin to a trick shot, a piece of fun or showing off that would never be seen in most Test-match situations. It would draw a gasp from the crowd, a snarl from traditionalists and a glare from the bowler. But over time,

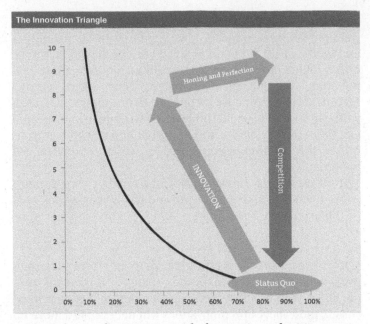

more and more batsmen started playing it as a legitimate way of targeting a largely unprotected area of the field – behind square on the offside. It was riskier than orthodox batting, but it could also be very effective, both at scoring runs and in forcing the opposition captain to move fielders from other areas to protect against it.

It was a high-risk/high-reward option. But those willing to play it had two big advantages:

1. It almost always came as a surprise to the fielding side.
2. It allowed the batsman to access the only area of the field that was poorly protected.

In the early 2000s, the dismissal rate in Tests was a wicket every 38 reverse sweeps, high compared to the wicket every 91 balls that fell when batting against spin in general. But although new and relatively risky, the rewards outweighed the risks. The shot scored at 8.9 runs an over, compared to 3 runs batting normally. It also unsettled bowlers and forced captains to move fielders.

This move formed the first part of the innovation triangle, going up and to the left: higher risks, higher rewards.

Then, over time, batsmen became better at playing the reverse sweep; through practice and refinement they were able to reduce the risks associated with it. The shot became safer and even more productive. So there was a steady increase in the number of times it was played. And as more batsmen became more proficient at it, the risk in playing it fell. For top-order batsmen in Test cricket between 2010 and 2013 the reverse sweep had an average of 122 runs per dismissal, and scored at 11.3 runs per over. No other shot against any type of bowling was anywhere near so productive. This was the second side of the triangle, honing and refining. The reverse sweep had moved towards the right-hand edge of the graph, becoming lower risk.

As it became safer and more effective, it became more attractive to far more batsmen, and was played more and more often by a larger and larger group of players.

And so, bowlers and fielders responded, learning how to counter it and reduce its effectiveness. Bowlers learned who reversed and who didn't and how to negate the shot when they anticipated it might be played. Captains developed field settings that hedged their bets, reducing the pay-off for playing the shot. This reduced the reward for playing the shot and so pushed it downwards on the graph, towards the bottom right-hand corner.

Since 2017 the reverse sweep has been played in Tests more often than at any time in the past, and has averaged 34.4 and scored at 9.2 runs per over. It has now entered the accepted range of shots for any top-order player in Test cricket, and like all the others sits either just above or just below the break-even line on the risk–reward curve depending on how well you play it. It has taken its place within the accepted canon of orthodox play on the bottom right-hand end of the risk–reward curve.

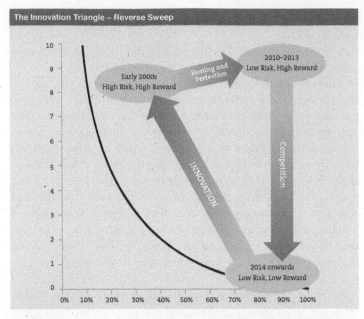

The Innovation Triangle – Reverse Sweep

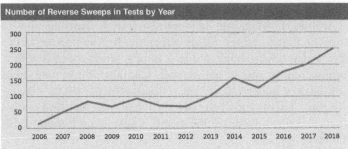

Number of Reverse Sweeps in Tests by Year

THE NEGATIVE METRIC

For Caspar, the key concept about innovation and risk taking is the idea of the negative metric. 'Whenever someone innovates in business or in life, they almost inevitably do so by accepting a negative metric that other people were unwilling to accept.'

The batsmen who started playing the reverse sweep (and the reverse hit) in Test cricket were not the players who invented the shot and first played it. Nor were they the only players of their generation who knew about the shot and could play it. The innovators were the ones who were willing to accept the negative metric that went with the shot. Initially this was the greater risk of failure, but more importantly the criticism that would follow if they got out doing it.

When Ryanair and the other budget airlines first brought low-price, low-frills air travel to the European skies they were able to do so because, unlike the major airlines, they were willing to accept that their customers might be unhappy with the service and that the number of complaints they received would probably be far higher than any regular airline would put up with. They aimed to be cheap, reliable and punctual. And that's what you got, no frills and none of the comforts and consideration that passengers had come to expect with air travel. Ryanair were successful in finding a profitable niche above the risk–reward line because they were willing to accept the public image that went with it.

Studies have shown that ice-skaters who fall more often in training are more likely to win. If they are willing to take more risks in training, ultimately it will make them better skaters. But the negative metric that they have to accept is the increased number of training accidents and the greater risk of injury that comes with it.

In many spheres of life, as with Ryanair, the negative metric is public criticism, or, in other cases, a negative impression of your competence among those that matter to your continued success or employment. The conservative instincts that buttress received wisdom are often very powerful. And this is particularly true in professional sport.

If you go against the traditional methods of success you may well be seen by many not as an innovator or pioneer, but merely as someone with suspect judgement, or someone who clearly doesn't understand the game very well. The very scrutiny and attention that professional sportsmen perform under puts pressure on them to conform.

Follow the accepted norms, 'play the percentages', and whether you win or lose you will be given credit for having tried to do the right thing. Strike out on your own, though, and if you fail you are likely to be criticised far more heavily than if you toed the line. And remember innovation almost inevitably involves greater risk.

Greater risks of failure carry a much greater chance that you will hit a losing streak. And it is sustained downturns or multiple failures that end careers.

So now it's important to consider what your ultimate goal is. Captains, players, coaches and selectors all need to keep the faith of those who have power over them. The batsman who fails playing a shot that is seen as a foolish and unnecessary risk; the captain who wins the toss and does the opposite of what everyone expects him to do; the selector who takes a punt on a player no one else rates; they all have to bear the magnified cost to their reputation if their bets don't come off.

We have mentioned already that where the theoretically optimal tactics differ from what the professionals do in practice, then the received wisdom almost always carries less risk. We are all loss averse, genetically programmed to be, and straying from the accepted path carries a twofold risk, firstly the increased failure rate of the innovation, and secondly the increased criticism and loss of standing that will accompany any failure.

It is no wonder that there are so many Tethered Cats still being tied up each night across professional sport. Any Tethered Cat you find might turn out to be one of Chesterton's Fences.

So what does this look like in other sports? As a rule of thumb, whenever there is a difference between what theory suggests is the optimal strategy and what the professionals do in practice, you will find that the professional strategy is more conservative than the statistically optimal. One of the keys to using analysis successfully to improve performance is a willingness to take risks, because the evidence-based approach is almost always riskier and more aggressive than the received wisdom.

There are any number of examples from lots of different sports, but some of the most well-documented are:

- shooting three-pointers in basketball;
- running on the fourth down in American football;
- we cover in Chapter 7 the sizeable, if counterintuitive, advantage of bowling first on flat wickets;
- we looked in detail at England's use of hitherto unseen levels of batting aggression to win a World Cup in the previous chapter. Eoin Morgan's willingness to accept the negative metric was the key to building the team that could do it.

The negative metric is where Caspar says that poker *does* differ from many areas of sport and business. And it is worth considering why.

'That is what's interesting about poker. You're not accountable to anybody. (So if you had to advise someone on how to play, and that person didn't understand what we're talking about in terms of risk, then it would be really difficult. Because you would have to advise them to do things that would increase their failure rate.) So that's the first thing, it's just us, we're not accountable to anyone.

'The second thing is that in poker . . . you *do* get to live in the long term. Pushing chips across a baize cloth becomes very meditative, and you don't have to do it for that long before you naturally start to live in the long term, because poker *allows* you to. No one's demanding to see your results.

'The third thing is that you're doing it for *your* money, and that will sharpen you. Ultimately, you realise that you have to adapt, because you understand that you are losing money if you don't. I try to make it clear that the type of decision-making you use is driven by context. But because the context for the poker player is *so* extreme – lone wolf, lots of time, your livelihood depends on it . . . when you are doing it really well . . . you get to a really unique point where you don't care about the result . . . (what matters) is just, "Did you solve the problem correctly? Did you play the hand right?"

'Context is crucial. There are areas in which people should move their lives more towards poker, and there are areas where they can't, and they shouldn't.'

Thinking like a poker player enables us to see more clearly the best way to maximise our expected returns when we have to make bets in an uncertain world. The perfectly valid question that follows though is, 'Are we willing or able to carry through on that thinking in the real world?'

UNKNOWN UNKNOWNS

When genuinely innovating, there is an additional layer of uncertainty. It is not just the success or failure that you are unsure of, it is also the level of risk you are taking. It is not a role of the dice, it is a role of something that may or may not be dice, and has an indeterminate number of sides.

Here we see why poker is such a good analogy.

Caspar says, 'The whole point about poker is that, at least in one way, there is a really clear delineation between what you can and can't control. And that is the cards that are yet to come. There are four uncertainties in poker. Number one is your opponents' hole cards. So that's things that you don't know about the current terrain. Number two is the cards that are yet to come. Number three is your opponents' actions in light of what you do. And that's actually something that early poker analysis massively underestimated, and it's something that's become fundamental to poker, your opponents' propensity to fold. And the fourth uncertainty in poker is what *you're* going to do, when you're actually faced with that decision. (You might think you'll know how you are going to react further into the hand, but you won't know for certain until you get there.)

'All of those four things will affect whether you win or lose the hand.'

The analogy Caspar uses to explain these different layers of uncertainty is of a salesman making cold calls from a list of contacts. He has been given two lists.

- He knows that the names on the first list are more likely to buy – he will make a sale roughly half the time – but that they are unlikely to spend much.
- The names on the second list are far less likely to buy anything – just 1 in 20 will be interested – but those that do will place much bigger orders than the first group, anything from 10 to 20 times as large.

The salesman knows that he will make more money in the long run by calling names from the second list. But he could also, very easily, not make a sale all day. Faced with a certain if slightly smaller profit from using the first list, or the real possibility of a long, fruitless day spent on the phone if he uses the second more profitable list, then the choice that the salesman makes will depend on his general disposition, and how he is feeling that day. We might not all come to the same conclusion faced with that choice, but this is a calculation that most of us understand.

Most real-world situations though, Caspar explains, don't involve this type of choice. They are more like a third list that the salesman is given. This list of contacts has no provenance; he knows that some of the names on the list will be interested in placing an order, but he has no experience by which to gauge how likely that is, or how big the orders might be.

This is, Caspar says, a much better representation of what real-world risk taking is like.

When genuinely innovating, there are multiple layers of uncertainty. It is not just the success or failure that you are unsure of, it is also the level of risk you are taking.

The advantage of orthodoxy is that you understand to a degree the odds of the bet you are making, and the possible pay-off. You may be selecting from the first list, or you may be selecting from the second list. But either way the list has provenance. Find a tall, athletic 17-year-old fast bowler with a good action, and you know the type of bowler he might eventually turn into. You also know that there is a chance he will succumb to injuries, or regress, or be unlucky, and never quite make it. But these are known risks and rewards. With enough experience you could give a reasonable estimate of the probability of success.

In taking a punt on the unorthodox player, the one of a kind who seems to be effective despite his physique and technique, you have far less idea what the chance of him succeeding is. Or of how effective he potentially is at the highest level. This, then, is one of the appeals of orthodoxy: it allows coaches to select using the first two lists. The question is, 'Is that the best way to discover and develop great players?'

THE ADVANTAGES OF BEING
DIFFERENT – LASITH MALINGA

One brilliant example of the advantages of doing things differently is the Sri Lankan fast bowler Lasith Malinga. If you have never seen him bowl, then it is difficult to describe him in a way that does him justice. When he bowls, his bowling arm is closer to the horizontal than the vertical throughout the delivery. The classical fast bowler's action is all vertical circles, straight lines as the batsman looks at him, and it is the precise angle and timing of these movements that batsmen have come to know, and use to anticipate the direction and speed of the delivery. Malinga, on the other hand, produces a rotational slinging motion that suddenly seems to explode violently out of a fairly conventional approach to the wicket.

This unique style has several effects on how the ball behaves and the challenges batsmen face in trying to play him.

The first and most obvious difference he creates is that batsmen find him harder to anticipate. He has similar advantages to those that left-arm bowlers possess, but to an even greater degree.

One of the advantages that left-arm bowlers have over their right-arm brethren is that batsmen find them harder to read, and so find it harder to anticipate where a delivery will land. This is because batsmen learn the anticipatory skills that make batting against fast bowling possible against predominantly right-arm bowlers. And these hard-wired skills are less effective when faced with a bowler who is left-handed.

The same effect applies when the bowler has an unorthodox delivery action. Batsmen find it harder to anticipate where the ball will pitch and so have to either initiate their movements later or adjust their shots to compensate for inaccurate initial movements. Either way, it makes the batsman look and feel rushed, and it creates more errors and false shots – the same changes that we see as delivery speed increases. If you have an unorthodox action, you are effectively quicker than you actually are. You feel quicker to the batsman than you look on the radar gun.

'Malinga, it's totally a different type of action. I don't think any other bowler in the world, I have seen at the international level, who comes even 50 per cent close to that,' Sachin Tendulkar has said in an interview with Pti Hyderabad in *The New Indian Express*.

'He's such a unique bowler you can't replicate facing him. You have to face balls from him to get used to playing him,' says Eoin Morgan.

Coupled with being difficult to line up against, Malinga has an entirely different release point. The average release position for a right-arm fast bowler is at a height of 204 centimetres and 46 centimetres to the right of middle stump as the batsman sees it. Malinga, from a similar position on the crease, lets the ball go 27 centimetres lower and 56 centimetres to the left. He actually lets the ball go on the far side of middle stump, almost as if he were bowling left-arm over the wicket. So not only are most of the cues the batsman is getting from his action misleading, but they also have to get used to looking for the ball more than half a metre away from where they would expect to see it released.

But picking up his release point is only the start of the challenges for the batsman. Spinners get sideways movement in the air from the spin they impart to the ball. This is not an option for an orthodox pace bowler because the natural mechanism of their release imparts predominantly backspin to the ball, and any small degree of sidespin they put on the ball has a negligible effect on its flight. Malinga, though, because of the extreme angle of his arm at release actually puts more sidespin than backspin on the ball, so he is able to get the ball to drift in exactly the same way that a spinner does. Particularly with the old ball, he can get it to veer sideways at high speed even when the conditions are not conducive to swing, which they now rarely are with an old white ball.

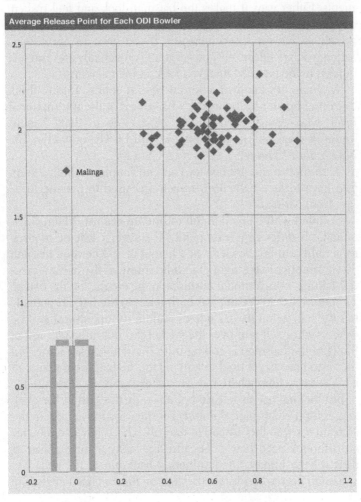

Average Release Point for Each ODI Bowler

In fact, largely because of this, Malinga has obtained far more sideways movement with the old ball in ODIs than any other bowler in the period since 2013 (when two new balls became the norm, drastically reducing the scope for reverse swing).

Degrees of Swing with Old Ball* ODIs since 2013	
	Swing angle average
S.L. Malinga	1.34
M.A. Stark	1.15
Hasan Ali	0.92
R.A.S. Lakmal	0.89
U.T. Yadav	0.83
N.L.T.C. Perera	0.80
K. Rabada	0.73
T.A. Boult	0.70
D.W. Steyn	0.70
Bhuvneshwar Kumar	0.67
Junaid Khan	0.64
Wahab Riaz	0.64
C.J. Jordan	0.64
Mohammed Shami	0.56
L.E. Plunkett	0.55
M. Morkel	0.50
B.A. Stokes	0.48
H.H. Pandya	0.46
C.R. Woakes	0.43
J.P. Faulkner	0.38
World Average	0.69

In the era of two new balls bowlers struggle to get any swing at all with the white ball after the PowerPlay overs, only 0.69 degrees on average. Malinga has averaged almost exactly twice that amount, and far more than any other bowler.

Thirdly, as well as being difficult for the batsman to line up and being able to get the ball to move sideways in the air when it won't for anyone else, there is also the fact that his deliveries fly differently to everyone else's. Spin bowlers impart topspin and pace bowlers impart backspin, getting the ball to dip and float slightly relative to a non-spinning projectile. Well, the fact that Malinga's full-pace deliveries have more sidespin on them also means that they have far less backspin. The backspin that an average international fast bowler imparts exerts an upward force on the ball equivalent to an acceleration of 3.3 ms^{-2}. That is the average, and most bowlers fall between 2.8 ms^{-2} and 3.8 ms^{-2}. For Malinga, the figure is almost half that, 1.7 ms^{-2}.

This results in one of Malinga's trademark dismissals when the batsman is bowled or LBW playing over the top of a yorker. To the batsman it looks like a low full toss, but then seems to dip on him late, passing under the toe of his bat as he frantically tries to adjust to the unexpected trajectory.

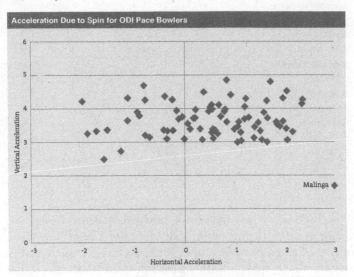

The chart shows the average acceleration that the bowler imparts to the ball due to spin and swing. You can see just how different, and how far outside the normal range of trajectory, Malinga's bowling falls. (All data is for ODI bowlers with the old ball)

On occasions when the conditions make getting the ball into suitable shape to reverse possible, Malinga has two more advantages. His unique delivery angle means that he can 'saucer' the ball through the air, causing it to land consistently on one side of the ball. On an abrasive pitch, conducive to reverse swing, this accelerates the degradation of the ball, but also crucially limits the damage to one side of the ball. Whereas conventional bowlers have to resort to cross-seam deliveries to scuff the ball, and take their chances with which side the ball lands on, Malinga gives his side an important edge in their efforts to get the ball into the necessary condition.

Then, once the ball is reversing, Malinga's extreme seam angle causes the ball to again behave differently to an orthodox bowler. Because the seam is canted over at such an angle he swings the ball not only sideways, but down. He can reverse the ball down into the pitch. This combines with his already greater levels of downward acceleration to make the ball dip sharply on the batsman.

So his deliveries are difficult to pick up, appear from an unexpected angle, appear to the batsman to swerve and dip, and when swing is available swing vertically as well as horizontally. And that isn't all. He has a final point of difference due to his unusual release angle. He is the most accurate and effective bowler of yorkers the game has ever seen.

Most Yorkers Bowled in ODIs	
	Yorkers
S. L. Malinga	607
M. A. Starc	259
K. M. D. N. Kulasekar	218
J. O. Holder	200
T. A. Boult	196
T. G. Southee	191
D. J. Bravo	171
Mohammed Shami	152
C. R. Woakes	147
N. L. T. C. Perera	140

IF YOU ARE OUTGUNNED, YOU ARE WISE
TO FIND A DIFFERENT WAY TO COMPETE

The musicians of the Sri Lankan stadium bands have the natural, inbuilt lack of orthodoxy of the autodidact. And they are mirrored on the field by players who have similarly retained the idiosyncrasies of the self-taught. The solutions they found for themselves do not always mimic the answers outlined in the coaching manual, but the game is the better and Sri Lankan cricket stronger for that fact.

No one is criticising orthodoxy. There is without doubt a huge amount of distilled wisdom in orthodox technique. And it works. For every successful unorthodox player there are a string of great players with classical techniques – Tendulkar, Kohli, Williamson, Root, Steyn, Rabada, Hazlewood. All we are trying to do here is point out the strengths and weaknesses of adhering to orthodoxy, and the possible advantages of sometimes embracing the extraordinary.

As training programmes improve around the world, and become ever better at giving young players secure basics and accepted models of success, the other thing worthy of consideration is this: *the comparative advantage of being unorthodox increases as the proportion of orthodox players rises.*

The more orthodox players there are, the bigger the advantage there is in being unorthodox. The more that players conform to an established model, the more similar they are, and therefore the more effective the unconscious programming of their opponents learned anticipation becomes. So the greater the extent to which orthodoxy becomes the norm, the better opponents' anticipation of their actions becomes, and therefore the greater the premium becomes on being different, playing in a way that negates those hardwired anticipatory skills.

God is on the side of the big battalions . . . but only if you fight them head on.

Zen and the Art of Fast Bowling

They say that before you have studied Zen, a mountain is just a mountain.

Then, as you study and gain greater insight, you slowly come to realise that it is more subtle and complex than that. A mountain is no longer just a mountain to you.

When you finally – after years or decades of study – achieve enlightenment, you discover that a mountain ... is just a mountain.

The path to mastery is the same in many crafts. It is the same for the monk, the teacher, the writer or the bowler. It is the path from simplicity, through complexity, to simplicity.

The beginner uses simple, basic techniques. He has no choice. They are all he knows and all he can cope with. As he learns and improves, he initially gains greater fluency in these core movements. Then, as he grows more adept, he embraces more and more technical complexity and masters a greater variety of skills and methods. He studies more deeply the intricacies of his art, and experiments with a wider and wider range of ideas.

But then the process reverses itself. After thousands of hours of immersion in the details and subtleties, and near endless refinements, slowly – over time – he comes to understand what works best for him and what doesn't. The range and complexity of the ideas on which he regularly relies starts to shrink.

The ultimate expression of this is the master craftsman, for whom true mastery of his art involves a return to simplicity, to a pared-down palette that he now wields to sublime effect. But it is a simplicity born of understanding his true form, and utterly different from the place where he started.

As the famous American poet and physician Oliver Wendell Holmes Sr said, 'For the simplicity on this side of complexity, I wouldn't give you a fig. But for the simplicity on the other side of complexity, for that I would give you anything I have.'

And moving from simplicity through complexity to simplicity, the path that leads from acolyte through adept to master is a good analogy for how we should seek to analyse the internal workings of cricket. Start with a simple question, then do your research, admitting as much detail and complexity as necessary, in order to arrive, in the end, at a simple answer to a simple question.

This then is the path that will be the substance and shape of this chapter. Indeed, many of the chapters that follow will describe a similar arc, from simple question through complexity and nuance to a simple conclusion. We take the time to describe it now because we suspect that at some point in reading this you are going to think, *You're making a simple game very complicated here!* Don't worry. We will always finish with simplicity. Cricket is a simple game, but one with endless subtleties that matter. We are allowed to take it apart to see how it works. Just so long as we can put it back together again.

WHAT IS THE BEST LENGTH FOR
PACE BOWLERS TO BOWL?

In England and other seam-friendly countries, there is a perennial talking point that periodically returns to the national cricket conversation: why don't fast bowlers pitch the ball up more?

Indeed, at times it seems to be an article of faith in certain corners of the commentariat that bowlers should, and they don't, and *no one knows why* (shrug emoji). An early version of this chapter was an article we wrote following the first Test of the 2018 England v. Pakistan series played at Lord's, when plenty was written and said about England again bowling too short.

England had batted first, and the admirable Pakistan pace attack took full advantage of helpful conditions to cut through the home team's batting line-up in just 58 overs. 'England, meanwhile, were shabby ... their bowlers did not succeed going full as Pakistan had,' reported Andrew Miller for CricInfo in a piece entitled 'Another England collapse opens door for Pakistan's nine-wicket rout'.

In reply, the England bowlers led by James Anderson and Stuart Broad had 23 overs at Pakistan that evening but could only manage to take one wicket. The second morning was no better for the home team's bowlers and the visitors declared with a first innings lead of 180 and went on to win by nine wickets.

There was the usual criticism of England's lengths, compared unfavourably to those of Pakistan (although ironically the data shows very little difference between the two).

It is both an easy and a safe charge to level at a team after the fact, when you know the results back you up. And is therefore a go-to comment for those with airtime or column inches to fill, made safe in the knowledge that its accuracy will not be challenged.

But we have a great deal of data available to us. With ball tracking, every ball bowled in a Test match becomes an independent experiment into how the game works. And we now have the results of over half a million such experiments.

So, it should be possible for us to see who is correct: the commentators who urge the bowlers to pitch it up, or the bowlers who stubbornly refuse to do so. Let's pull the game apart, use the wealth of data we have available to find out how it works, and progress from there to some basic principles we can agree on. As we have said, we are allowed to take it apart so long as we can put it back together. Through complexity to simplicity.

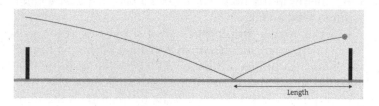

85

To start with, what do we mean by length? For our purposes, the *length* of a ball is the distance from the batsman's stumps to the point where the ball bounces (measured in a line perpendicular to the crease). In Test cricket, the average length is 7 metres (give or take a few centimetres), and the vast majority of balls land between 2 metres and 10 metres.

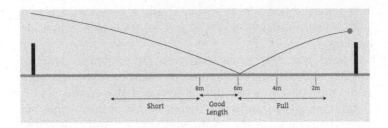

The length of a ball has two main effects. Firstly, it dictates the height that the ball will arrive at the batsman, and secondly, it determines the amount of time he has to react after it bounces. Each of these has an impact on the danger that the ball poses to him and the opportunities that it presents.

A delivery from an average fast bowler comes off the pitch at about 32 metres/second. The fastest recorded human reaction to a visual stimulus is 120 milliseconds (most people struggle to beat 200 milliseconds, even with training), although there is some evidence that actions already underway can be refined in a slightly shorter period of time than that.

It is safe to assume that top-order Test batsmen are in the 1 per cent who can get close to the lower end of that range (120–200 milliseconds). This means that the ball will travel roughly 4 to 5 metres in the time that it takes a batsman to react and adjust to what he sees.

Determining the path of the ball after pitching requires at least a metre or so of flight (small deviations of about 1 degree are enough to induce a miss or an edge). So anything that pitches within 5 to 6 metres of the batsman doesn't leave him enough time to adjust his shot. If the batsman is on the front foot, his interception point is around 2 metres away from the stumps, so this puts the minimum length at which the batsman can start to react at about 8 metres.

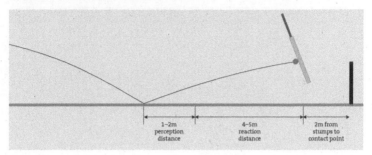

| 1–2m perception distance | 4–5m reaction distance | 2m from stumps to contact point |

And we see exactly this in the performance figures. In Test cricket, balls pitching in the 6–8-metre zone average 22.6 against top-order batsmen (that is they take a wicket for every 22.6 runs they concede), whereas in the 8–9-metre zone wickets are nearly twice as expensive, averaging 40.1 runs per wicket.

This is the main reason that a traditional 'good' length for a quick bowler is the area roughly 6–8 metres from the stumps. It is the length for an 80–85 mph bowler that gives the ball the most room to deviate and beat the bat, without giving the batsman time to adjust to that deviation.

Averages and economy rates

Throughout the book we will be using a variety of indices to measure the effectiveness of different strategies, and different types of player. Most are simple and almost as old as the game itself.

AVERAGE is simply the number of runs scored per wicket. If we say that good-length balls *average* 22, then it means that typically 22 runs will be scored off that type of ball for every wicket that falls.

ECONOMY RATE is the number of runs scored off each over. An *economy rate of* 4.2 means that each over costs the fielding side 4.2 runs.

A bowler's *STRIKE RATE* is the number of balls per wicket taken.

Lengths and their Characteristics

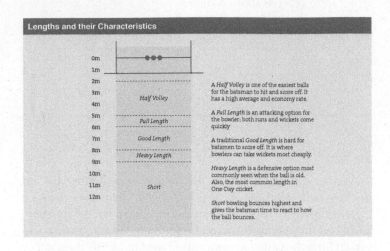

A *Half Volley* is one of the easiest balls for the batsman to hit and score off. It has a high average and economy rate.

A *Full Length* is an attacking option for the bowler; both runs and wickets come quickly

A traditional *Good Length* is hard for batsmen to score off. It is where bowlers can take wickets most cheaply.

Heavy Length is a defensive option most commonly seen when the ball is old. Also, the most common length in One-Day cricket.

Short bowling bounces highest and gives the batsman time to react to how the ball bounces.

Averages by Length

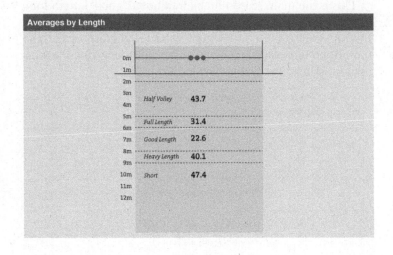

Outcomes for Different Lengths in All Tests		% Balls bowled	Average	Economy Rate	Strike Rate
Half-Volley	Under 5m	10%	43.7	5.5	48
Full length	5–6m	13%	31.4	4.0	48
Good length	6–8m	43%	22.6	2.0	67
Back of a length	8–9m	15%	40.1	3.0	81
Short	Over 9m	7%	47.4	4.3	66

Aware of the danger these balls pose, batsmen generally avoid attacking deliveries of this length. The harder you swing the bat, the smaller the margin for error, so playing an attacking shot significantly increases the chances of edging or missing the ball. They will, for the most part, leave or defend good-length balls and wait for a ball that is safer to attack.

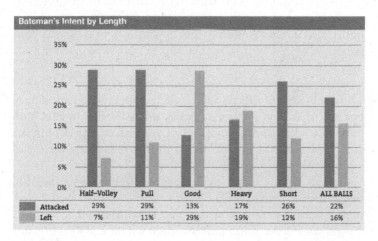

Batsman's Intent by Length	Half-Volley	Full	Good	Heavy	Short	ALL BALLS
Attacked	29%	29%	13%	17%	26%	22%
Left	7%	11%	29%	19%	12%	16%

Clearly, we are making some hefty generalisations here, but it is still a useful exercise in understanding the basic principles involved. For example, length is only one factor – a half-volley on the stumps averages 25 in Tests, one outside off stump averages over 72. Later in the chapter, we will try to unpick the complex interdependence of line and length. For now, let's treat our different lengths as homogenous blocks.

In general, the evidence is clear. Averaged across a whole match there can be no dispute over the optimum length to bowl. Around 6–8 metres from the stumps, a traditional 'good length', costs fewer runs per wicket than any other length. There are other lengths that take wickets more often, but this is more than compensated for by the much higher run rates from those lengths. In England, a top-order wicket costs you a smidge over 24 runs on a good length. Move a metre fuller, and those wickets now cost you 30 runs apiece, raising the opposition's expected total by 20 per cent.

The arithmetic is simple enough then for any team with the accuracy and the patience to make use of it. Hit this length (6–8 metres) as often as you can and you will bowl the opposition out as cheaply as possible. In most situations the fielding team will happily spend 20 more overs in the field if it means bowling the opposition out for 40 runs fewer.

LORD OF LORD'S

The apotheosis of this type of bowler is one of the greatest pace bowlers of all. In his three matches at Lord's, Glenn McGrath took 26 wickets at an average of 11.5. In all 62 per cent of the balls he bowled at Lord's landed in that 6–8-metre area, and virtually nothing was fuller than that.

Overall, for the matches in his career that we have data for, he hit a good length with 58 per cent of the balls he bowled, higher than any other bowler in the Hawk-Eye era.

And we see the same pattern when we look at Test bowlers who are playing now. Of the bowlers who have delivered over 1000 balls since the start of 2016, the four bowlers with the highest 6–8-m length percentage have the four lowest bowling averages.

One interesting aspect of these four bowlers is that, although we think of them as 'pitch it up' bowlers, Mohammad Abbas, Vernon Philander and Bhuvneshwar Kumar actually have the three lowest percentages of balls bowled fuller than 5 metres. They don't bowl half-volleys, they bang out length.

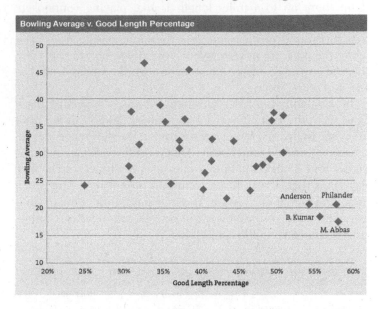

SO WHY EVER PITCH IT UP?

Why then do you hear ex-players and commentators urging the bowlers to pitch it up – bowl a fuller length landing closer to the batsman?

Well, what they understand is that not all periods of a match are equal. There are times when the conditions are in the bowler's favour, when taking wickets is easier and cheaper. At the start of the innings when the ball is new, for example. In particular, it is the case on the first morning of the match when the pitch is often at its most helpful to the bowlers. 'You need to take advantage of these conditions,' runs the argument, 'don't worry about conceding runs, bowl to take wickets. Capitalise fully on the conditions NOW while they are in your favour.' (There is an extreme strand of thinking that says 'fuller is better regardless – all day, in all conditions'. There is little or no evidence for this argument. On average, across most conditions, a good length is the *best* length.)

Going that metre or so fuller accelerates the game: you get both more wickets and more runs. So for the bowler, throwing it up there on to a fuller length is like playing your joker. Rewards and penalties are doubled. You are backing yourself to win this round of the game and therefore raising the stakes while the odds are in your favour. And if you had to play your joker at any point during a match, you would probably do it at the start of the innings.

In England, top-order batsmen average 33 against pace bowlers in the first 30 overs of an innings, and 39 in the next 50 overs. In the first innings of the match the difference is even greater, 32 and 40 respectively. That is quite a difference; wickets become 25 per cent more expensive after lunch on the first day. This then seems like a sound argument for being more attacking in that first session. You may pay a little more in runs per wicket, but you will take your wickets much faster, capitalising on the favourable conditions.

Bowling Averages in English Tests		Overs 1–30	Overs 30+
Half-Volley	Under 5m	48.1	55.0
Full length	5–6m	28.8	34.4
Good length	6–8m	24.5	27.9
Back of a length	8–9m	38.1	62.9
Short	Over 9m	53.7	67.5

There is also an argument in favour of patience. We need to make sure that the price we are paying for our wickets on a full length before lunch (on special offer though they are) is better than the price we will pay after lunch on a good length. And in fact, there is little difference between the two.

The full ball before lunch averages 28.8, the good length ball after lunch averages 27.9. As such a small difference is not enough to distinguish between the two, neither strategy is demonstrably superior across the board. So we need to look more closely at different conditions. To do this we need to understand how different lengths affect the batsman, his options and his likely success in different circumstances.

WHAT ARE THE KEY DIFFERENCES BETWEEN A FULL LENGTH AND A GOOD LENGTH?

Looking at the physics of the ball's flight through the air and impact on the ground offers some insights into the key differences between those two types of delivery.

- Firstly, it is common sense that a fuller ball will swing further. It is in the air for longer, and therefore has more time to deviate. And you see exactly this in the data: the fuller the length the larger the average deviation in the air. (The causality doesn't all run one way in this relationship, but the gradient of the graph suggests that we can accept the above statement.)
- Secondly, fuller balls deviate less off the wicket. That is, they hit the ground with a smaller vertical component to their velocity, and so are less likely to deviate off the pitch, and do so to a lesser degree. A ball banged into a hard length (8 metres) hits the ground 30 per cent harder than a half-volley (3 metres) and deviates on average about 15 per cent more. This is then exaggerated by the fact that any deviation on pitching will have a greater effect the further the ball travels afterwards.

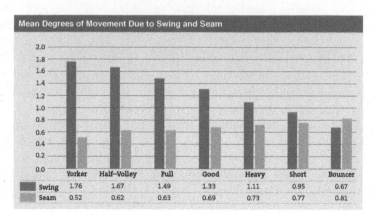

Mean Degrees of Movement Due to Swing and Seam

	Yorker	Half–Volley	Full	Good	Heavy	Short	Bouncer
Swing	1.76	1.67	1.49	1.33	1.11	0.95	0.67
Seam	0.52	0.62	0.63	0.69	0.73	0.77	0.81

- Thirdly, fuller lengths bring the stumps into play more. On most English pitches, a ball landing in the 6–7-metre range will either hit the top of the stumps or bounce just over them. Balls fuller than that are unlikely to bounce higher than the stumps, so full balls are over twice as likely to hit the stumps as length balls.
- Lastly, the batsman plays the different lengths in different ways. This turns out to be a key difference, to which we will return.

Let's examine these points further.

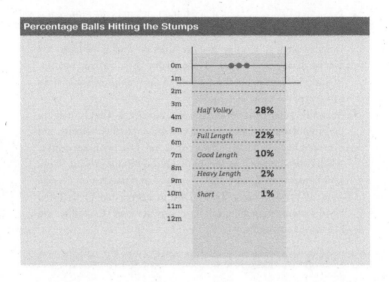

Percentage Balls Hitting the Stumps

Half Volley	28%
Full Length	22%
Good Length	10%
Heavy Length	2%
Short	1%

Firstly, what effect does swing have on our length equation?

If the ball swings less than 1.5 degrees then good length still beats full length (so McGrath, not a big swinger of the ball, was pursuing exactly the right approach for his style of bowling).

Even in England with the Dukes ball, over two-thirds of balls bowled swing less than 1.5 degrees, so this is the default situation. Once the ball is moving extravagantly, though, as you can see, the fuller length has a better record not only in strike rate, but also in average.

Bowling Average by Degree of Swing						
		≤0.75	0.75–1.50	1.50–2.25	2.25–3.00	>3.00
Half-Volley	Under 5m	56.4	54.9	36.1	4.3	61.1
Full	5–6m	33.7	47.5	19.6	20.9	29.3
Good	6–8m	25.7	25.0	26.3	24.0	34.0
Heavy	8–9m	48.0	61.8	40.3	31.3	35.5
All BALLS		43%	25%	13%	10%	9%

There is an added complication for swing bowlers, though. Because of the unpredictable nature of their art they find it harder to hold a consistent line. They are more likely to let the ball slide on to the batsman's pads, or to give him width outside the off stump, than a bowler who doesn't swing it. Length then becomes their only defence against being hit. (As we shall see later, a good length offers more margin for error in your line than a full length does.) So, the swing bowler is more incentivised to pitch the ball up, but also more dependent on not doing so to maintain control of the scoring rate.

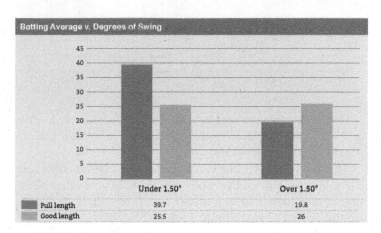

	Under 1.50°	Over 1.50°
Full length	39.7	19.8
Good length	25.5	26

Next, let's take a look at movement off the pitch.

Most wickets in Test cricket (nearly 70 per cent) occur when the batsman edges or misses the ball. As a rule of thumb, one edge in seven will produce a wicket. The biggest predictor of whether a ball will be missed, edged or hit successfully is the degree to which it seams (deviates sideways on bouncing).

We have heard bowlers counter the 'pitch it up a bit' advice by saying that they bowl a good length because 'it's the length the batsman nicks'. There is some truth in this. Whether he is attacking, defending or trying to rotate the strike, the batsman is more likely to edge or miss a good-length ball than one on a full length.

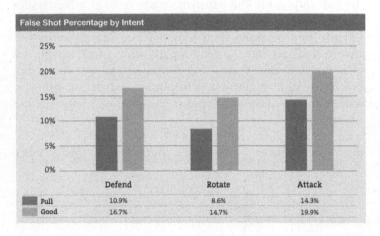

False Shot Percentage by Intent			
	Defend	Rotate	Attack
Full	10.9%	8.6%	14.3%
Good	16.7%	14.7%	19.9%

However, as we saw earlier, a batsman is more likely to leave and less likely to attack good-length balls. This means that the overall figures are less clear cut.

This then is why fuller length balls have a better strike rate. They induce more edges and, although they generate fewer misses, the balls that *are* missed are more likely to hit the stumps and so produce more wickets.

If these distances sound large – after all, a metre sounds like a big target to hit, *surely they don't miss that very often*

– it is worth remembering that these areas are effectively much smaller due to the angle at which the ball lands. The difference in release angle from a ball that will land 6 metres away from the stumps and one that will land 5 metres away is about 0.8 degrees. This is the same angular difference as between the top and bottom of the bullseye for a darts player. And darts players don't have to launch their projectile at 85 mph.

Try it. Mark out two lines a metre apart on a fullish length and see how many balls you can land between the two. And remember that the faster you bowl, the smaller the target becomes, because the flatter trajectory of the ball makes the target effectively 25 per cent smaller at 85 mph than it is at a club bowler's 65 mph. Pace and accuracy are not mutually exclusive, but for a number of reasons each makes the other considerably harder to achieve. Even for the most skilful bowlers, the levers they have at their disposal to adjust things such as length are not as finely tuned as they might wish. Therefore we aren't talking about putting every ball into any of these areas: it probably wouldn't be possible and, anyway, variation is a valuable part of the bowler's armoury. We are merely looking at the relative merits of moving some of the balls bowled from one length to another.

LINE AND LENGTH

We have so far been guilty of ignoring an equally important aspect of bowling accuracy, and that is the ball's *line*. (For our purposes we will consider the line to be the horizontal position that the ball passes the stumps, as for various reasons this is the most important aspect after length in determining how the ball is played by the batsman and the threat that it poses to him.)

Take a look at the chart below of 'Economy Rate' broken down by line and height as the ball passes the stumps. The figure in each little square gives you the runs per over scored from balls in this area. The lighter areas are the balls the batsman finds it easier to score off, and they form three main areas: balls on the batsman's pads, half-volleys outside off stump, and cut balls – short and wide.

Economy Rate – First 30 Overs

	Wide			Offside				Channel				Stumps				Legside	
1.5m	2.5	3.1	3.7	3.4	3.0	2.4	2.9	3.4	3.0	2.7	1.9	1.8	2.0	1.8	1.7	1.4	1.2
	2.6	2.7	3.7	4.3	4.0	3.5	3.6	3.7	3.4	2.5	2.1	2.3	2.4	2.4	2.4	2.0	1.9
	3.4	3.4	4.0	4.9	4.9	4.0	4.0	3.5	3.3	2.8			2.7	2.9	2.7	2.6	2.6
	4.3	4.3	4.8	5.3	5.1	4.8	4.1	3.9	3.5	3.1			3.2	3.4	3.0	3.0	
	5.1	5.9	5.8	5.9	5.6	5.1	4.6	3.9	3.5	3.0			3.5	4.0	3.5	2.9	
	5.6	6.3	6.5	5.9	5.9	5.4	4.8	3.9	3.2	2.7						3.8	3.3
	5.5	5.8	5.8	5.6	5.3	5.0	4.2	3.4	2.7	2.3				3.1	3.9	3.8	3.5
1m	4.0	4.4	4.7	4.6	4.5	4.1	3.6	2.9	2.3	1.9	1.6			3.0	3.9	3.7	3.2
	2.8	3.2	3.7	3.6	3.5	3.2	2.9	2.4	1.9	1.6	1.3	1.5		2.5	3.0	3.7	3.1
	1.9	2.2	2.6	2.6	2.6	2.5	2.3	2.0	1.7	1.4			3.0	3.9	5.8	3.3	
	1.3	1.6	1.9	1.9	2.0	2.0	2.0						3.0	4.0	3.9	3.6	
	1.2	1.4	1.8	1.9	2.1	2.3	2.3	2.3	2.0	1.7	1.6			3.8	4.9	4.6	4.3
0.5m	1.6	1.9	2.4	2.7	2.8	3.1	3.2	3.0	2.7	2.4		3.5	4.1	4.3	5.1	5.4	5.2
	2.4	2.8	3.4	3.9	4.2	4.5	4.4	4.1	3.6	3.3	3.1	3.5	4.0	6.2	6.2	6.3	5.9
	2.9	3.5	4.6	5.3	5.6	5.8	5.6	5.2	4.6	4.2	4.0	4.3	4.9	6.0	6.8	6.8	6.5
	2.6	3.6	5.0	5.7	6.3	6.5	6.2	5.7	5.0	4.3	3.9	4.1	4.7	5.8	6.9	6.7	6.3
	1.8	3.3	4.6	5.4	5.4	5.7	5.1	5.0	4.1	3.6	2.8	2.8	3.3	4.6	5.7	6.4	5.9
	1.9	3.4	4.3	4.3	4.3	4.4	4.4	3.9	3.4	2.9	2.7	2.5	2.8	4.1	5.2	5.8	5.4
0m	2.5	4.5	7.0	6.1	6.3	7.0	6.4	5.0	4.1	3.8	3.6	3.6	4.3	5.9	6.9	5.8	5.8

Economy Rate – First 30 Overs

	Wide			Offside				Channel				Stumps				Legside	
0m	3.1	6.1	8.8	9.5	10.2	11.7	10.0	6.5	5.2	5.4	4.8	6.0	6.1	6.7	7.1	8.2	7.4
	2.7	4.5	7.8	7.1	8.6	8.4	7.8	5.8	5.0	4.7	5.0	4.6	5.0	6.2	7.7	7.9	7.0
1m	1.0	2.6	3.3	4.0	3.3	3.8	3.6	4.2	3.5	3.2	2.7	2.7	3.1	4.8	6.0	5.9	5.9
	2.4	2.7	3.8	3.2	3.4	2.9	3.2	2.9	3.0	1.8	1.2	1.9	2.3	3.0	3.9	5.4	4.4
2m	2.4	3.7	4.5	4.9	4.7	5.0	4.4	4.3	3.3	2.4	1.6	2.0	2.1	3.5	4.4	5.0	4.9
	2.7	4.3	6.0	6.3	6.5	6.6	6.1	5.7	4.9	4.3	3.6	2.9	3.7	5.0	6.4	6.3	6.1
3m	3.3	4.6	6.5	7.8	8.2	8.2	7.5	7.0	6.5	5.9	5.4	4.8	5.3	6.5	7.3	6.6	6.1
	3.5	4.7	6.3	7.5	8.3	8.5	8.1	7.5	6.9	6.3	6.1	5.9	6.3	7.0	8.0	6.6	6.1
4m	3.7	4.4	6.0	6.8	7.4	7.8	7.8	7.1	6.3	5.8	5.5	5.9	6.2	7.3	8.0	6.8	6.4
	3.4	4.0	5.1	5.8	6.3	6.7	6.7	6.0	5.2	4.6	4.5	5.2	5.8	6.8	7.8	6.9	6.5
5m	2.3	2.8	3.8	4.2	4.7	5.0	5.0	4.6	4.0	3.6	3.4	4.1	4.7	6.0	7.0	6.5	6.1
	1.7	1.5	2.1	2.7	3.0	3.2	3.4	3.3	2.9	2.6	2.4	2.8	3.5	4.8	5.9	5.9	5.7
6m	0.7	0.9	1.2	1.5	1.7	2.0	2.1	2.2	2.1	1.9	1.7	1.9	2.5	3.7	4.7	5.2	4.9
	0.7	0.8	1.0	1.1	1.1	1.3	1.5	1.6	1.5	1.4	1.3	1.5	1.9	3.0	3.9	4.2	4.0
7m	1.0	1.0	1.1	1.2	1.2	1.3	1.4	1.4	1.4	1.2	1.1	1.3	1.8	2.7	3.4	3.6	3.3
	1.4	1.7	1.8	1.9	1.8	1.9	1.8	1.7	1.5	1.2	1.1	1.3	1.8	2.7	3.5	3.4	3.1
8m	2.4	2.8	3.3	3.2	3.1	2.9	2.6	2.2	1.8	1.4	1.2	1.5	1.9	2.9	3.7	3.5	3.2
	3.6	4.3	5.1	5.1	4.8	4.2	3.5	2.8	2.2	1.7	1.4	1.6	2.2	3.1	4.1	4.1	3.6
9m	5.2	5.9	6.5	6.4	6.3	5.6	4.6	3.5	2.8	2.2	1.8	2.0	2.3	3.3	4.3	4.3	3.9
	6.3	7.0	7.3	6.8	6.8	6.3	5.4	4.2	3.3	2.6	2.3	2.3	3.0	3.9	4.7	4.4	3.7
10m	6.5	7.3	6.9	6.4	6.4	6.2	5.4	4.5	3.5	3.0	2.7	2.7	3.0	3.9	4.4	3.7	3.1
	4.3	4.5	4.9	4.8	4.8	4.5	4.3	3.9	3.4	2.9	2.6	2.5	2.7	3.0	3.2	2.7	2.4
11m	3.4	3.4	3.9	4.5	4.1	3.5	3.6	3.8	3.3	2.8	2.5	2.4	2.4	2.6	2.8	2.5	2.2

(Row groupings at left: Half-Volley, Full, Good Length, Heavy, Short)

The second chart gives the same information broken down by the length the ball pitches and the line that it passes the stumps. Again, you can see light areas where the batsman can attack, and dark areas where he either defends or leaves. These charts will make sense to anyone who understands cricket (once they've got their head around them). But the next charts showing the bowling average of balls by area are a little more surprising.

Average	Wide				Offside			Channel				Stumps				Legside	
	36	33	22	54	25	17	23	27	28	16	17	11	19	30	23	18	14
	28	16	18	32	21	23	16	23	21	21	16	17	23	44	37	22	24
	16	15	16	37	36	28	26	19	20	19	19			36	32	25	25
1.5m	17	19	24	47	40	36	24	25	20	19	19				38	30	28
	33	40	55	64	43	33	25	23	23	20	22			41	51	38	40
	57	86	70	65	47	35	26	22	20	22	23			39	49		42
	67	67	62	58	48	39	28	21	18	19	24			46	60	50	41
	45	67	61	53	49	44	34	25	19	17	19	26			62	68	45
	52	68	69	52	46	41	32	23	18	16	18	26	45	74	139	83	64
1m	67	68	61	53	49	39	29	21	17	16	18	28	50	102	167	127	62
	49	43	44	48	40	32	23	20	17	18	19	28	60	101	111	79	74
	29	28	32	39	37	32	27	23	22	23	24	10	13	33		72	74
	35	32	35	36	35	38	34	30	29	31	34	12	14	17	14	76	75
0.5m	39	42	38	37	40	49	50	47	41	49	51		16	17	17	95	99
	36	49	52	43	44	55	69	64	68	69	105	22		21	78	82	102
	26	47	56	52	50	68	92	104	96	129	134	20	22	22	47	97	82
	86	219	303	129	62	92	110	99	81	69	68	8	11	14	45	125	127
	46	105	136	84	69	89	308	159	80	42	38	6	7	15	21	233	244
0m	19	61	85	84	96	158	164	155	63	34	26	8		20	30	94	94

Batting Average – First 30 Overs

Again, you can see light areas where batsmen pile up the runs with relatively little risk, and dark areas where the bowlers take their wickets at bargain basement prices.

Here you can see why hitting a good length is more forgiving in terms of line than bowling fuller. The area where wickets cost 20 or less is pretty big on a good length, well over half a metre wide. Whereas up in the 5–6-metre zone it is largely confined to the width of the stumps. To make that fuller length pay off you must bring the stumps into play. Not just bowl fuller, but also straighter and more accurately.

Batting Average – First 30 Overs																
		Wide			Offside				Channel				Stumps				Legside	
Half-Volley	0m				139	81	248				172	59	25	40	42	20	77	174
	1m				134	176	228			179	63	48	23	29	28	29	176	168
									146	49	31		7	9	13	13		
	2m				90	124	131		169	94	31	21	4	6	8	9		
				74	43	38	82	175	82	55	43	37	6	6	9	11		
	3m	100	107	77	42	34	56	91	94	70	67	80	13	13	16	19	112	117
		24	41	50	53	44	44	70	78	86	83	128	26	27	26	23	73	63
Full	4m	24	33	62	58	47	55	70	80	74	86	125	51	40	29	26	75	70
		27	32	41	42	45	52	61	61	56	70	96	44	38	32	28	90	117
	5m	32	29	25	32	39	46	48	44	47	53	64	29	29	30	29	122	145
		30	27	27	26	34	41	36	35	35	41	45	21	23	24	23	75	81
	6m	37	34	28	32	32	33	31	26	25	29	33	16	17	20	19	62	64
Good Length		81	36	41	39	33	30	22	20	19	21	23	12	14	19	21	70	67
	7m	29	31	30	52	35	26	19	16	15	15	15	10	13	20	25	74	74
		39	38	50	57	42	30	21	16	14	13	15	10	14	23	29	74	63
	8m	54	78	60	53	44	35	24	19	15	15	16	13	17	27	38	77	67
Heavy		52	79	85	56	45	37	29	23	20	18	18	18	22	32	45	86	90
	9m	48	71	80	68	50	42	36	29	25	22	20	22	28	40	56	89	79
		58	69	86	73	58	56	46	37	30	28	23	25	32	44	68	76	94
Short	10m	58	81	84	58	62	64	54	40	34	33	36	32	40	59	101	69	47
		51	67	53	52	54	60	46	37	31	36	36	37	33	56	83	51	32
	11m	34	31	28	42	39	39	33	38	36	30	29	27	33	41	47	32	30
		33	21	23	35	34	26	31	40	36	30	22	24	31	40	35	32	29

The converse is, of course, true, which is why the batsman's strengths and weaknesses need to be taken into account, along with how the bowler is trying to dismiss him. If the bowler is trying to get the batsman to nick-off then he may prefer the greater margin of error that a good length gives him, for example.

SO, HIT A GOOD LENGTH WITH THE NEW BALL OR PITCH IT UP? WHO IS RIGHT?

In summary:

Full (5–6 metres) gives the ball more time to swing, induces more attacking shots, brings the stumps into play more, generally has a lower strike rate (balls per wicket), but requires more accuracy in terms of line.

Good (6–8 metres) produces more seam movement, gives the ball more time to deviate, generally has the lowest average (runs per wicket) and economy rate (runs per over), and is more forgiving of line.

So there you have the basic facts from which you can draw your own conclusions on the matter. For our part, we would just say that there seems to be a reasonable amount of truth and good sense on both sides of the argument, and more doubt than the more entrenched prognosticators allow.

There are many moving parts in cricket, interconnected in a way that is at least partially opaque. To find your way to the truth, you have to be admitting of nuance. As in many areas of cricket there are strong arguments running in both directions, so it is not sufficient to repeat your own opinions louder and more clearly. To solve the problem, you must accept the strength of the opposing viewpoint and argue away its force.

Going fuller in favourable conditions is one answer, one very valid tactic. But it seems clear that it is not the only possible approach, nor is it demonstrably more effective than other alternatives except under certain conditions.

If that answer is too fence-straddled for your tastes, then we will come down far enough to say that we think the evidence justifies the following approach:

1. If you are not a swing bowler then do as the master did. McGrath's 560 wickets at 21 and all the evidence above suggest he wasn't wrong.
2. On the other hand, if swing is part of your arsenal, then you have a slightly subtler calculus.
   a. If the ball is swinging big, pitch it up.

    b. If it is not swinging but it's seaming around, then either strategy is valid, so long as you think that this seam movement is going to fade.

    c. But, if the pitch is likely to offer help throughout the innings, then you are better off being patient and holding length.

    d. Finally, if there is little sideways movement in the air or off the pitch, then hold a good length . . . and good luck.

3. Adjust according to the individual batsman and his weaknesses.

There is a rule of thumb in analysing sport: where the received wisdom differs from the mathematically most efficient strategy, then generally what the maths suggests is riskier and more aggressive than what the pros do in practice. The stats say you should shoot 3-pointers, run the ball on a fourth down, bowl first on a flat Test-match pitch, and attack the new ball in One Day Internationals (ODIs). All of these feel like gambles, though. And so they have traditionally been seen as cocky, over-aggressive or foolish.

We are all naturally risk averse – it is hardwired into us for good evolutionary reasons – but those instincts work against us when evaluating even fairly simple strategies in many sporting situations. You will miss more of those 3-pointers, you will fail more often than if you take the easier shots. So you choose the more conservative strategy. Stats, on the other hand, are bloodless and fearless, and they don't hear the crowd groan as the ball bounces off the rim . . . again. They just know you will average more points in the long run by taking the greater risk.

Then again, there is also the momentum of the contest that none of these stats can capture. The bowlers don't want the batsmen to get away to a good start. They would rather establish control early. This is the control that enables them to keep the close catchers in, so that when the edge comes it is caught, rather than flying into the vacant third slip area (the vacant area from which the captain just moved a man to plug the hole in the covers through which the ball had been disappearing for four). And there is a selfless aspect. The pressure they are creating by hammering length helps the bowler at the other end, makes his job easier.

ENLIGHTENMENT

There are few crafts more punishing than bowling fast in Test cricket. Few sporting roles more cursed with long, bitter, toil-laden days in the heat and the dirt. The raw and aching joints, the ruined feet, the fractured vertebrae. And it is this that shapes the bodies and minds of those who endure bowling through lengthy careers.

They don't need the finely parsed statistical analysis above because they have bowled those thousands of overs in Tests and lived with the pain and joy that have resulted. They have learned their methods the Aeschylus way. In Greek mythology, Zeus decreed that mortal man could only learn truth through bitter experience; that wisdom must come through suffering.

> Even in our sleep, pain which cannot forget
> falls drop by drop upon the heart
> until, in our despair, against our will,
> comes wisdom through the awful grace of God.
>
> (Aeschylus, *Oresteia*, 458 BC)

This, then, is what we see when we watch Stuart Broad, James Anderson or Vernon Philander – or Glenn McGrath, Curtly Ambrose, Courtney Walsh – in late career. We are look-ing at the pared-down palette of the master craftsman. It is not lacking in subtlety, in fact the opposite; there is 100 Tests-worth of pain-scoured wisdom behind every small adjustment of pace or line. There is undeniably consummate skill. But each last ounce of unnecessary complication has been burned away. It is not the crude simplicity of the novice, but the deadly elegance of the master. That is what drives the cost of their wickets steadily down, point by unforgiving decimal point. It is the difference between knowing something and having it burned into every last neuron.

It is also worth noting that it is what they do on their good days, and it is what they do on their bad days. Broad and Anderson were slammed for bowling too short in that first Test against Pakistan in 2018. But compare Broad's lengths then, when he and Anderson were castigated, with his lengths when he took 8 for 15 to win the Ashes at Trent Bridge in 2015, and you will see they are near identical.

Stuart Broad's Lengths, 1st 10 Overs		Trent Bridge v. Aus, 2015	Lord's v. Pak, 2018
Half-Volley	Under 5m	9%	10%
Full length	5–6m	22%	21%
Good length	6–8m	49%	53%
Back of a length	8–9m	16%	12%
Short	Over 9m	5%	4%

Or compare the lengths Anderson and Broad bowled at Lord's versus Pakistan with those they bowled at Lord's five years earlier when they bowled out New Zealand for 70, taking all ten wickets between them. You will see that they bowled fuller when they were thwarted than when they triumphed. Or indeed, compare them with Mohammad Amir's lengths in the opening spell in the same match, which drew so much praise. They are certainly no shorter.

Broad and Anderson Lengths, 1st 10 Overs		Lord's v. NZ, 2013	Lord's v. Pak, 2018	Amir Lord's, 2018	McGrath Lord's, 2005
Half-Volley	Under 5m	7%	9%	8%	3%
Full	5–6m	9%	19%	9%	7%
Good	6–8m	56%	52%	62%	62%
Heavy	8–9m	19%	14%	17%	25%
Short	Over 9m	9%	6%	4%	3%

They are just doing what has brought them their greatest successes, and over a thousand Test wickets.

Because they know that, when all is said and done, a mountain is just a mountain.

Why Don't Indians
Bat Left-Handed?
....

It could well be the finest moment in the history of coaching.

From a clear Majorcan sky the sun bounces waves of heat off the clay court. Face slick with sweat, eyes burning with frustration, he glares out from under a mop of dark hair at the latest ball he has failed to bend to his will. His uncle approaches, bends forward, calmly lifts the boy's right hand off the tennis racket and resettles it into just his left hand, then goes back to feeding him balls. The transformation, from right-hander who hits two-handed on both sides into a leftie with a two-handed backhand, starts to take root. The intentional conversion from right-handed to left-handed is not a well-trodden path in tennis as it is in some sports, but in this case it pays dividends . . . and how.

Scant years later, and that left-handed forehand, by now developed into something unprecedented, powers him to his first French Open title. The still boyish Rafa Nadal stands at the centre of Philippe Chatrier Court and bites the corner of the trophy cradled in his arms. It is a photocall we will see often. Eleven more French Opens, and 19 Grand Slams in total, and Uncle Toni's decision looks like a moment of genius. On clay it has helped create something close to perfection, the greatest there has ever been by a distance. He wins slams on all surfaces, but on clay he is utterly imperious.

Even the greatest tennis player ever to pick up a racket is tamed. Again and again that sledgehammer forehand, whipped with a pace and venom that must be seen to be comprehended, explodes off the court at Roger Federer's one-handed backhand, relentless and uncontrollable. The great man is matched on all surfaces and dismantled on clay.

Which takes us back to that moment on a hot Balearic tennis court, when right-hander became left-hander. It is not an obviously beneficial move in tennis. Although there has long been a suspicion that left-handed players are over-represented at the highest level, careful analysis across a range of eras has suggested that this is not actually the case.

In cricket, however, it is a more widely held belief, and one that seems to have more substance behind it. Many an astute cricketing parent has done the same thing as Uncle Toni did, turning their son or daughter round to create a left-handed batter from a right-handed youngster. For the vast majority it will make no difference to their success within the game. But to a tiny, tiny percentage, it will make the difference between success and failure, between having a Test career and not doing so.

At least, that is the case in England, Australia and much of the Test-playing world. But not so in India. In India the ambitious father will gain nothing from his sinister intervention, because in India there seems to be no advantage to being left-handed at the highest level. At least not as a batsman.

When India lined up to play England at Lord's in 2018, and lost the toss on a well-grassed pitch, one right-hander after another emerged from the famous pavilion. Both openers, then Cheteshwar Pujara at three, Kohli at four, and on they came – the entire top eight were right-handed. It wasn't a day for batting and the England seamers entirely in their element were unstoppable, but to an English or Australian eye that uninterrupted flow of righties was almost as remarkable as the carnage at the crease.

A year earlier, it was an equally right-handed top six that lined up for India to win the series against Australia in Dharamsala, the most beautiful cricket ground in the world high in the Himalayas. As it had been in 2013 in Chennai for the first Test of the series and on each occasion, and countless others, Australia in contrast had four lefties in their top six. The Australians suffered in 2013, and the Indians cantered home then too. The infamous 'Homework-gate' incident, in which four Australian players were dropped for not complying with the coach's request for ideas to improve the team's performance, was to follow.

These are far from isolated instances. Left-handed batsmen are hugely overrepresented in England and Australia Test teams, but barely feature in Indian sides. And the explanation as to why that is the case illuminates one fascinating aspect of how cricket works.

But first, let's start at the beginning.

A SHORT HISTORY OF CACK-HANDEDNESS
At the very beginning of Test cricket, the left-handed batsman didn't really exist. Of the first 72 players to play Test cricket, only 7 batted left-handed, and they were all primarily bowlers.

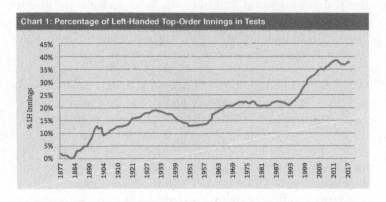

Chart 1: Percentage of Left-Handed Top-Order Innings in Tests

It wasn't until William Scotton opened the batting at The Oval in 1884 that Test cricket had its first top-order left-hander. Then, over the next 30 years, left-handed batsmen established themselves as the fairly stable minority that they would remain for nearly a century. If you look at the underlying proportion of left-handed batsmen in cricket, it varies across different playing populations, but typically falls in the range 15–25 per cent (made up of both naturally left-handed players, and naturally right-handed players who bat left-handed), and this was similarly the proportion of left-handed batsmen in Test cricket for most of Test history.

Left-handedness in the general population

According to a meta-analysis of 144 studies, the best estimate for left-handedness in the general population is approximately 11 per cent of men and 9 per cent of women, and 10 per cent overall.

But then, around 1990, we start to see a steady increase in the overall numbers of left-handed batsmen at Test level. There doesn't seem to have been any noticeable rise in the base level of left-handed batsmen within cricket as a whole. There is no concomitant increase in bowlers who happened to bat left-handed, for example. But there was, between 1990 and 2010, a sharp surge in the proportion of top-order innings played by left-handed batsmen. More interestingly, this rise happened mainly in certain countries, and in particular at one position in the order.

It seems unlikely that this overrepresentation was due to fashion or tactics. Looking at the performance figures, it seems left-handers merely outperformed right-handers during this period. That is to say that they were selected not because they were left-handed but because they were successful. And yet, so pervasive and exaggerated has this trend been that it is hard to imagine that it wasn't their left-handedness that was giving them an edge in performance, an advantage that they still seem to enjoy today.

So why is this the case? Where does this advantage come from?

It is surprising, because if we were extrapolating from how left-handers fare in other sports we would expect to see an overrepresentation of left-arm bowlers but not expect left-handed batsmen to have any edge at all.

LEFT-HANDEDNESS IN OTHER SPORTS

At one time it was thought that the reason left-handers were overrepresented in sport was due to the way in which the brain controls movement and certain types of spatial tasks. It was known that particular areas of the right hemisphere of the brain were overdeveloped in left-handed people, and so it was believed that this could lead them to have an innate advantage over right-handers when it came to sport.

Further research disproved this idea by showing that in professional sports where there was no interaction between competitors (such as darts or snooker) there was no apparent advantage to left-handedness. The theory that then followed was that being left-handed is a tactical advantage because opponents find it unusual and have to use different angles of attack and so on. In particular, it was felt that the anticipation skills that elite performers use to predict where the ball will go next might be reduced when facing left-handed opponents.

In time this was shown to be the case. Indeed, there is compelling research that shows that the shorter the time players have to react, the more overrepresented left-handed players are in that sport. A study of six sports by sports scientist Florian Loffing compared typical reaction times in each sport with the proportion of elite players who were left-handed. It showed that players in fast-reaction sports were 2.6 times more likely to be left-handed than those in slower reaction sports. This ranged from just 9 per cent of squash players, who had the longest time to react, up to 30 per cent of pitchers in baseball, the sport with the fastest average reaction time.

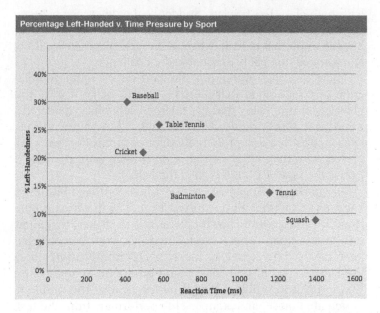

Percentage Left-Handed v. Time Pressure by Sport

To explain why this is the case we need to explore a little how the brain works when playing fast-reaction sports.

Sporting actions are hardwired into the brain through thousands of hours of training. And those actions that take place the quickest involve the least conscious awareness and involvement. Think of the way in which you flinch automatically if a blow is aimed at your face. You react before you are even aware that you intend to do so. The same is true of a high-class player in a high time-pressure sport, their movements and reactions become automatic and unconscious.

For example, take a talented schoolboy batsman and put him in a practice net next to a Test player. Then take a couple of bowling machines and fire balls at them both at 80 mph. The Test player will probably perform better, but after a while the schoolboy will also do pretty well. You will be surprised that there is not a bigger difference in how well they bat. At least, there isn't when they know roughly where the ball is going to land. Now take the bowling machines away and replace them with high-class Test bowlers. Suddenly, the difference between the two players is chalk and cheese. The schoolboy will hardly be able to put bat on ball, whereas the Test player looks, if not comfortable, then at least equal to the challenge.

There is a high minimum standard for eyesight, coordination and technique that must be met to make it as a Test player. But it is likely that the talented schoolboy meets that standard in most regards too. What makes Test players special, what makes them so profoundly different from the best club players who may otherwise be quite similar, happens largely before the bowler even lets go of the ball.

When performing close to the limit of their abilities, a batsman (or tennis player, or goalkeeper) will pick up cues from the action of the bowler (or server, or striker) that allow him to anticipate where the ball will go, even before it has been released (or struck, or kicked). This anticipation allows the batsman to hit balls that would otherwise be too fast for him to react to. And, among other things, it is this ability to anticipate that separates super-elite performers from the rest.

But this anticipation is learned almost entirely unconsciously and is therefore finely tuned to the types of bowlers the batsman has faced in his career, most of whom will have been right-handed. So those hardwired skills that allow the player to anticipate where the ball is going to be, even before it has been released, are tuned mostly to right-handed opponents. They are therefore noticeably less efficient when used against opponents who play 'the wrong way round'. Technique and reflexes that have self-optimised to right-handed opponents are less effective when dealing with a left-handed player.

When players in a number of sports watch temporally occluded* footage of right- and left-handed opponents, they are significantly worse at predicting where the ball will go from left-handed opponents than they are from right-handers.

---

* Temporal occlusion means stopping the footage at various stages so that the batsman doesn't see the whole delivery.

The faster the sport, the less time the batsman has to adjust to the flight of the ball, and therefore the more he must rely on this anticipation. It is in these sports, therefore, that left-handedness pays its biggest dividend.

The same is true of the level at which you are playing. In most ball sports, the higher the level that you reach, the faster the ball travels and the less time you have to react.

In school and club cricket, for example, players are still able to ball-track: they can wait for a ball to be bowled, pick up the direction of its flight and have time to move and hit it. But as the level gets higher, the speed of the bowling increases, and ball tracking becomes a smaller and smaller part of the key decision-making process. It is at this point that left-arm bowling starts to gain an edge. And we can see that clearly if we look at the proportion of left- and right-armers. There are roughly 50 per cent more left-arm pace bowlers in First Class cricket than in the general population (16.6 per cent compared with 11 per cent in the underlying male population), which is in line with what you would expect given the pattern in other time-pressure sports.

Cricket seems to fit this pattern as far as pace bowlers are concerned, but not when it comes to the overrepresentation of left-handed batsmen, because none of the theories so far really apply to batting. No fielder has to react to a batsman's actions within the period of time that would be required to generate the overrepresentation of left-handers that exists in cricket (even slip fielders generally get around two-thirds of a second to react to edges). So there should be roughly the same number of left-handed batsmen at every level of the game. But there demonstrably aren't.

SO WHERE DO ALL THE LEFT-HANDERS COME FROM?

As you move higher and higher through the levels of cricket, the number of left-handed batsmen increases markedly.

LH % Since 1 Jan 2000, England Only	
Test Batsmen (1–6)	43%
First-Class Batsmen (1–6)	33%
First-Class Non-Batsmen (9–11)	19%

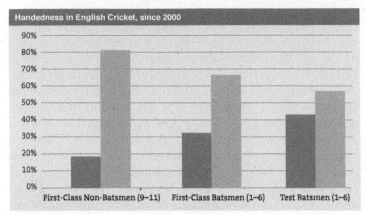

Throughout this chapter, the main measure we will use to measure the prevalence of LH batsmen is the percentage of innings played by a left-hander, and for bowlers the percentage overs bowled by a left-arm bowler.

The proportion of left-handed batsmen rises as the standard of batting rises. And this pattern of the percentage of left-handers increasing as the level rises is repeated, to varying degrees, in almost every country. India, and since 2010 Pakistan, are the only exceptions. But for every other major nation, the Test team contains more left-handed batsmen than their First Class system.

Percentage LH Batsmen by Country			
	Test Batsmen	Domestic Batsmen	Domestic Non-Batsmen
West Indies	52%	36%	26%
Australia	48%	40%	17%
Sri Lanka	45%	35%	26%
England	43%	33%	20%
South Africa	34%	31%	13%
New Zealand	34%	28%	19%
India	22%	26%	18%
Pakistan	22%	30%	20%

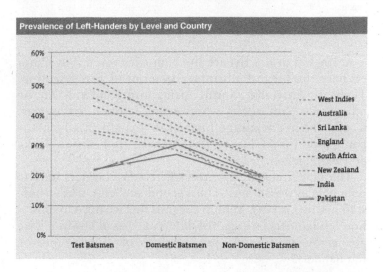

Prevalence of Left-Handers by Level and Country

And if we look at the degree to which left-handers are over-represented amongst Test batsmen, then there is a clear clue to the reason for the difference.

Ratio of Test Top Order LH to Domestic Tail LH			
	Ratio	Test Batsmen	Domestic Non-Batsmen
Australia	2.90	48%	17%
South Africa	2.61	34%	13%
England	2.14	43%	20%
West Indies	2.01	52%	26%
New Zealand	1.81	34%	19%
Zimbabwe	1.81	22%	12%
Sri Lanka	1.76	45%	26%
Bangladesh	1.35	35%	26%
India	1.22	22%	18%
Pakistan	1.09	22%	20%

At the top of the list are the countries where left-handers have the biggest advantage in terms of Test selection. They are Australia, South Africa and England. At the other end of the scale, where being left-handed appears to offer little advantage (and even a slight disadvantage going from First Class to Test cricket), are Pakistan, India and Bangladesh.

The first group are countries where fast bowlers tend to dominate proceedings. The second are countries where spin bowling is king. Which suggests that we need to look at how left-handers fare against different types of bowling if we are going to unpick the mystery of India's missing left-handers.

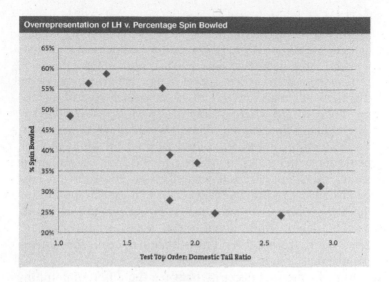

LEFT-HANDED BATSMEN V. PACE

There is an advantage to being a left-armer when you bowl pace, but ironically it *doesn't* come when you are bowling at right-handers. To understand why this is the case, and to unpick the various forces that are creating these asymmetries, let's look at the records of right- and left-arm bowlers against right- and left-handed batsmen.

Batting Average		Bowler	
		Left-Arm	Right-Arm
Batsman	LH	35.6	39.0
	RH	37.1	36.1

Symmetrical   Goofy

The first thing to note is that 'symmetrical' combinations (LA-LH or RA-RH) favour the bowler more than 'goofy' combinations (LA-RH or RA-LH). Overall, in symmetrical combinations the batsman averages 36.1, and in goofy combinations 38.5.

The second thing we notice is that left-arm bowlers do slightly better than right-arm bowlers in each type of match-up. Their record when symmetrical (against left-handers) is slightly better than right-arm bowlers' record when symmetrical (35.6 compared to 36.1). And their record when goofy is markedly better (37.1 compared to 39). As we explained earlier, this slight edge is down to their novelty value, the left-handed player's advantage that occurs in most ball sports. And this is the reason why there are 30 to 50 per cent more left-arm pace bowlers in professional cricket than one might expect given the background level of left-handedness in the general population.

But why the first disparity between the different combinations? Why does a symmetrical combination favour the bowler, and a goofy combination favour the batsman?

To answer this question, we must introduce one of Test cricket's most persistent Tethered Cats (or Chesterton's Fences), namely Law 36 – leg before wicket (LBW).

Much could be written on the vagaries of the LBW law that we have inherited from previous generations, but for now we are only interested in the fact that the batsman cannot be out LBW to a ball that pitches outside the line of leg stump. In goofy combinations, this includes a large proportion of the balls that will hit the stumps, whereas this is not the case with symmetrical combinations.

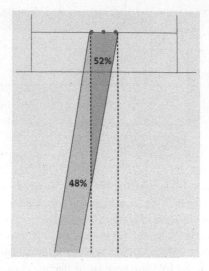

When right-arm pace bowlers bowl over the wicket, 48 per cent of their deliveries that would hit a left-hander's stumps pitch outside leg stump and therefore cannot result in LBW. When right-armers bowl to right-handed batsmen this happens only 0.5 per cent of the time. Therefore, you would expect goofy combinations to produce significantly fewer LBWs than symmetrical combinations, and the evidence bears this out.*

---

* There is also a small clue in the LBW data about other advantages that left-handed batsmen are getting. Whenever a batsman plays a defensive shot near the line of the stumps, he is weighing two competing risks – one is that the ball will seam away from him and he will edge it, the other is that it will nip back into him and he will be bowled or LBW. Without the same threat from LBWs, left-handers are free to set themselves up so as to reduce the risk of edging the ball. This is a possible reason why the left-arm to left-hander combination, which is unusual for a left-hander to face, produces higher rates of LBWs than the right-arm to right-hander combination where the batsman is facing off against his main threat..

% LBW		Bowler	
		Left-Arm	Right-Arm
Batsman	LH	20%	13%
	RH	14%	18%

| Symmetrical | Goofy |

- Left-armer to left-hander has the lowest batting average, because the bowler has both the advantage of the symmetrical combination and the novelty value of bowling left-handed.
- Right-armer to left-hander has the highest batting average, because the batsman has the advantage of the goofy combination to reduce his exposure to LBW, plus he is facing the type of pace bowler that he spends 80 to 90 per cent of his time playing and practising against.

Batting Average		Bowler	
		Left-Arm	Right-Arm
Batsman	LH	35.6	39.0
	RH	37.1	36.1

| Symmetrical | Goofy |

To summarise, left-handed batsmen have an advantage when facing right-arm pace bowlers because of the LBW law, and as over 80 per cent of fast bowlers are right-armers this gives them a significant edge in pace-friendly conditions.

THE NEW BALL
It seems clear that there is an advantage to being a left-handed batsman in a world dominated by right-arm pace bowlers. And

this advantage is magnified if you happen to bat mainly in conditions in which the biggest threat to your wicket is from fast bowlers. So if you are an opening batsman and so always face the new ball, for example.

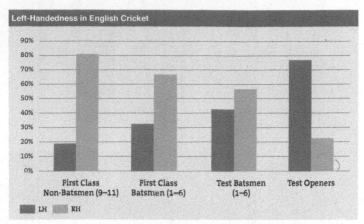

So if this is one of the reasons for left-handed batsmen's success, we would expect a particularly large overrepresentation in seam-friendly countries and among opening batsmen. And indeed, if we look at the proportion of left-handers by position in the batting order we find that in every Test-playing country there are more left-handers among the openers in First Class cricket than there are among the non-opening batsmen, who have in turn more left-handers than you find among the tailenders.

This is repeated to an even greater degree in Tests. Openers around the world (with the single exception of India) are disproportionately likely to be left-handed. Indeed, in some countries they completely dominate those positions. In Australia, for example, 84 per cent of the innings played this century by opening batsmen have been by left-handers. In England the figure is 77 per cent. And every single country on the list has a higher proportion of left-handed players in the opening positions than from three to seven. In Pakistan the contrast is particularly stark: 52 per cent of their openers have been left-handed, whereas a mere 5 per cent of their other top-order batsmen have been.

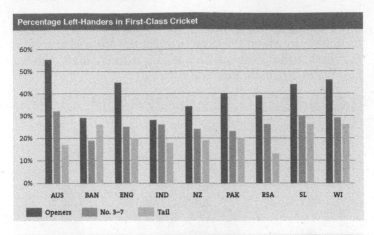

Percentage Left-Handers in First-Class Cricket

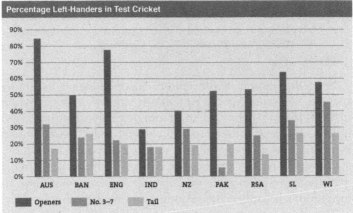

Percentage Left-Handers in Test Cricket

So why is this the case? Why does the apparent advantage of being left-handed sharpen from club to First Class to Test level? And from tailender to top order to opener?

There has always been accepted thinking within the game that a left/right combination opening the innings is a nice thing to have. But it is nowhere near a strong enough or widely enough held belief to have created this disparity.

It is hard to see any reason for this other than performance. Left-handers simply perform better at the top of the order, and that is why they are selected, not because of a belief in left-handers' innate superiority.

For example, if we break left- and right-hander's records down by the phase of the innings, looking at the first 30 overs compared with the periods after that, we see a marked advantage to left-handers in the new-ball period that then completely disappears for the remainder of the innings. It appears that, averaged across all Tests, it is a huge advantage to be left-handed for the first two hours of a Test innings, but has no apparent benefit after that.

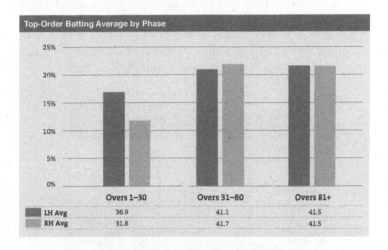

	Overs 1–30	Overs 31–80	Overs 81+
LH Avg	36.9	41.1	41.5
RH Avg	31.8	41.7	41.5

This is what leads to that preponderance of left-handed openers, and a top order that still has a slight but reduced left-hand bias. (It also shows you why openers carry a roughly five-run penalty on their batting average compared to other batting positions. If a good player averages 40+ and a very good player 45+, then for openers those categories should be 35+ and 40+.)

BUT WHY *DON'T* INDIANS BAT LEFT-HANDED?

So, if that is such a consistent pattern across all countries, why is it so clearly not the case in India? Why did eight consecutive right-handed batsmen walk out of the Lord's Pavilion on that extraordinary day in 2018?

The answer becomes clear when we look at the type of bowling that takes wickets with the new ball in each country. In most countries, the major threats to your survival as an opening batsman come from right-arm pace. And as we have seen, left-handers have a clear advantage against this type of bowling due to their ability to use the bowler's angle of attack, plus the LBW law, to negate some of the threat that they offer.

This is where Tests played in India (and now the United Arab Emirates) are different, particularly in the second innings of a Test match. The major threat to a batsman's wicket does not come from right-arm pace in these conditions: it comes from spin. And this is the case even with the new ball.

Top-Order Batting Average		Bowler	
		Pace	Spin
Batsman	LH	38.3	41.6
	RH	36.3	45.4

And just as there is a difference in the way that left- and right-handed batsmen perform against pace bowlers, there is also a difference in how they perform against spin. Only in this instance, the advantage falls the other way round. Across all Test cricket, right-handed batsmen have a better record against spin than left-handers do (as we can see in the table below).

Phases of the Innings in Test Cricket				
Over 1–30	LH	RH	LH–RH diff	%SpinW
Australia	41.5	35.4	6.1	13%
England	35.4	29.2	6.2	14%
India	37.6	39.7	-2.2	45%
Pakistan	42.6	36.7	5.9	25%
South Africa	34.0	30.3	3.8	10%
UAE	34.0	33.1	0.9	48%
Over 31–80	LH	RH	LH–RH diff	%SpinW
Australia	44.4	42.1	2.4	37%
England	39.2	42.4	-3.2	28%
India	33.1	43.4	-10.4	66%
Pakistan	48.8	48.1	0.7	48%
South Africa	39.5	38.3	1.2	23%
UAE	35.9	51.5	-15.6	56%

So now let's look back at those relative performances against the new ball in each country. Given that left-handers fare better against pace and worse against spin, as the percentage of wickets taken by spin rises towards 50 per cent, left-handers lose their comparative advantage. Once it is above 50 per cent, they are at a disadvantage to right-handers. That is why in India, where 45 per cent of new-ball wickets this century have fallen to spin, opening batsmen are no more likely to be left-handed than are tailenders.

And in both India and Pakistan, where the majority of wickets with the old ball fall to spin, left-handers are actually *underrepresented* from numbers three to seven, only 18 per cent and 5 per cent respectively of the Indian and Pakistan non-opening specialist batsmen being left-handed.

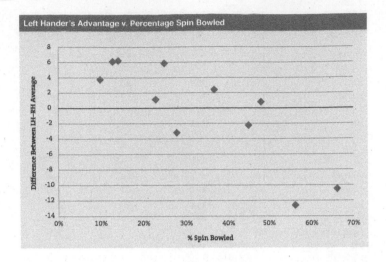

But if the LBW law seems the prime candidate for the left-handers' edge over right-handers against pace, what is the reason for the reversal of that advantage once the spinners come on?

EVERYONE WANTS A LEFT-ARM SPINNER
Anyone who has ever coached or captained a cricket team, at any level, will know that one of the nicest commodities with which to find yourself is a good left-arm spinner. They are a type of player where demand always seems to exceed supply. Unlike batting, where a player's natural handedness does not necessarily determine which way round they will choose to bat, the vast majority of players bowl with their dominant hand. This means that left-arm spinners will come from a mere 10 to 13 per cent of the population, rather than the nearly 90 per cent who will choose to bowl right-handed. You are rarely at a loss for an off-spinner, whether it be a specialist or a part-timer who can roll some out when necessary. Left-arm spinners, on the other hand, are far more precious.

Spin to Top-Order Batsmen in Tests	
Direction of Turn	Batting Average
No Turn	93.1
Away	35.6
In	47.4

As has long been well known, the ball turning away from the bat offers more of a threat than the ball turning into the bat. Left-arm spinners spin the ball away from the right-handed batsman, whereas right-arm (finger) spinners spin the ball *into* the right-hander. (There is more good news for the left-arm orthodox spinner as the game progresses, as most of the rough created by the right-arm pace bowlers is outside the left-handed batsman's off stump.)

Spin to Top-Order Batsmen in Tests		
Direction of Turn	LH	RH
No Turn	85.6	97.9
Away	29.5	40.1
In	42.6	50.2

As you can see, the ball turning in to the batsman has a significantly higher average (at least 10 runs per wicket higher) than the ball turning away. As you would expect, this is reflected in the records of each type of spinner against left- and right-handed batsmen.

While left-handers have a superior record against left-arm spin, however, it is a much smaller margin than the deficit they face in how well they play off-spin. And this contributes to their far poorer performance against spin overall.

*Most modern leg-spinners can turn the ball both ways and so can choose to take the ball away from both left-handed and right-handed batsmen. In all these pieces of analysis, we have tried to use as large a sample size as possible, so for the most part in this chapter we have considered all Test cricket since 2000. In closely analysing the performance of spin, however, we will take a smaller, more recent sample. It is worth looking at the current situation of the game, because changes to the level of scrutiny on bowling actions along with the increased prevalence of the Decision Review System (DRS) have altered the balance of power between bat and ball substantially. Unfortunately for left-handers, it seems to be exaggerating their problems rather than mitigating them.

% Spin Faced		Finger-Spinners	
		LA	RA
Batsman	LH	28%	57%
	RH	38%	45%

From the table, you can see the problem left-handed batsmen face. Not only are they worse than right-handers at both playing the ball turning in to them and at playing the ball turning away, they also face far more bowlers who turn the ball away from them. They face off-spin 57 per cent of the time, compared to right-handers, who only receive 38 per cent of their deliveries from left-arm spinners.

Top-Order Batting Average		Finger-Spinners	
		LA	RA
Batsman	LH	41.9	31.2
	RH	38.4	51.7

To summarise, the relative proportions of left- and right-handed players in Test cricket seems to make sense once we understand the relative strengths and weaknesses of each type of player.

Left-arm pace bowlers have an advantage because of the difficulty batsmen have in reading their bowling actions and anticipating where the ball will arrive.

Left-arm batsmen have an advantage at the top of the order because the LBW law gives them an edge over right-arm pace bowlers.

Right-handers, on the other hand, fare better against spin because of the relative scarcity of top-class left-arm finger-spinners.

WHAT ABOUT WHITE-BALL CRICKET?

So far, so good.

We seem to have unpicked the various forces at play in Test cricket that are influencing the prevalence of left-handers with bat and ball. But what does this imply for the shorter formats? If we are correct about what is happening in Test cricket and why, what can we expect to see in white-ball cricket?

Well, the arguments that we have so far put forth would seem to imply that bowlers and batsmen will move in different directions as we move to shorter matches.

As we saw earlier, the left-arm pace bowler's advantage comes from being harder to anticipate, and across a number of sports this advantage increases in proportion to the time pressure the opposition player is under. The shorter the format, the more attacking the batsman will be, and there is ample research to show that attacking shots necessitate an earlier decision by the batsman on where the ball is likely to be. The more attacking the batsman is, the more reliant they are on anticipation. This effectively increases the time pressure on the batsman, so increases the reliance on anticipation, and therefore increases the left-arm bowler's advantage.

So white-ball cricket, because of the greater attacking intent, is effectively a faster-reacting sport from the batsman's perspective than Test cricket is.

On the other hand, left-handed batsmen gain the majority of their advantage in Test cricket by being harder to dismiss. Their partial protection, via the LBW law, means that their dismissal rates are lower, and this is the main reason that their averages are better against pace bowling.

As the format shortens and the scoring rate increases and becomes more important, the value of this LBW protection diminishes sharply. So we would expect to see both the percentage of left-handed batsmen and their relative performance levels diminish as we reduce the number of overs.

And indeed, this is what we see.

(We have taken matches between the Test-playing nations so that we are comparing the same player pools in each format.)

Percentage LH by Format and Position			
	Openers	Top 6	No. 3–6
Test	58%	37%	26%
ODI	44%	34%	29%
T20	37%	31%	28%

Among opening batsmen there is a fall in the number of left-handers from 58 per cent in Test cricket to 37 per cent in T20s.

The percentage of left-arm pace bowlers rises from an already overrepresented 17.8 per cent in Tests to 23.5 per cent in T20 Internationals, double the naturally occurring rate, and actually more in line with what we would expect to see, given the pattern displayed in other sports.

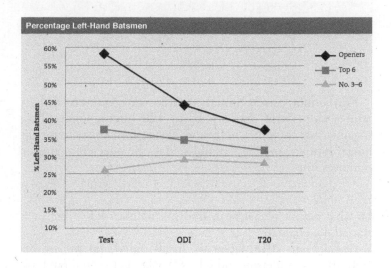

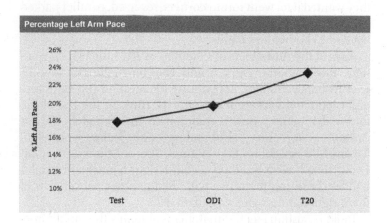

Fast Bowler Performance in T20Is		
	Average	Economy Rate
LA	24.7	8.0
RA	26.6	8.3

Furthermore, even though they are overrepresented, left-armers outperform right-armers in T20 Internationals. This suggests that there is a selection bias against them from the longer formats, and they should actually be selected in greater numbers still.

LORD'S AND CHENNAI

So what *did* happen next in the two matches with which we started the chapter?

At Lord's in 2018, faced by an all right-hand Indian top eight, Broad, Anderson and Chris Woakes between them took 18 wickets for a little over 9 runs apiece. The ball did anything they wanted it to, went round corners, reversed, parallel-parked and then set off again before generally finding the edge of the bat and a slip fielder's hands.

Against the Australians in Chennai in 2013 the two off-spinners, Ravichandran Ashwin and Harbhajan Singh, took 15 wickets between them, accounting for seven of the eight top-order left-hand wickets at a cost of 17 runs. In the rest of the four-match series, Ashwin maintained his stranglehold over Australia's top-order left-handers and India won 4–0. Meanwhile Australia's best spinner, the outstanding Nathan Lyon, toiled away manfully against right-hander after right-hander, finishing the series with 11 top-order wickets (10 of them right-handers) at a cost of 43.4.

India v. Australia in Test matches is arguably the most home-team-dominated fixture in international cricket. Between 1970 and 2015, only one series was won by the away team and it took the all-time great Australian side of 2004 to do it. In 45 years, each team has totalled just five Test wins apiece away from home. And while there are any number of contributing factors in this, one of them must be the fact that Australia keep turning up with their left-hand-dominated line-ups to play in India, and then India travel Down Under to the home of leftie advantage with their almost completely right-handed batting order.

So, though we now understand the overrepresentation of left-handers at the top of the order, we still haven't explained why it has been a feature of increasing prevalence since the mid-90s. What was it that caused the proportion of left-handers in Test cricket, that had stayed relatively constant for decades to rise so inexorably from that point on? What unseen hand has steadily increased left-handers' advantage for the last twenty years? In the next chapter we will discover exactly that.

UNCLE TONI

So what was the reason, those 20 or so years ago in the Mediterranean sunshine? Why did Uncle Toni turn Rafa into a left-hander? After all, there have been rumours ever since of an enforced change by a ruthless and ambitious coach.

'No! That's a legend,' Toni explained in an interview to *Tennis* magazine in October 2010. He went on to explain that at the start, Rafa had played with two hands but used one hand to direct. But he, Toni, had the impression that he was stronger on his left side than on his right.

Even if Rafa happened to write and eat with his right hand he was nevertheless fairly ambidextrous. Toni didn't feel that on the tennis court Rafa was naturally more right-sided than left, if anything the opposite. Nor did he feel that there was any inherent advantage in being left-handed in professional tennis.

'At no point did I tell him he needs to play with his left hand because that way, he will be much stronger.'

He simply advised him, at the age of 10, to stop playing his forehand two-handed, because there were no top male players who played the shot with two hands.

So that seems to be the real story behind the legend. Less

Machiavellian than the myth perhaps, but still one of the most intriguing moments of decision in sporting history. Would Rafa have been just as good if he had settled on playing right-handed? We will never know.

Sachin's Helping Hand

Manchester United are 1–0 down to Sheffield Wednesday. It's April 1993, the business end of the Premiership season, and Alex Ferguson's side is deep into a title race against Aston Villa. Every win is crucial.

After 86 minutes, United's captain Steve Bruce powers home a brilliant header from the edge of the box to bring his team level. United's players celebrated but knew the job was only half done; as the eighty-ninth minute ticked past, the assistant awarded seven minutes stoppage time in which to find the goal. Steve Bruce scored again. United won the title.

It was called 'Fergie time', and it stuck. For the next 20 years, Ferguson's United developed an enviable reputation for scoring late goals, and for plenty of them coming in generous periods of stoppage time. If United needed a goal at Old Trafford, they would get time to score one.

Part of the reason 'Fergie time' came to resonate so deeply was because it was both a cause, and a consequence, of United's winning habit. There are numerous studies that show the unconscious influence the crowd has on referees' decision-making. Away teams receive more yellow cards than home sides. If the home team is behind, the officials give more stoppage time; if they are ahead, they give less. The ability of the home crowd to influence officials is well documented across a wide variety of sports.

Cricket is by no means immune to bias of this kind. And while there are numerous interventions that an umpire must make throughout a game, the most contentious moments often surround LBW appeals. Umpires must take in a lot of information in a very short space of time, then make a predictive judgement. It is a difficult task, and an unenviable one – but when it comes to these decisions, the presence of home-team bias is disappointingly clear.

Throughout Test cricket's history, umpires have consistently given more touring batsmen out LBW than home batsmen. With the exception of the 1940s (an anomaly, given that due to the Second World War only six Tests were played), every decade up to the 1990s saw LBWs make up a greater proportion of dismissals of away batsmen than home batsmen.

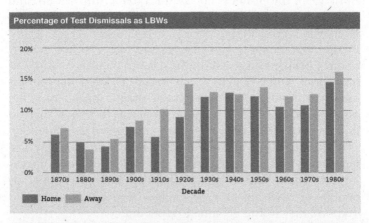

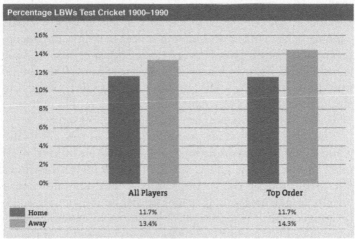

And for much of cricket's history, the explanation for that bias required little imagination. Up until 1992, Test umpires came almost exclusively from the home country. A Test between England and West Indies at Lord's would be officiated by two Englishmen, a Test in Lahore overseen by two Pakistani umpires, etc. It seems, with a modern eye, a remarkably strange flaw to accept.

Of course, in a slower and less globally mobile world, it made sense. When travel was an altogether longer and more stressful endeavour, having matches officiated by home umpires was an obvious convenience.

What's more, a sport that built its self-image on fairness and honour could surely rely on the most morally upstanding of all involved in the game – the umpires themselves – to put aside national loyalties and play fair. Couldn't it?

In practice, no, it couldn't.

Some stories of scarcely believable bias are well known. Perhaps the most infamous concerns the dismissal record of Pakistan legend Javed Miandad, who played 34 Test matches in his home country before being dismissed LBW. Across his entire career, 9.3 per cent of his knocks at home ended in being given out LBW; abroad, it was 24.2 per cent. Pakistani umpires did not give Miandad out, and it became the go-to reference point for the discussion, held up as a textbook example of home-side bias.

Osman Samiuddin, in *The Unquiet Ones*, his excellent history of Pakistan cricket, addresses the topic from a different angle: 'By the time [Nur] Khan took over, moans about Pakistani umpiring had become as much a part of the touring subcontinental experience as an audience with the head of state.'

There's little doubt that much of the Miandad-narrative is tinged with bigotry. He was not, after all, the only player whose statistics show this discrepancy between home and away LBW rates. Yet he is the one to whom the story was attached. Allan Border was out LBW 6 per cent of the time he batted in Australia, but 22 per cent away from home; for Desmond Haynes, it was 7 per cent to 29 per cent; Ken Barrington, 7 per cent to 15 per cent. Of the leading Test run scorers between 1950 and 1990, the overwhelming majority had a lower LBW percentage at home.

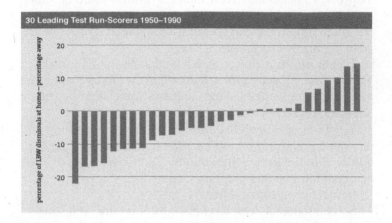

Almost everywhere had this bias. There were only two exceptions. From 1950 to 1990, the only countries where home players were given out LBW as often as visitors were New Zealand and England – it appears no one likes the English, not even the English. Every other country, with conditions as different as Australia and India, gave touring batsmen out LBW more than they gave their own batsmen out. It was, as Samiuddin puts it, 'a global blight'. (Global blight it may have been, but you have to admire the splendidly one-eyed extremism of the Sri Lankans. Prior to neutral umpires, home top-order batsmen were dismissed LBW 6 per cent of the time. For visiting top-order batsmen the figure was 30 per cent.)

Key members in Pakistan cricket and India cricket were aware that this was the case. Nur Khan, as head of what is now the Pakistan Cricket Board, addressed the issue directly: 'You come to my country and call us cheats because of the umpires. We go to your country and have the same issues. It can't be this way. True or not, it doesn't matter, it is the perception. So how can you carry on like this?'

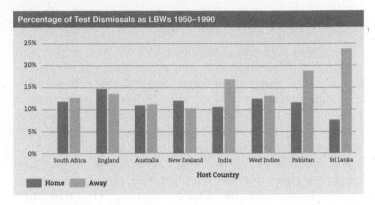

Percentage of Test Dismissals as LBWs 1950–1990

Host Country

Home Away

In public, at least, this was as much about accepting the flaw in the game's infrastructure as it was about apportioning blame. Shortly after taking his position in 1980, Nur Khan introduced a handful of 'neutral observers' for the home series against West Indies, officials whose presence had no purpose beyond informally reviewing decisions made on the field. Checks and balances – almost entirely for show, but there nonetheless.

More visible cricketing figures were getting involved as well. 'Imran Khan was becoming a notable and charismatic advocate', writes Samiuddin in *The Unquiet Ones*. Imran perhaps saw it at least in part through a self-serving lens – 'We drew 1–1 [against the West Indies in 1988] but with neutral umpires we would have won 2–0' he later claimed – but such was his charisma and fame, his voice was always likely to be heard above others'. Aggrieved by his achievements being tainted by Pakistan's reputation, Imran was broadly in favour of anything that allowed the focus to fall more squarely on his players and, perhaps more pertinently, on to him.

When the West Indies arrived in Pakistan for the following tour, two neutral umpires were used for the first time in Test cricket. The move was a declaration of intent, showing that Pakistan was the most serious nation when it came to the issue of removing home bias, far more serious than the nations hurling the insults. A four-Test series between India and Pakistan, in 1989, was umpired by two Englishmen, John Hampshire and John Holder.

The pressure, perhaps intensified by the increased broadcasting of matches and an increase in standards elsewhere, was growing. The integrity of local umpires was debated with increasing frequency. And so, after all the wrangling behind the scenes, the International Cricket Council (ICC) arrived at a compromise. In 1994, they introduced the practice of every Test being overseen by at least one neutral umpire.

For once, the effect of a major rule change in sport had largely the effect that was intended. The arrival of a neutral umpire immediately decreased the bias. The difference between home and away LBW percentages dropped, from 2.3 per cent to 1.6 per cent. Then in 2002 the ICC introduced the practice of having *two* neutral umpires, and that difference disappeared almost entirely.

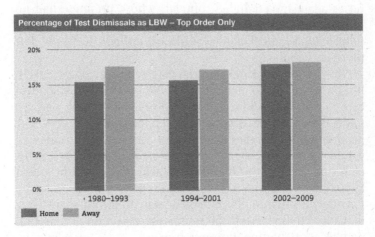

That was fortunate. This was a significant ideological shift for cricket to undertake and the results probably needed to be immediate and obvious for the measures to stick. Structurally, questioning the integrity of umpires by prising them away from their own sides was a big step for cricket as a culture to undergo. Very few decisions have left a previous era looking quite so

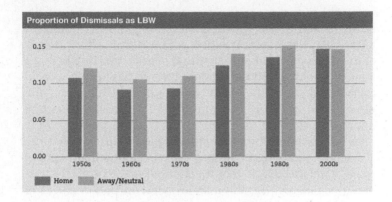

anachronistic, so fundamentally flawed; the move to umpires untethered from national interest is arguably the most *symbolic* cricket has seen, abandoning the model of the honourable amateur for one of professionalism. Umpiring, and the role of the umpire in the culture of the sport, was changed.

But less obviously, and less immediately, fundamental aspects of the sport were also changed. Improvements in the quality and impartiality of umpiring were to have a profound impact, changing the game in ways that absolutely no one could have anticipated.

HARDER, BETTER, FASTER, STRONGER

Beijing, 2008: 'A fair start, Asafa Powell, Usain Bolt also out well, here they come down the track, Usain Bolt, sprinting ahead, winning by *daylight*, and setting a world record, 9.68.'

London, 2012: 'They're away, and Gatlin got away brilliantly, and he's ahead of the field at the moment, Bolt going brilliantly, here comes Usain Bolt, Usain Bolt storming through, he takes it again, Blake takes the silver, 9.64 – oh, he's retained his title in the most *emphatic* way.'

Rio de Janeiro, 2016: 'Gatlin got a good enough start. Bolt is a bit slow to begin. He's got some work to do. Gatlin's in front. Bolt's stretching out now. He's coming after him – he's *immortal* now.'

141

In athletics, the march of progress is obvious. Across the board, in all the different disciplines, comparing performances today with performances from 40 years ago makes that progress clear. Times get quicker, weights get heavier, and distances get longer. The Men's 100-metre sprint record has been beaten in every decade since the 1890s (save for the 2010s), among the most clear and visible yardsticks for proving sporting improvement.

As standards improve (conditions, sports science, professionalism) so do performances, but the other thing that happens when standards rise is that the amount of variation falls. As overall standards rise, the margins between performances of elite athletes get smaller.

When Jesse Owens won Olympic gold in the 100 metres in 1936, amid the backdrop of Nazi rule in Berlin, the American was 0.6 seconds quicker than Lennart Strandberg, the Swede in sixth place. When Bolt won in 2016, that gap was 0.15 seconds.

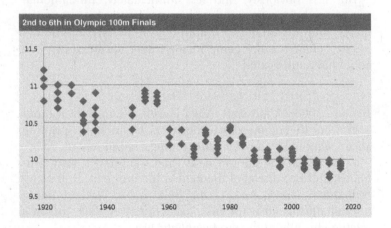

2nd to 6th in Olympic 100m Finals

In sports such as swimming and athletics, we can see the improvement in times and distances. But, in other sports, such as football and rugby, it is harder. The raw score tells us little about the standard of performance. A rugby match finishing 20–12 could just as easily be a Premiership final as an Under-15s school match. For those sports, the more obvious indicator of increasing standards is the decrease in variance.

You can see a very clear example of this in baseball. Scoring levels have stayed relatively constant in baseball for 100 years. A good batting average in the 1930s is still a good batting average. But if you look at the standard deviation (a measure of variance, of how spread out the individual scores are) of players' batting averages by season, it has fallen steadily year on year and decade on decade. Players have collectively averaged the same, but the averages of the best and the averages of the worst each year have got closer and closer together.

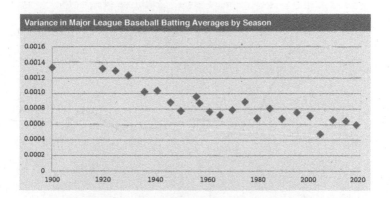

It is exactly the same effect that causes Olympic sprint times to crowd together. The better you get at something, the harder it is to improve further. As you push closer and closer to the limit of what is humanly possible, each incremental improvement becomes smaller and smaller and harder and harder to make.

As the whole of baseball gets better, the standard becomes more uniform, the gap between the best and the rest closes. Only 20 players have ever averaged over .400 in a baseball season. And the last person to do it was Ty Cobb in 1941. Since then players have got steadily further and further away from it, and it is highly unlikely that anyone will ever do it again. The standard has got too high for anyone to lift themselves that far clear of the rest. It would be like running a sub eight-second 100 metres.

You can see a similar pattern if you look at the distribution of batting averages in Test cricket. Although overall scoring levels have not changed much since the 1930s, the variance between players' averages has fallen steadily. As the standard of cricket improved, the difference in batting average between the best and the rest in the Test game has fallen.

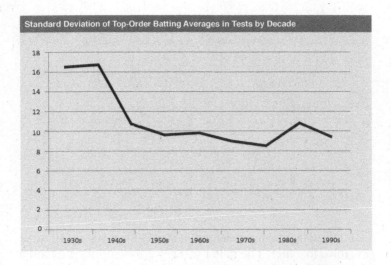

This pattern of declining variance as standards improve is the reason why it is unlikely that anyone will ever beat Don Bradman's career batting average of 99.9.

Decade on decade it got progressively harder for a batsman to average over 50 in Tests. That is, until about 1996. Then suddenly there was a reversal in the trend, and variance in Test batting averages increased. This, however, wasn't a sudden reversal in the march of progress. The increase was most likely the first unforeseen consequence of the improvement in the quality of umpires and their decisions.

To illustrate why this is the case, let us conduct a thought experiment. Let's imagine that for 12 months of Test cricket, we tell umpires that instead of trying to get their decisions right they are allowed to make them completely at random. Whenever there is an appeal, they choose an outcome at random. No biases in play, no skill either. Just luck. All we need them to do is keep the overall proportion of their decisions the same. Same number of outs and not outs.

Umpires are involved in around 40 per cent of dismissals in Test cricket: all LBW decisions, naturally, but also around half of all caught-behind dismissals, almost all bat-pad catches, and a chunk of stumpings and run outs. All of these will be given out or not out at random.

Let us further assume that the players don't notice and continue to play as they otherwise would. The same number of appeals, same number of balls bowled at the stumps, the game essentially carrying on in identical fashion, save for the umpiring change.

We can see the effect this will have on player performances by following the fortunes of three players. Firstly, Player A – the median player. His batting average is the same as the typical top-order batsman in Test cricket, around 36. Second, we have Player B – a superstar. His batting average is much better than most, a soaring 54. Finally, we have a weaker batsman, Player C. His batting average of 24 is significantly lower than average. Those are their individual averages in a world where every decision made is perfect. So what will happen to their records when those decisions are made at random?

No need to worry about Player A. He is absolutely fine, in this new reality – he averaged 36 before, and he averages 36 now. He bats for the average length of time, endures the average number of appeals and so is given out just as frequently as he normally would be.

And Player C is OK too. He is actually doing better than before. With our random umpires, a greater proportion of the times he gets rapped on the pad, plumb in front, he is being given not out. So he is on average surviving for longer, and his average has actually risen from 24 to 28.

Things don't work out so well for our superstar. Because he is a better batsman, Player B stays longer at the crease – and is therefore the subject of more appeals. As a result, he is more likely to get himself on the wrong end of a stinker. The longer you are at the crease, the more likely you are to get a bad decision. So his average has fallen from 54 to 45.

What this 'experiment' shows is that poor umpiring is a leveller. It makes it harder to distinguish statistically between good and poor batsmen. It reduces the variance in measured performance between the best and the worst.

And as you would expect, the converse is true as well. Good umpiring increases variance. The better the umpire, and the more accurate their decision-making, the wider the gap between Player B and Player C appears. If you improve umpiring, the best average more and the worst average less. Which, of course, is exactly what happened when neutral umpires were introduced.

In the 1980s, 7 per cent of Test batsmen averaged over 50. In the 2000s it was 15 per cent. At the same time the standard deviation in players' batting averages, which had fallen steadily since the 1930s, suddenly went back up.

It looked like cricket was seeing its greatest generation of batsmen since the war. Actually, of course, it was seeing its greatest ever generation of umpires. Better umpires and better decisions were making the best batsmen better and the worst batsmen worse.

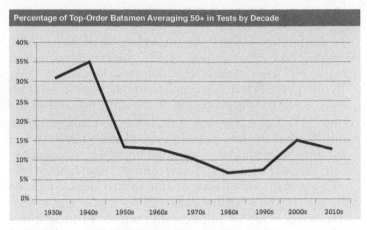

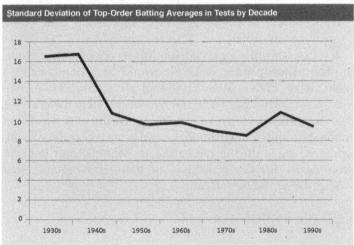

It's all there in macrocosm – but microcosms are rather more fun, are they not? And so, we turn to Sachin Tendulkar. One of the finest batsmen to ever play the game, Tendulkar is also a remarkable example of longevity. He averaged 50+ in the 1990s, the 2000s and the 2010s, his performance only falling short of excellence for brief periods at the start and end of his career. The way he made that average, however, changed significantly as the umpiring changes took effect.

In the first half of the 1990s (including his debut in 1989), Tendulkar had a Test average of 52.7, broken down into an average of 72.9 in India and 43.9 away from home.

By then established as a superstar, from 1995 to 2000 his average went up slightly again, 59.92 until the end of the century. The home and away split, however, changed significantly. In that five-year period, Tendulkar averaged 53.4 in India and a staggering 66.3 away from home. He made centuries in England, Australia, South Africa, New Zealand, Sri Lanka, Pakistan – he fell short of a ton in the Caribbean on the 1997 tour, but he still came away with a series average of 58.

Tendulkar made 13 Test centuries outside of India in the 1990s. A number only bettered by Ken Barrington and Sunil Gavaskar, both of whom registered 14 outside their home countries in the 1960s and 1970s respectively.

It is barely worth saying that Tendulkar was, of course, entering his prime in these years. He would have dominated no matter what. Players such as him find a way not just to survive but to excel. The difference was that compared to the previous era, Tendulkar was working with a tailwind – a wind that started blowing from the north, several years before. Nur Khan, Imran Khan, even the reputation of Miandad, all laid the groundwork for the generation of dominant batsmen that emerged over the next decade.

VERTICAL STRIPES ARE SLIMMING

'The stumps have got shorter and wider'

Paul Hawkins

Winchester College has a richer cricketing history than most. One of the oldest schools in Britain, teaching pupils for well over 600 years, its prestigious halls have seen many notable alumni pass through. Few schools can claim to have produced two Test captains, but even fewer can claim to have produced two who would go on to lead different nations; Mansur Ali Khan Pataudi and Douglas Jardine captained more than 50 Tests for India and England respectively. Combined, they made more than 30,000 runs, each playing more than 250 matches for various teams throughout their careers. Both left legacies, on and off the field; it is rather surprising then that neither of these men are the most influential contributors to cricket to come out of the city of Winchester.

Having played minor counties cricket for Buckinghamshire, Paul Hawkins had always been a keen sportsman, counting rowing and tennis among his other passions. Part of the reason he had opted for Durham University over other establishments had been its excellent record on the sports field, as well as in the classroom – yet it was in the latter where Hawkins would find his groove. Completing a PhD in artificial intelligence, he was more than aware of the way technology could impact and improve a range of sports. In an era of increased commercialism, of advertising money beginning to flood into broadcasters' pockets, the opportunity for sport and technology to fuse more closely was greater than it had ever been. Around the turn of the millennium, Hawkins became a founder of the technology company Hawk-Eye Innovations – headquarters just outside Winchester.

Using a multi-camera set-up, Hawk-Eye's team was able to track the flight of an object through the air with extreme precision and accuracy, and then use that information to *predict* what would happen to the object next.

Hawk-Eye's ascent within cricket was rapid. The ball-tracking set-up was part of the award-winning Channel 4 coverage during the 2001 Ashes series. At the time, the channel's coverage was gaining a serious reputation among sports broadcasting for being at the forefront of innovation and analysis – Hawk-Eye was a central, indispensable part of that reputation. The predictive element of the technology meant that the programme makers could display the expected flight of the ball for LBWs *after* the point of impact, determining if the ball was going to hit the stumps. It's a luxury that most modern viewers take for granted, but 20 years ago it was a ground-breaking step forward in what television analysis could provide.

Naturally, such capabilities began to attract the attention of coaches and administrators, who wondered if such technology could have an even greater role to play in sport. Hawk-Eye was subsequently introduced into tennis, where it was used to determine whether balls had landed in or outside the tramlines.

The 2006 US Open was the first grand slam tournament to fully integrate the system into its officiating. The process, where players directly challenge calls and replays were shown almost instantly, was about as slick and efficient as any referral system in sport. It made demonstrative, obvious improvements to the sport, and the spectacle. 'The greatest Wimbledon Final ever – Nadal v. Federer in 2008 – would have been over in three sets had it not been for a Hawk-Eye call,' Hawkins asserts, proudly. 'Hawk-Eye's contribution to sport is that conversation is about the game and the players, not about the officiating.'

In 2008, however, that contribution was still limited to tennis. Cricket, where the technology had made its name, took a little longer to get everyone on board.

There had been a trial introduction of a Decision Review System in 2008, when India took on Sri Lanka. Getting Indian cricket to agree is the key to making any change in the modern game, and there were more than a few nervous administrators watching on. As the game unfolded, you can imagine heads were starting to droop. There were 12 decisions that were overturned due to the new system – but only one benefited India. Eight years would pass before India agreed to use DRS in a bilateral series.

Sunday 11 March, 2001, Kolkata: Harbhajan Singh is stood at the top of his mark. He runs in and pins Ricky Ponting, the young Australian, playing across the line. Gone. Next ball, Adam Gilchrist is stood facing up to Harbhajan, who bounds in from over the wicket, the same angle that has snared Gilchrist's right-handed teammate. Gilchrist, himself left-handed, watches the ball pitch outside leg and skid on into his pad, maybe even via the edge of his bat. Given. Shane Warne falls next ball. Harbhajan Singh has a Test hat-trick.

Saturday 30 July, 2011, Nottingham: Stuart Broad pitches a ball much fuller than his usual zone of attack, and Indian captain M. S. Dhoni edges to the slips with an ugly swipe. Next ball, Broad goes very full again but this time much straighter, right at the pads of the newly arrived Harbhajan Singh. It hammers him on the pad, and he's given out – though replays show he got a considerable amount of bat on it. With no LBW reviews allowed in the series at India's request, Harbhajan has to go. Broad goes full and straight again to the new man Praveen Kumar, and bowls him with one that keeps low. Stuart Broad has a Test hat-trick.

With full DRS, neither hat-trick happens.

The rest of the world moved rather more quickly than India. The first Test with a version of the Decision Review System as a fully incorporated part of the officiating set-up was held between New Zealand and Pakistan, in November 2009. It went without a hitch, and the stage was set. The age of DRS had begun.

The practical elements were significant, and initially undermined the project to an almost fatal extent. The burden of cost for the new systems fell on the hosts, and with the finances of cricketing boards varying massively in terms of security and size, some boards felt it was a burden they could not bear. In 2010, the technology was due to be used in Bangladesh's tour of England, but was abandoned two days before the match after the ICC and Sky Sports were unable to decide who should pay for it. In 2011, the Board of Control for Cricket in India (BCCI) vice-president Niranjan Shah observed that 'last year, about 65 Tests and 170 ODIs were played around the world. Multiply those numbers with $60,000. It would be a staggering amount for one or two decisions in a match.'

It wasn't just the practical elements of the process that plagued its introduction. The opposition wasn't only from boards. As Hawkins puts it, 'There was half an idea that using it as an officiating tool could be bad for business. The broadcasters enjoyed the controversy.' That slight gap between what happened in the game as determined by the umpires, and what 'really' happened according to the technology, was where a lot of impassioned debate among fans and pundits took place. That debate was valuable.

Elsewhere, there was a far more emotional debate taking place. Rather than questioning whether the new system was affordable, many were questioning whether it was *right*, not on a scientific level but a philosophical one. Cricket has always wrestled with how much to trust the umpire. In a bygone era, complete trust was necessary, given the absence of any means of redress. Without trust, there was anarchy. The entire system was predicated on the belief that one man – always a man – had mastered an understanding of the laws of the game, and could be trusted to deliver a correct verdict often enough to fall in line. It makes sense, then, that the first wave of raising umpiring standards was focused on improving the umpires themselves. The introduction of neutral umpires allowed that trust to stay unmoved, perhaps even strengthened. Bringing in neutral umpires still centralised the power and authority over the game, but strengthened the trust in that authority.

But what if the players could challenge that authority directly? How would that change cricket?

In theory, the introduction of DRS should not inherently have benefited batsmen over bowlers, or vice versa. The process simply lets players review decisions they don't think have been adjudicated correctly, increasing the number of correct decisions. Justice is blind – and so it proved. From 2005 to 2009, the batting average for top-order players in Test cricket was 38.92, a figure that only dropped by 0.3 in the next five years, as DRS was introduced across the game. The overall balance between bat and ball remained unchanged.

There were some key elements of the game, however, that DRS seemed to *directly* change. For one, the frequency of LBW appeals. In 2007, there was an LBW appeal roughly every 65 balls, but by 2015 this had risen to almost 95 balls. Perhaps this was a result of wider lines, more defensive bowling, seamers and spinners less keen to target the stumps; or perhaps it was a drop in the speculative appeal – the 'don't ask, don't get' appeal. The latter seems to have been the case, because while LBW *appeals* got rarer, the frequency of LBW *dismissals* barely changed. In the 2000s, an LBW dismissal came once every 378 deliveries; in the 2010s that fell only slightly to 363. Fewer appeals were bringing essentially the same number of dismissals. Again, a broad equilibrium had been maintained.

What is more revealing is *how* that equilibrium was maintained. The two main bowling types experienced the change in very different ways; for seamers, LBWs became rarer; for spinners, they became more common.

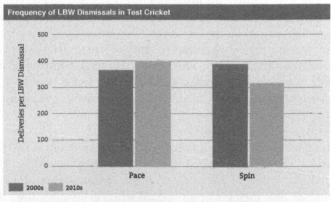

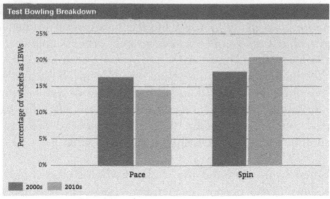

One possible reason for this would be that the introduction of the DRS had 'corrected' decisions made previously, and put things back in their rightful place. Spinners must have been the ones making the most use of the new system, reviewing lots more LBW decisions, with plenty of those reviews being successful.

Review Success Percentage		
	Pace	*Spin*
Caught	34%	29%
LBW	16%	18%

Yet since 2010, spinners have reviewed unsuccessful LBW appeals 15 per cent of the time, exactly as often as seamers. What's more, they're only marginally more successful in overturning those decisions when they do review. No, rather than letting spinners unleash their inner umpire and get wrong decisions overturned, the impact came elsewhere. The biggest impact of the DRS was not about changing the umpire's mind after he had made his decision. It was about changing the initial decision itself.

ELIMINATING THE HOWLER

The most commonly quoted aim of DRS was to 'eliminate the howler'. Bringing in any form of technology would, so the argument goes, get rid of those horrible moments just a few minutes after a wicket or an appeal when everyone knows the batsman *hasn't* nicked it to slip, or that he *was* plumb, and the umpire looks like a fool. Giving the batsmen an immediate form of redress would ensure nobody had to endure this particular sporting faux pas.

Yet the way the system is set up prevents this. If the aim was to eliminate the howler, then one review per side would suffice. If the primary intended use was for situations when the batsmen knows they are not out, then there is no need for a system that protects the batsmen when he gets it wrong.

Nathan Lyon is around the wicket to Ben Stokes. England need two to win. Seconds earlier, Lyon had failed to gather the ball for a very straightforward run out, which would have sealed the match for Australia, securing the Ashes.

Stokes, down on one leg, attempted to slog sweep Lyon's straight, quicker delivery – he misses. It strikes Stokes on the pad, and Lyon almost falls to the ground imploring the umpire to give it out. They don't. If they had reviewed the decision it would have been overturned, three reds that would have won the match – they were unable to review it because they had wasted a speculative review in the previous over. Stokes remained.

On radio commentary for the BBC, Glenn McGrath fumed: 'I always said DRS will cost you. If you use it badly, you will lose a Test match – if you use it well, you win it. It has cost them this match.'

Ben Stokes hit Pat Cummins for four through cover and England won the Test.

The series was drawn and Australia's quest to win a series in England was extended to at least 22 years.

*   *   *

Initially, when the system first came in, bowlers were reluctant to review LBWs. They, and their captains, sent less than 10 per cent of their LBW appeals upstairs. The next decade would see a lot of changes to the rules, which encouraged them to be more speculative, but the first and most effective of these was in September 2013, when it was decided that reviews would be 'reset' after 80 overs. In other words – have a swing as you get them back in a bit. This seemed to be the push captains needed to send more decisions upstairs, particularly when the spinners were bowling, because in 2014 the proportion of appeals reviewed shot up dramatically. The pattern continued. The years 2015, 2016 and 2017 each saw another considerable increase – given the opportunity to review more, captains were doing so.

Percentage Unsuccessful LBW Appeals Reviewed	
2010–2013	9.6%
2014	16.7%

In November 2017, it was decided that they would *not* be reset after 80 overs, but that very close LBW reviews (those involving Umpire's Call) would not be punished by the loss of a review. This reduction, in real terms, of the number of reviews at a captain's disposal did not send the DRS-rate back down to 10 per cent. Having been shown this brave new world, captains were cannier, more confident in their beliefs, and more informed than ever about when those umpiring mistakes came. The long and the short of it is that by 2018 about a quarter of all LBW shouts were being reviewed.

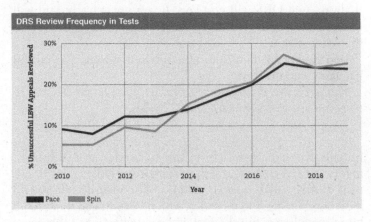

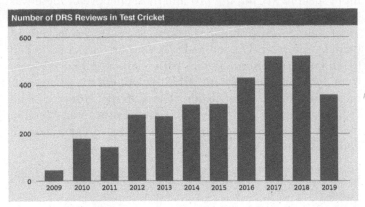

There has been a school of thought that focuses on how DRS changes have had a profound effect on what umpires will and won't give out on the field. Specifically, that umpires are more likely to give batsmen out LBW on the front foot against spinners, compared to previously. Hawk-Eye data was showing that more deliveries were hitting the stumps when batsmen were well forward, which pushed them to give more dismissals out.

This stands up. If you were a spinner in the years before DRS, you had a less than 15 per cent chance of getting a batsman LBW if appealing when he was on the front foot. By 2018, that had risen to over 20 per cent.

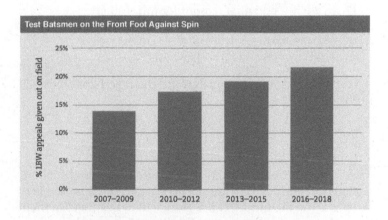

This is a trend, however, that began to take hold a few years after DRS was in place, and it is a trend for all bowling types. From 2014 onwards, the proportion of LBW appeals given out just goes up, and up, and up. In the initial years of DRS being in place, an LBW appeal was given out by the on-field umpire around one in five times; by 2020, it was almost one in three.

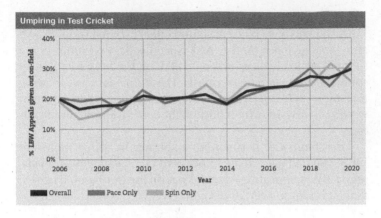

There are two potential reasons for this. Either:

a) There were more appeals that *deserved* to be given out.
b) Umpires were keener to give appeals out.

Well, there's a third option as well, which perhaps holds the truth:

c) Both.

WHAT GOES AROUND, STAYS AROUND

The retirement of Shane Warne in 2007, alongside fellow legends Glenn McGrath and Justin Langer, was a more obvious marker in the history of the sport, a hard line that signified the end of arguably the greatest side Test cricket had ever seen. However, the retirement of fellow spin-great Muttiah Muralitharan in 2010 marked the end of an era in a broader sense. 'Murali' was a bowler so unexpected and outrageous as to be unplayable to hundreds of batsmen – and scarcely describable to just as many writers, commentators and pundits.

The Sri Lankan had reinvented the art of 'finger' spin, embellishing layers of nuance and mystery, taking numerous hits to his reputation that, in theory at least, left the door open for similar successors. He changed what it was to be a spinner, unequivocally.

And yet, in 2010, what it was to be a spinner was about to be changed *again*, and this time on a deeper level. Big, cultural changes tend to happen as power shifts from one generation to the next, and the departure of the grand masters of spin was no different.

The leading finger-spinners at the turn of the decade – those who played a reasonable number of Tests in both the 2000s and the 2010s – all chose to make one clear tactical change.

When comparing their records in the latter part of the 2000s and the early part of the 2010s, they had all clearly come around to a global trend. The trend of, well, coming around.

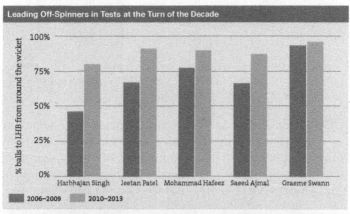

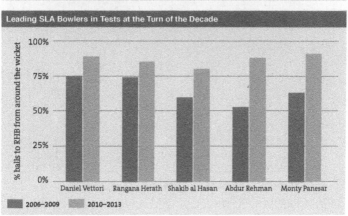

Every single one of the best finger-spinners in the world suddenly started doing the same thing. When faced with batsmen who they naturally took the ball away from, the best finger-spinners in the world all went round the wicket.

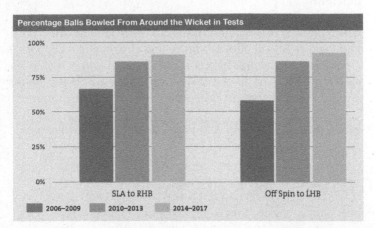

The effect of this was obvious and pronounced. The proportion of deliveries for finger-spinners that would permit an LBW dismissal – pitching 'in line' or outside the off stump, and going on to hit or clip the stumps – increased substantially around the turn of the decade. For other bowlers, it remained stable.

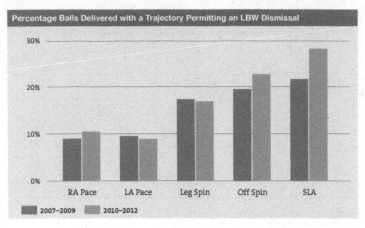

One fundamental reason why spinners – particularly finger-spinners – got more LBWs after the introduction of DRS is that they simply bowled more balls that *could* dismiss batsmen LBW. In a five-year Test career, Graeme Swann dismissed 43 left-handers LBW; in the entire 2000s, Muralitharan had only taken 33 such wickets. In part, a consequence of Muralitharan's ability to dismiss batsmen in any number of different ways; in part, a sign of a generational strategic shift.

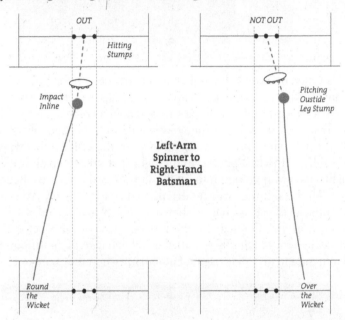

What's more, the pattern became self-perpetuating. Progressively across the decade, finger-spinners bowled more and more deliveries that were able to dismiss a batsman LBW, i.e. pitching on the right line, hitting in line, and projected to either hit or clip the stumps. It just kept going up, and up, and up.

Since the introduction of the DRS, there has been an ever-increasing number of deliveries bowled that *could* be 'out' LBW. Finger-spinners have bowled more and more balls on the right trajectory to keep LBW in play.

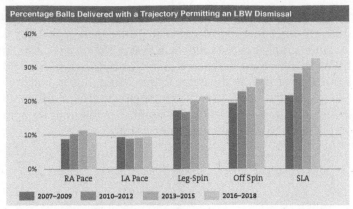

Yet each of those balls could have been met with the firmest of front-foot defences, blocked with the very middle of the middle of the bat. By combining ball-tracking and contact data recorded by analysts, we can do an umpire's job for them – on paper about a decade late, and with no way of influencing the action either way, but still . . . If a ball pitches in the right spot, hits the pad in the right spot and is going on to hit the stumps, it should have been out. All those things can be determined retrospectively. What's fascinating to see is that as shown in the charts '"Out" LBW Appeals in Test Cricket', for the first five years of DRS being in place, there was actually remarkably little change in an umpire's willingness to give players out. Particularly when they *were* out.

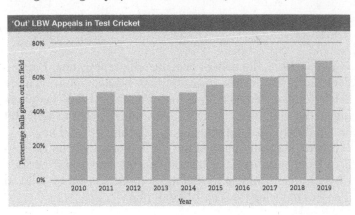

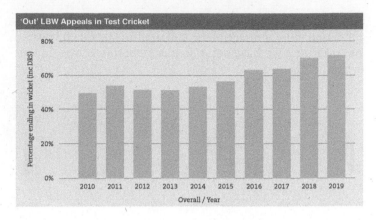

There is a 'retraining of human perception', a sort of cultural process where everyone in the game has to reconsider what they had always assumed to be true about LBWs. Hawkins says, 'In terms of the line, the human eye naturally follows the middle of the ball, so when the middle of the ball is missing by three centimetres, and the edge of the ball is hitting the stumps, that's where perception gets it wrong. You've almost got to make the stumps half a ball wider, for your *brain* to project whether the ball will hit the stumps.'

In terms of height, the issue comes from the fact that everyone watching on telly, every umpire, every non-striking batsman, is in the wrong place to determine the height of the ball: 'Even from a standing umpire's perspective, when the ball hits the front pad, you're still looking down on it. Look at umpires from the 1950s – they are crouched *right* down. You'd have to think they all ended up with terrible back aches,' Hawkins offers sympathetically. It isn't hard to see why umpires would have adopted this stance: 'If you get two umpires, one stood up and one sat on a chair with their eyes at stumps level, then ask them to officiate 50 balls and mark where the height of the ball was . . . the one sitting will show it higher (and more accurately) than the umpire who's stood up.'

Except, of course, modern umpires don't crouch low, and neither does a television camera from behind the bowler's arm. That has changed the game. The result is that we all have a distorted mental image of the ball we think has been bowled, and over time we have come to place enormous trust in that image.

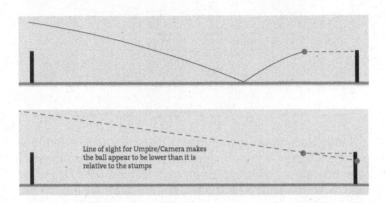

Line of sight for Umpire/Camera makes the ball appear to be lower than it is relative to the stumps

For those present at the early Hawk-Eye experiments, this was old news: 'We knew about shorter-wider back in 2000 when we were doing our testing.' That knowledge had been slowly dripping through into the mainstream while Hawk-Eye was being used in TV analysis, but without anything as systematic and attention-grabbing as the DRS to focus people's minds, much of that knowledge dissipated. For most people – umpires included – this news was disorientating enough that it took the introduction of DRS fully to comprehend what was going on, and it took several years to get used to it. Cricket has internalised this inaccurate version of how the ball moves. It's hard to remove it.

This is the 'retraining of human perception' to which Hawkins is referring. The lag of people growing to understand what they do not understand. As the decade has progressed, umpires have given more and more legitimate LBW appeals out on the field, because their own knowledge about what is and isn't out has changed. 'If Hawk-Eye disagrees with your own perception, it's very difficult to challenge your own beliefs, and what your own eyes told you.'

Plenty of column inches are filled by criticising the technology that drives DRS. There are particular instances of misalignment or misapplication, or even issues with the process on-field, but the technology itself is almost entirely reliable in a sample this large.

*   *   *

The semi-final of the 2011 World Cup, and India are playing Pakistan in Mohali. India's reputation has grown throughout the tournament, and they are closing in on a first home win in a 50-over World Cup. Pakistan's star weapon, the beautifully deceptive Saeed Ajmal, is the jewel in the crown of the opposition's attack.

Tendulkar is on 23 not out (off 26 balls), with India off to a flier thanks to Virender Sehwag. Ajmal pins Tendulkar, hammering him on the pad. Ian Gould gives it out on the field. Tendulkar walks calmly down to the other end of the cut strip, speaks to Gautam Gambhir, and reviews it. The process is new enough, recent enough, for the novelty of seeing the man most associated with old-style values to ring out, clear and peculiar.

The DRS process is followed. The ball pitched fine, the impact was fine – and the ball went down leg. Tendulkar is reprieved. Pakistan are incensed. He will go on to make 85 (115) in a match that India won by just 29 runs.

It was the only review in which Sachin Tendulkar was ever involved.

*   *   *

It was the rise in the accuracy of umpiring decisions that caused the simultaneous rise in the proportion of left-handed batsmen that we looked at in Chapter 4. As umpires improved, left-handed openers became more and more common, their numbers rising from the 20 to 25 per cent that had held steady for decades, to over 55 per cent.

The LBW law should give left-handers some protection against right-handed seamers, but pre-1994 it was not being enforced accurately enough nor fairly enough to afford them much advantage. So as standards of umpiring rose steadily, so did the performance of left-handers at the top of the order. And so, of course, did the performance of the best batsmen relative to the rest.

The improvements eradicated home bias, increased the number of left-handed batsmen, persuaded finger-spinners around the wicket, changed the way batsmen defended against the turning ball, and stretched the batting averages of the best batsmen further away from those of lesser players.

Cricket is not inclined to leaps of faith. It stumbles over its own deference to tradition, its own reservations about sweeping changes to itself. Few sports tweak their own rules as often, yet few sports do so with such subtlety, in such gentle increments. Big changes are not cricket's thing. That applies as much to issues of power and authority, and questioning either of those things, as it does to the colour of the ball and the size of the boundary.

Accountability for those in power does not ruin trust. It improves performance of the people in charge, it improves that trust, it amplifies the positive elements of the relationship between ruler and ruled and it adds to the game as a whole. All sport grapples with this; cricket has far too often paraded its own relative indifference.

Fundamentally, DRS has changed the game, and what we think about the game. Some people like that, some people don't like that, and some people don't believe it. The arrival of any challenge to trust in the umpire was always going to be controversial, and so it proved. The introduction was cricket's enlightenment. There have been plenty of moments when cricket changed fundamentally on the pitch; none have seen the game change more in the mind of the players. The introduction of DRS was possibly the single most revolutionary moment in the recent history of Test cricket.

Oppenheimer and Duality

....

'What do they know of cricket who only cricket know?'

(*Beyond A Boundary*, C. L. R. James)

Anyone who has spent any time in a professional dressing room must have, at some point, been confronted by the essential paradox of the whole endeavour. On the one hand, the result is everything. It is the only thing. We are all being paid, and we are being paid to win. The result is all. We aren't expected to win every match, but we are expected to *try* to win every match. Indeed, to do our utmost to do so, or what is the point of the venture? We collect a paycheque at the end of the month on the understanding that this is what we have endeavoured to do.

And the scale of the enterprise is huge. The budget for a typical Test match runs north of £20 million, and that is simply the direct expenditure, taking no account of the surrounding blizzard of coverage, comment and advertising. When we play India, 500 million people are watching live. When India play Pakistan the TV audience is larger than the population of Western Europe. The sheer weight of desire aimed at a favourable result is scarcely possible to conceive.

They used to say England would rather lose a battleship then a Test match. We have no battleships left to lose. But losing a home Test is still an event of weight and significance, something that haunts, and in some cases ends, careers.

And matches can turn on the outcome of a single ball. The invested imaginings of millions of people then hang on that instant, and the margin between success and failure cannot be excised by the thickness of a razor. And so, the details, the nuances, the trivialities, anything that might possibly influence the result, matters; matters like the weight and heft of a guillotine. The sheer bulk and tonnage of what will be said and believed about any major international match could sink a battleship.

And yet, in the same breath, it all means nothing. Sport is *not* real. It does not matter. It is at best a charming distraction from the real business of living. No sporting result changes the sum total of human happiness. Sometimes we are happy, sometimes they are. The only sane response to a poor result is to look at the celebrations of the opposition fans and say, 'Well, at least they're happy, and we will be back again tomorrow.'

We are akin to fictional characters, no more or less real. Our hopes and dreams, our triumphs and failures, are flickering shadows on the cave wall of real people's lives.

It has to matter enormously to make any sense, yet at the same time it is an essentially trivial activity compared to most of life's endeavours.

ROBERT OPPENHEIMER

Each year at the BBC, a series of lectures is given in memory of the corporation's founder Lord Reith. In 1953, it was the turn of Robert Oppenheimer to deliver the annual Reith Lectures. He had been for decades one of the foremost names in nuclear physics but was nevertheless better known as the mastermind of the 'Manhattan Project' and hence the father of the atomic bomb. He was a lifelong student of Hindu philosophy (his quoting of the *Bhagavad Gita* while reflecting on the first successful nuclear test had become his most famous remark, 'I am become Death, destroyer of worlds'). As such he had an agreeably Eastern, non-linear view of human affairs.

In these quite brilliant and extraordinary lectures, he laid out across a wide range of topics his hopes and beliefs about the future. He also discussed at length, and in detail, the nature of scientific thought and the advantages of having submitted one's mind to its rigours.

In particular, he argued that one of the benefits of scientific study was that Nature forces you to think in a certain way. You have to learn to align your thinking with the way that Nature actually works in order properly to understand it. You can't have an opinion on how something *should* be. For example, you can't have an opinion on what the structure of the atom is – or you can but it is a profoundly pointless thing to have. Nor can you have an opinion on gravity; if you step off a cliff you will fall and hit the ground, regardless of your predisposed thoughts on the matter.

Oppenheimer used the example of wave-particle duality in quantum mechanics to illustrate this point. A sub-atomic particle such as an electron often behaves like a point-mass, like a minuscule ball-bearing that bounces around, colliding with things. And this type of behaviour is easily shown to be true through experiments that an A-level student could carry out. In other situations it doesn't behave like a particle at all, but rather like a long, distributed object such as a wave. Again, this is provable experimentally at a basic level and causes easily observable phenomena such as interference patterns, and the fact that certain atomic orbits are stable and others are not.

An electron is a particle and behaves like one, and it is also a wave with all the properties you might expect of a wave. Nature forces you to hold both of those contradictory ideas in your head at the same time in order to understand how sub-atomic particles behave. It is *both* at the same time, and it is neither. And quantum theory is not the only area where such dualism exists; there are similar antinomies across science. Such as in the way we must think about time in general relativity.

Oppenheimer saw the value of applying the scientist's fluency in dualism to problems that occur outside of science. As an example, he suggested that there was a similar paradox of duality between the rights and freedoms that should be granted to each and every individual, and on the other hand the need for a safe and cohesive society, which necessitates infringing upon those freedoms. Both are logically consistent points of view that are clearly true, and yet they contradict each other.

Millennia before, Buddhist thinkers had come to a similar conclusion on a number of topics. In traditional Buddhist theory, the mind and the body are neither separate nor are they one. They exist as discrete objects and they are at the same time indivisible. They are at once different and the same, both of those things and neither. It is only possible fully to comprehend the mind–body duality by accepting this antinomy, by holding these conflicting ideas in your head at the same time.

We find in sport in general and in cricket in particular that similar situations that require duality of thinking often arise. You often find that it is possible to argue quite logically from one point of view to a sane and sensible conclusion, but that this reasoning is nevertheless completely incompatible with a different and *equally valid* point of view. Sometimes the data helps us and tips the balance in favour of one argument or the other. But often we are working from too small a sample size for the available data to ever definitively arbitrate the matter. At which point we must resort to dualism fully to understand the problem and its solutions: we must accept the force of both arguments, accept that both contain elements of truth and that neither is a complete solution. Balance and nuance must remain legitimate tools for a useful understanding of many areas of the game to emerge. This is not a failure of reason, but a triumph of its highest sense.

The opposite of this is the level of thinking that you find all too often within cricket. Which is, to reduce it to its basic form, *I can create a valid argument for this to be the case, therefore it is true, therefore I am right.* So: 'The batsman keeps playing and missing, therefore the bowler is bowling too short'; 'It's a good wicket, so we should bat first'; 'He's our best bowler so we'll save him till the end', etc.

You could easily write down ten of your own without difficulty. Perfectly plausible arguments that within their own limits make perfect sense. But once the exercise becomes about winning the argument, rather than discovering the truth, it is incredibly unlikely that you will achieve the latter.

As Oppenheimer tells us, along with his great contemporary, the theoretical physicist Richard Feynman, if the history of science has been anything, it has been a battle fought for the right to doubt. For the right to question and challenge established truth. Feynman talked of 'the great progress that comes from a satisfactory philosophy of ignorance' in *What Do You Care What Other People Think?*. There can be no progress in any craft while the Elders of the Guild are allowed to declaim the 'truths' of their faith without fear of contradiction.

Humility, doubt, nuance, opening ourselves to challenge, admitting the paradox of duality, these are necessary tools.

So for those of us that are close enough to the coal face for these things still to sting, the result of the match is everything, and yet in the same instant, within the same breath, trivial.

The Cat That Turned
Into a Fence

....

The hardest ground in the world to win at as an away team is Brisbane Cricket Ground (otherwise known as the Gabba), the Australian citadel. No visiting team has won there in 32 years. Of the last 31 Tests played at the 'Gabbattoir', there have been 24 home wins and 7 draws.

Let's go back to 2002 and the first Test of the Ashes. An unfancied England team under Nasser Hussain is about to launch their campaign to win back 'the urn' from Steve Waugh's powerhouse Australian team.

As usual, the first match of the series is in the unforgiving heat of Brisbane. At the toss, the sound the coin makes as it hits the bone-hard pitch is enough to tell any Englishman he is a long way from home. Nasser calls correctly, unaware that he is about to go down in cricket history. Unfortunately, for all the wrong reasons.

Now roll forward two-and-a-half years to Edgbaston in 2005. This time Ricky Ponting is the visiting captain who wins the toss.

At this point, Australia have held the Ashes for the last 18 years. It feels longer. Already 1–0 up in the series, the whole of Australia knows the urn is tucked safely in Ponting's back pocket. But he is about to join Nasser on the Ashes Captain's Naughty Step. Australia will go on to lose the Ashes, and have not won a Test series in England since.

In the introduction, we introduced the story of 'The Tethered Cat', in which a habitual action outlived the conditions that created it, and mentioned that cricket is particularly well-resourced in such habits. And possibly the most pervasive of them occurs before a ball is even bowled.

THE TOSS

Cricket is an unusually asymmetric game in a number of ways. In particular, one side gets the opportunity to bat first, and can bat for as long as they choose.

The side that wins the toss at the start of the match gets to choose whether to bat first or bowl first. This clearly gives them an advantage.

But how much of an advantage do you think it gives them in a Test match? How many more matches do you think the team who wins the toss wins than the opposition? Five per cent more? Ten per cent more? Without looking the exact numbers up, that feels about right doesn't it?

But it isn't.

When we first started to look at these figures for Test cricket in 2010, we noticed something very strange. In recent Test history, the toss didn't seem to be much of an advantage at all. Indeed, in the previous 1000 Test matches played up until that point, the side who won the toss had won 338, and the side that had lost the toss had won 342. And looking in more detail at the previous 40 years of Test cricket, there was no period where the toss was a statistically significant advantage to the team that won it. We now believe there have been three distinct phases in the history of Test cricket and that the decisions that captains have made at the toss has had a different effect in each of them.

Winning the toss in the modern era appeared to give a side no advantage at all. But how could that be the case? It was an asymmetric situation where you got to choose the better option. If this choice wasn't having an impact on the results, then there was only one possibility. Teams must be making the wrong choice as often as they made the right one. There must be a fundamental misunderstanding of how Test matches are won and lost.

UNCOVERED PITCHES

It wasn't always so. Up until the 1970s almost all cricket was played on uncovered pitches.

On uncovered pitches, batting first in almost all instances was a robustly successful strategy. If it rained during the match, the pitch would deteriorate, affecting the side batting second disproportionately. Until 1970 the side batting first in a Test won 36 per cent of matches and lost only 28 per cent.

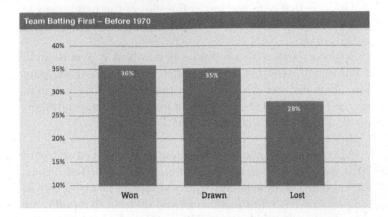

Understandably, the vast majority (89 per cent) of captains who won the toss chose to bat, and this resulted in sides who won the toss having a markedly better chance of winning. The small number of captains who chose to bowl first should probably have batted as well, as they lost more than they won.

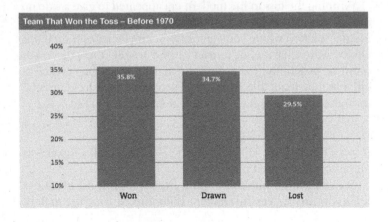

But in the modern era, the advantage of winning the toss seems to have disappeared. This is, of course, very counter-intuitive. After all, one team bats first, then the other, and the two teams' chances of winning are not equal. The team batting first has different requirements for victory to the team batting second, and the pitch changes over the course of the match, affecting the balance of power between bat and ball. Therefore, we would assume, teams that win the toss can choose the best conditions and so gain an advantage. But they don't. How can that possibly be?

This is the problem with Tethered Cats. Sometimes, a perfectly reasonable response to current circumstances becomes a habit, then a tradition, then an article of faith that outlives the circumstances that created it. We rarely question what we know to be self-evidently true, particularly when everyone else is doing the same thing. And so the bias towards batting first seems to have outlived the circumstances that created it by several decades.

'If you win the toss, nine times out of ten you should bat. On the tenth occasion you should think about bowling and then bat.'

That was a very successful strategy to adopt for the first century of Test cricket. And one that is still the default setting for most captains. In the Tests played between 1980 and 2010, nearly twice as many captains have batted first than have chosen to bowl. Is it still successful?

Well, in a word, no. In that period, the side batting first won 31 per cent of those Tests, the side bowling first 36 per cent. The bat-first bias at the toss would seem to be neutral at best, and probably counter-productive.

Even so, it is still hard to believe that captains weren't able to use the toss to their advantage. There are venues where the evidence is stark. Some pitches clearly favour the side batting first, some the side batting second. In the 40 Tests played in Lahore, the team batting first has won just 3.

Adelaide, by contrast, is a classic bat-first venue. It starts as a batsman's paradise, consistent and true, with little sideways

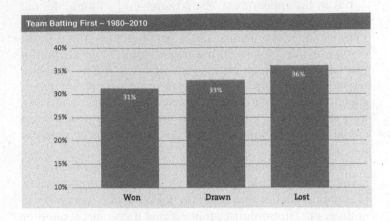

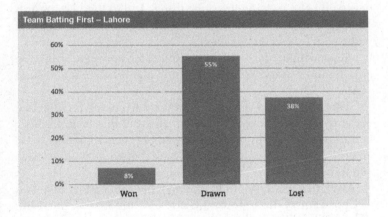

movement, but by the fifth day can be very tricky to bat on, with uneven bounce and considerable turn for the spinners. In the 73 Tests played at the ground, the side batting first has won 35, the side batting second 19. Since 1990, averages in the first innings are 44.6, second innings 38.9, third innings 30.1 and fourth innings 27.1, and, as you would expect, in that period 25 out of 26 captains have chosen to bat first, gaining a considerable advantage in doing so.

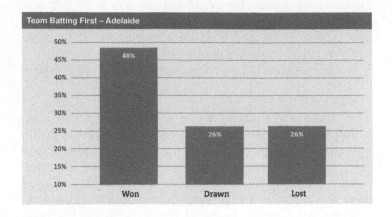

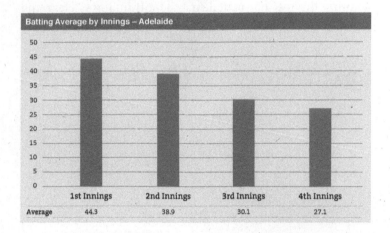

These are not isolated cases. Many pitches have similarly skewed characteristics. Galle and Old Trafford, for example, both have similar records to Adelaide. Karachi is as bowl-first friendly as Lahore.

So, there are grounds where winning the toss hands a clear advantage to one team, others where the difference is smaller, and some where it is negligible. A strategy where you did the obvious at the venues that were no-brainers and chose at random everywhere else would net you a 5 to 10 per cent advantage. So why didn't international captains get any advantage at all from the toss? Were there specific situations where captains tend to make the wrong call?

Well, yes. Let's take one particularly clear example: India.

TESTS IN INDIA

The breakdown of when the toss is an advantage, and when it isn't, is an interesting one. Home teams, surprisingly, do no better than away teams in using the toss to their advantage. Teams also do quite differently in different countries. India is a particularly extreme case. In the 93 Tests played there this century, captains have been almost unanimous in knowing what to do. In 86 of the 93 matches the team winning the toss has batted first. The thinking is clear and simple.

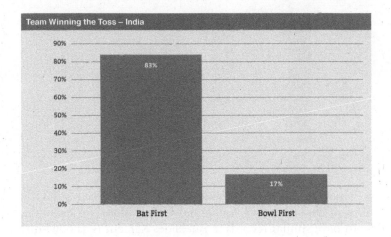

Most pitches in India start flat and true and deteriorate steadily as the match goes on. Bat first and not only do you get first use of a fresh pitch, you are also bowling in the final innings when batting is hardest. The thinking may be simple;

however, it also seems to be flawed. In those 93 matches, the team batting first has won 28 and lost 38.

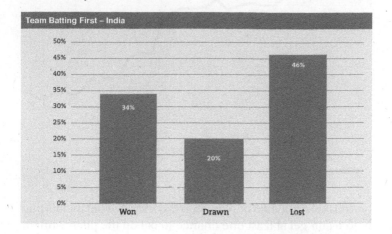

Now, India win most of their matches at home, and so if they had ended up batting second more often than the visitors this might account for some of this bias. And indeed, India *have* batted second more often, but it turns out their performances are also slanted towards bowling first. When they bat first, they win 55 per cent of matches, when they bowl first, they win 60 per cent. (India incidentally chose to bat first on 38 of the 43 occasions when they won the toss, and their record when they won the toss was 55 per cent wins, compared to 59 per cent when they lost the toss.)

So what is going on?

Well, there are two effects at play. Firstly, although the pitches deteriorate, they generally take three or so days to do so. The graph shows a comparison of batting averages against time in Tests.

Pitches in India start more batsman-friendly than Test pitches in general, and they also deteriorate more than most. But this only starts to make a marked difference around 18

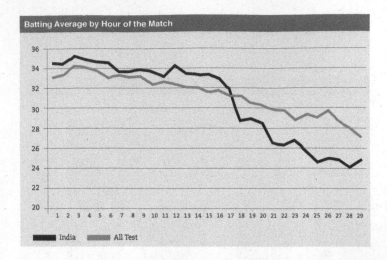

Batting Average by Hour of the Match

India   All Test

hours (three full days of play) into the match. That means that both teams get at least one chance to bat on the pitch while it is still flat. The effect of the deterioration is not to hand an advantage to one side or the other, but rather to magnify the advantage of a first innings lead for whichever team gets one.

What happens once you have a first innings lead is then the key to understanding the most efficient route to victory. Generally, the side batting last can use the time left in the game more efficiently than the team batting first, who must bat to make the game safe before they can start the task of bowling the opposition out.

The mechanics of winning the match are much simpler for the side batting second. Bowl the opposition out, and then knock off the requisite runs, with no time wasted.

In India, where there has historically been a high proportion of draws and forcing a result can be difficult, this difference is particularly important. It hands an advantage to the side batting second who can use the limited time remaining in the game more efficiently when hunting the win. And the evidence seems to support this supposition. In those 93 Tests, when the team batting first got a lead, they went on to win 50 per cent of those matches. The team batting second, however, converted 70 per cent of their leads to victories. Although there were marginally fewer first innings leads for the team batting second, there were overall more wins.

PERCENTILES AND PROBABILITY SPACES

For those who are interested in the mechanisms of Test wins we are about to get really geeky. First, there are a couple of concepts we need to get our heads round.

First of all, percentiles. If you are in the 40th percentile for height, you would expect 40 out of 100 people to be your height or shorter. If you were in the 95th percentile for height then you would expect only 5 in every 100 people to be taller than you.

Similarly, if we look at the possible range of scores for a Test we can use percentiles to measure how likely a team is to make a certain score. For example, for an average team batting second in a Test match, a score of 420 is in their 70th percentile. So they will score more than 420 roughly 30 per cent of the time.

Secondly, we need the idea of sample spaces. Imagine we each roll a six-sided die and add the two numbers together. There are 36 equally likely outcomes, which we can illustrate in a chart like this:

Your Roll							
6		7	8	9	10	11	12
5		6	7	8	9	10	11
4		5	6	7	8	9	10
3		4	5	6	7	8	9
2		3	4	5	6	7	8
1		2	3	4	5	6	7
		1	2	3	4	5	6
				My Roll			

181

As you can see, the total 8 occurs five times, so we can say that the probability of getting a total of 8 is 5 in every 36, or 14 per cent.

We are now going to play a game. The rules are as follows, we each roll our dice and . . .

1. if your score is greater than or equal to mine, then you win;
2. if my score is greater than yours, I win;
3. however, if we both of us throw a 4 or higher, then it is a draw.

How likely is each of the three results? We can look at the probability space to tell us:

Your Roll		My Roll					
6	7	8	9	10	11	12
5	6	7	8	9	10	11
4	5	6	7	8	9	10
3	4	5	6	7	8	9
2	3	4	5	6	7	8
1	2	3	4	5	6	7
	1	2	3	4	5	6

Your win | Draw | My win

In 15 of the 36 possibilities you win. So you will win 42 per cent of the time. I will win 12 out of 36 or 33 per cent of the games, and 25 per cent will be draws.

We can take the same approach with Test matches by creating a sample space based on how well each team scores during the match. Let's take a look at the probability space of a Test match between two well-matched teams on a typical modern pitch, with no weather interruptions. Team A is always the team that bats first.

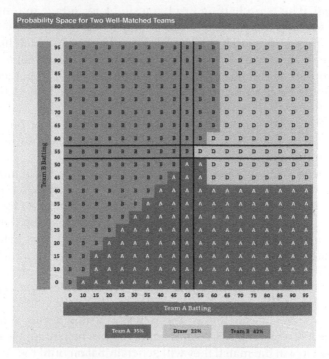

Here the batting performances of each team form our axes. The numbers are how well they scored, measured from 0 to 100 in percentiles. So the left-hand side are low Team A scores, the right-hand side are high scores. The top half of the chart shows good Team B batting performances, the bottom half are poor performances. As you can see, when both sides score highly (top right-hand corner) we get a draw. When one side or the other scores poorly, they tend to lose.

So, if Team A's scores are in the 70th percentile then we are looking at the column above the number 70. And we can see by looking up and down this column that they won't lose if they bat this well. The result now depends on Team B's batting.

If they perform better than their 40th percentile then they will save the match, otherwise Team A will win.

One thing you will notice is that the chart is not symmetrical. The team batting first has a slight advantage in terms of scoring; the pitch tends to be more batsman-friendly in innings 1 and 3 than in 2 and 4. So in low-scoring matches, where there will be a result, Team A has a slight edge. If you look at the hundred squares (from 5th to 50th percentile for each team) in the bottom left-hand section of the chart, you will see that 53 of them areTeam A wins, and 47 are Team B wins. However, the overall balance of power lies with Team B, who will win a fifth more matches than Team A.

So, if Team A scores more runs, why does Team B win more matches? Well, the key is what happens in relatively high-scoring games. As we have said, it is far easier for Team B to force a result in matches where they bat well. Look at the top right-hand corner of the chart where both sides have batted better than average. You can see that the light squares extend into this space where as the dark squares don't. There are no wins to the team batting first in matches where both sides score relatively highly.

We can see what this means in reality by thinking about the effect of a first innings lead. If Team A gets a first innings lead, then to win the match they will generally bat on until they can make the game safe and declare. Then they try to bowl out the opposition, who in turn know just what they have to do to save the game. On the other hand, if Team B get a first innings lead, they just have to bowl Team A out and chase down the resulting total. They are able to use the time left in the match far more efficiently to force a result.

The advantage to the side batting second is at its greatest when the draw is most likely. So the model seems to suggest the following as a framework.

When there is a high probability of a result, because the bowling attacks are stronger than the batting line-ups or because the wicket will favour the bowlers, then the question is simple: which side will get the best conditions on this pitch? Generally that means you should bat first, unless you think the wicket will do appreciably more on day one and then improve. The rule of thumb is that you want to bat most of day two, either by bowling out the opposition in under four sessions or by batting first for five or more sessions, and you choose whichever course gives you the best chance of doing so.

So far so orthodox. Where the stats diverge from traditional thinking is in matches where there is a good chance of a draw. As we've seen, this skews things slightly in favour of batting second. On pitches that deteriorate markedly, such as Adelaide and Galle, the advantage of first use of the wicket still wins. But, on pitches that start flat and stay fairly flat, or deteriorate late in the game, there does seem to be evidence that the side batting second has an edge. This is where we part company with received wisdom and practice.

Let's revisit our two examples of bowl-first friendly wickets. Lahore and Karachi have records heavily slanted in favour of the team batting second (see the table 'Team Batting First'). Both also have high draw percentages, and have tended to deteriorate slowly or not at all.

Team Batting First				
	Played	Win	Draw	Loss
Lahore	40	3	22	15
Karachi	43	7	18	18

By now it will come as no surprise to you that even at these two venues, the two most bowl-first friendly venues in Test history, the large majority of captains have chosen to bat first (70 per cent in Lahore, 80 per cent in Karachi). And as a result, teams' chances of winning there improved by over a half if they lost the toss.

So captains' behaviour at the toss, in particular in subcontinental conditions, seems to be a particularly clear example of a Tethered Cat. In truth, there are many such examples in cricket, where received wisdom doesn't concur with the evidence: where what teams do doesn't seem to maximise their chances of winning. Why is this the case? Large numbers of supremely talented people are dedicating their lives to playing and coaching international cricket, and the game is followed by millions. There is no shortage of effort and thought going into the game, and the rewards for success are large.

Well, part of the story involves how our brains handle information. There has been a great deal of research into memory and perception, and the results are both surprising and illuminating when it comes to our decision-making in sport. For a start, our memories don't work as you might expect. They are not akin to a videotape; we don't record a series of events and then play them back as and when they are needed.

The disturbing truth is that our unaided recall is not very good. The human brain encodes less than 10 per cent of what we experience; the rest it simply makes up. Our minds construct a narrative around the coded memories we do have that fills in the gaps with a plausible story. Faced with a huge number of random or near random events (a cricket match, for instance) our brains pattern-spot, even when there is no pattern. Our minds look for those events that they can form into a pattern or story, and that becomes the meaning or lesson that we take away from the match. Even if the vast majority of events that occurred didn't fit the pattern, we disproportionately remember the ones that did.

At their best, our memories work like Albert Camus's description of fiction; they are 'the lie through which we tell the truth'. What we remember didn't actually happen; what we remember is a story that our brains have fabricated, but one that we hope contains the essential truth of what happened in a way that we can understand and retain.

Let's use the thought experiment of an international rugby match. You head off to Twickenham to watch England play Australia, and in the bar after the match a friend asks you how you thought Owen Farrell played. If you saw him making a great tackle and a scything break, then you will probably have it in your head that he played well. If you remember instead a tackle he missed, and a couple of balls he knocked on, then you will say he had a poor game. And yet you know perfectly well that you watched 30 players in continuous motion during 80 minutes of rugby, and that Farrell has in all likelihood touched the ball 20 or so times, made a dozen tackles, hit a similar number of rucks, tracked back, organised defensively, and been making an almost endless stream of low-level decisions and adjustments. You know that you didn't see the vast majority of what he did, and can't remember most of what you did see. Yet you still feel you have a clear impression of how well he played.

And it's not just our recall that is faulty. It's also our perception of events. We see everything through the prism of our previous experiences and beliefs. We look for what we expect to see and we are far more likely to spot examples that agree with our expectations than contradict them. There is a wealth of hard scientific data showing just how easily manipulated our perceptions are by context and emotion. We are, unfortunately, very poor witnesses to our own lives.

For example, you may not know this, but we are both excellent drivers. We know this to be true because we have seen ouselves drive a lot. We could quote you endless examples of us driving well. We would say we are certainly in the top half of drivers on the roads. The only thing that slightly shakes our faith in this assessment is that everyone else thinks the same. Over 90 per cent of us think we are above-average drivers. The same holds true in a range of different areas. We have a strong tendency to significantly overestimate our own abilities. And in particular, we hugely overestimate the accuracy of our own memories and perceptions.

Yet even knowing these fallibilities doesn't seem to shake our faith. Even though we understand how our memories fool us. Even though we have seen endless examples of matches being misremembered by people, ourselves included. Even so, we still come away from games with the certain belief that we remember it right, that our memory of it is the correct one, and most other people do too.

This is how data can help us when used well. It acts a bit like a video camera. Video analysis, with slow motion and freeze frame, has enabled coaches and players to see things they couldn't otherwise see. It reveals aspects of technique that the unaided eye can't spot. Used well, statistics can do the same, revealing patterns and trends over seasons and decades that would otherwise be all but impossible to spot.

The 'used well' is crucial there. If our memories can trick us, then data is equally adept at doing so. But used well, evidence-based analysis becomes one more tool. One more source of evidence to draw on when trying to understand the game we love.

But now we are drifting into still waters, and in danger of being plucked away by a different current. So, back to the toss.

Our fallible memories are only part of the reason captains and coaches behave the way they do. There is another, far more powerful reason to make the choices they make and one that is harder to argue against. For this we need to go back to Brisbane in 2002, and Nasser Hussain choosing to bowl.

'The test of a first-rate intelligence is the ability to hold two opposed ideas in the mind at the same time, and still retain the ability to function' – F. Scott Fitzgerald

It was the first Test of the Ashes, and a powerhouse Australian team were at the peak of their powers and playing at home in 'Fortress Brisbane', the hardest ground in the world to win at as an away team. Hussain won the toss and chose to bowl. Australia were 364 for 2 by the close of play and went on to win comfortably.

It is no use looking back with hindsight and using that to determine whether a decision was right or wrong. I am sure that if Nasser had known that choosing to bowl first would bring a host of dropped chances, the loss of a key bowler to injury and Australia piling up the first innings runs, then he would have chosen to have a look behind door B and strapped his pads on.

But he didn't know and, in evaluating a past decision, we shouldn't know either. We need to remain behind the veil of ignorance, aware of all the potential paths the match could have taken, but ignorant of the one that it did.

One way we can do that is to simulate the match. There are various models that allow us to simulate matches, given the playing strengths of the two sides, and give probabilities for the outcome. When we do this for that Brisbane Test, we get the following probabilities for England.

England Win Probability – Brisbane 2002			
	Win	Draw	Loss
Bat first	4%	3%	93%
Bowl first	4%	10%	86%

Every batsman in Australia's top seven finished his career averaging over 45 (three averaged 50 plus). None of the English players did, and only two averaged 40. England had a decent bowling attack. Australia had Warne, McGrath and Gillespie with 1000 wickets between them already.

England were a pretty good side: they had won four, lost two in their previous ten matches. But the truth is that on that day they were hopelessly outgunned, and in alien conditions. Steve Waugh, the Australian captain, said later that he would also have bowled first if he had won the toss. If he had done, then Australia would almost certainly have won that match as well. Australia were almost certainly going to win regardless of who did what at the toss.

But none of that made any difference. Hussain's decision to bowl first was castigated by the public and press of both countries. It was described in *Wisden Cricketers' Almanack 2013* as 'one of the costliest decisions in Test history'. The *Telegraph's* Derek Pringle wrote that the decision should prompt the England captain 'to summon his faithful hound, light a last cigarette and load a single bullet into the revolver' in an article entitled 'England's day of horrors'.

At the time of writing, if you Googled 'Nasser Hussain

Brisbane', the first article that comes up is titled 'Hussain's coin toss horror-show'.

For Nasser in Brisbane, read Ricky Ponting at Edgbaston in 2005. Another decision to insert the opposition that has never been lived down.

Yet, if either of them had batted first and lost, no one would ever remember their decision at the toss. You will rarely if ever be criticised for choosing to bat. Batting is the default setting; bowling first is seen as the gamble. And remember, the side that batted first during that period of history lost significantly more than it won.

Test cricket is one of the greatest contests in sport, a brilliant, multi-faceted contest for mind and body. On the one hand, a series of individual contests; on the other, a game that challenges a team's unity of purpose to the utmost. An intensely technical, endlessly tactical battle that is, at one and the same time, a brutal five-day arm-wrestle of mental and physical endurance.

But it is also a game of numbers. The technique, the teamwork, the mental and physical strength are all essential, and are the vast majority of what decides the result of any match. But if you can tilt the numbers slightly in your favour, get them working for you, not against you, plot a slightly more efficient path to victory, then you are always working slightly downhill rather than toiling against the slope.

As we have seen in a number of different ways, on flat pitches, the numbers tell us that the counterintuitive choice is the right one. That bowling first improves your chances of winning. And yet . . .

We all do it. We look at a pristine wicket, flat, hard and true, and batting seems the only option. It is written into our cricketing DNA. So imagine yourself as a Test captain at the toss, gazing down at a bone-hard surface on which you could land light aircraft. You know there is nothing at all in it for your bowlers. There is no point leading where they won't follow and, unless there's a glimmer of interest from your attack, putting the opposition in is asking for trouble. Plus, you know you'll never be criticised for batting first.

The evidence may suggest there is a small marginal gain in bowling. But small margins be damned. If the marginal gain erodes your credibility and authority, then that is probably not an exchange you are willing to make. There are tides you can't swim against. Just listen to the commentariat describe 'the modern way' as if they are holding something that's died under their floorboards between a rubber-gloved finger and thumb. Risk taking and unorthodoxy are popular just so long as you win.

In 2015, Alastair Cook and Misbah-ul-Haq stood together at the toss in the baking heat of Abu Dhabi. Both are men of considerable character; brave, implacable and preternaturally determined to win. Each has withstood the slings and arrows of captaining their country through some fairly outrageous fortunes. Each is ready to bat first without a second thought. Because while they are certainly brave, they are not stupid. And you would have to be really stupid to make the right decision.

And there of course you have the central problem of much decision-making in cricket. This pitch is slightly different to all the other pitches that there have ever been. And you don't know for certain how it is going to play, or how that will influence the balance of power in the match. There are those who would argue that this is why stats are useless, or at best very limited.

We would agree entirely that stats are never sufficient to make a decision. There is nuance and subtlety to weigh; the brain and eye have access to information that the laptop doesn't. The feel and instincts of coaches and players, the hardwired learning from decades in the game, contain incredibly valuable information and will always be the mainstay of decision-making that must be flexible and fluid through changing match situations. But if we are honest, we must also accept that the sheer weight and tonnage of what we don't know about how cricket works would sink a battleship. To use stats and nothing else to make decisions would be incredibly foolish, and as far as we are aware no one ever has. But equally, to insist on making decisions on incomplete information, without ever reviewing the effectiveness of those decisions, would seem almost equally perverse.

Misbah won the toss in Abu Dhabi, and over the next two days Pakistan compiled a huge first innings total. England then did the same. At which point only one side could possibly win. Pakistan duly collapsed and England would have cantered home but for bad light curtailing the fifth day's play.

We are not saying that everyone was wrong in Abu Dhabi. We are not saying that Misbah should have bowled. The hostility of the conditions on that first morning, where it was well over 45 °C in the shade, would have decided anyone. Any captain asking his bowlers to field first on that joyless pitch, under the hammer of the desert sun, would have faced a mutiny. Any captain who did that and lost would have become instant tabloid chum. The weight of opprobrium heaped on him doesn't bear thinking about. It's the sort of decision that ends captaincies. No, Misbah had only one option and he took it.

But maybe there will come a time when it isn't such an obvious choice. Maybe one day we'll stop tying up that particular cat.

TEST CRICKET'S THIRD PHASE

If we had tried to write this book a few years ago then we would have ended the chapter here with that call-back to the idea of the Tethered Cat. And everything we have said so far still holds true for the two periods we have described, the era of uncovered pitches running up to the 1970s, and then the modern era from 1980 until 2010. But there is now compelling evidence that a tipping point was reached and at some point in the last decade something fundamental shifted. As a result we have entered a new era, a third phase for Test cricket where the balance of power between batting and bowling is different again.

Test cricket is a remarkably stable format. Through decades of evolving tactics, techniques and playing conditions, the underlying dynamics of the game have remained largely unaffected. The balance between bat and ball in Test cricket has shifted a little back and forth, but it has stayed broadly the same since before the war (unlike in One Day cricket).

Likewise, the fundamental fairness of the format has remained unchanged for 40 years. There are some good tosses to win, but in general the two teams start the match with the same chance of victory. In the period from 1980 to 2014, the team batting first won 32 per cent, and the team batting second won 36 per cent, and in no decade during that period did the ratio drift far away from equality.

Recently, though, a trend has emerged that, although it initially looked like a blip, now looks like it could be a profound shift in the balance of the game. Since the start of 2014, the team batting first has won 156 (56 per cent) of the 280 Tests played and lost only 82 (29 per cent).

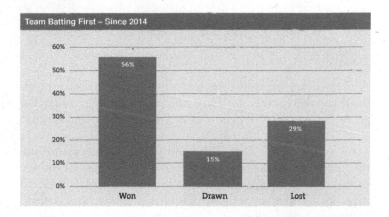

Some of this discrepancy could be natural variation, but it is vanishingly unlikely that all of it is.

To understand what has changed we need to understand the forces that held everything stable for so long.

A GAME IN BALANCE

Since the advent of covered pitches, the rough equilibrium between batting and bowling has been maintained by two opposing factors. On the one hand, the team that bats first has slightly better batting conditions. Although the second innings is generally the best time to bat, the fourth is by far the worst, and so, if time were not an issue, you would expect the team batting first to win more than they lose.

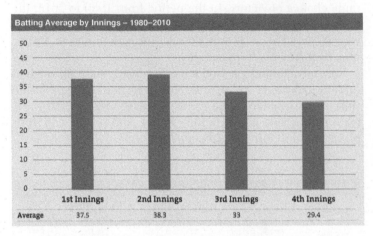

Batting Average by Innings – 1980–2010			
	1st Innings	2nd Innings	3rd Innings	4th Innings
Average	37.5	38.3	33	29.4

Time, however, *is* an issue, and this tilts things back towards the team who bat second. They can use the limited time in the game more efficiently when converting strong positions into wins.

As we have seen, batting second allows a team to use the time left in the game more efficiently. And this is what you see in the results. Historically, a first innings lead of a hundred runs has resulted in roughly 50 per cent wins for the team batting first. But, when it is the team batting second with a hundred-run lead, their win rate is over 70 per cent.

The more likely a draw is, the more of an advantage it is if you use the remaining time efficiently. So the more draws there are, the stronger the bat-second advantage in forcing results.

THE DECLINE OF THE DRAW
As you can see in the first graph, the proportion of draws in Test cricket has been in steady decline since the start of the

nineties. As scoring rates have risen, a greater proportion of matches have ended in a result.

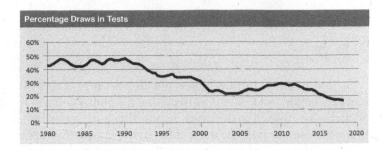

Although not everyone's favourite outcome, the draw is an important balancing force within Test cricket and has always acted as a counterweight to the team batting first's other advantages. And so the draw's slow decline seems to have contributed to a tipping point. If one of the disadvantages of batting first has traditionally been that you draw more matches from a position of strength than the team batting second, then when these draws turn into results, they break disproportionately in favour of the team batting first.

THE RISE OF THE SPINNER

The decline of the draw alone, though, is not enough to have skewed the figures so far. Something else has magnified the effect, and while it is always hard to definitively attribute cause to effect in something as complex as Test cricket, there is a compelling suspect.

It is clear for a start that the relative advantage that innings one and three hold over innings two and four has widened significantly.

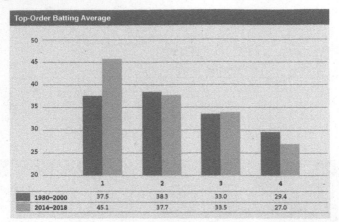

Top-Order Batting Average	1	2	3	4
1980–2000	37.5	38.3	33.0	29.4
2014–2018	45.1	37.7	33.5	27.0

So, are pitches starting better and deteriorating faster? It may be a factor, but it seems unlikely that the global behaviour of pitches has shifted so decisively in one direction, and we can find no reason for it in the data, either in the raw performance numbers of runs and wickets or in the detailed ball-tracking information about how the pitch is behaving.

The most likely cause is not a change in the pitches, but who bowls on them. For various reasons (the DRS scoring system for one) spinners are bowling more and more of the overs in Test cricket. (In the early 1990s spinners bowled 30 per cent of Test overs; in the last four years it has been 42 per cent.) And unlike pace bowlers, spinners become uniformly more effective as the game goes on, as the pitch wears and the bowlers' footmarks develop.

So as the proportion of overs bowled by spinners has increased, the profile of scoring across the average Test match has shifted accordingly. This has increased the average advantage that the side batting first gets, and without the coun-terweight of a number of matches being drawn this has swung results hard in one direction.

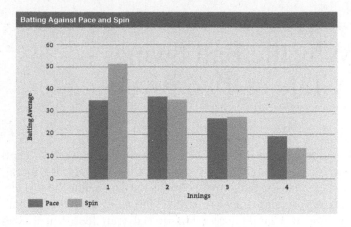

It is very hard to apportion cause and effect with any confidence, so these may not be the reasons for the shift in results that we are seeing. But whatever is causing it, unless it is a blip, it threatens the very validity of Test cricket. A sport where a coin toss makes one side twice as likely to win would lose a lot of its appeal.

It is ironic that one of our favourite examples of a Tethered Cat seems to have turned back into a successful strategy without ever being recognised as sub-optimal, despite having been so for decades. Of course, Test matches in any era are not some homogenous block where the same decision is the right choice at each and every toss. Every ground is different, every combination of teams is different. In every decade there have been matches where the right thing to do was bowl, and there have been matches where the right thing to do was bat. And in deciding which of those is the case, it is important to understand the forces we have outlined in this chapter.

It is possible our favourite Cat just turned into a Fence.

But the fact is that throughout the history of Test cricket, captains have shown a distinct bias towards batting first. This worked against them between 1980 and 2010 but seems to have benefited them in the period since. The Cat does seem to have turned back into a Fence.

....

Why the Ball Swings –
A Tale of Two Rivers

....

Imagine you are standing by a wide, shallow river. It is a still day, and the calm water is glass smooth. Through it you can see clearly to the flat gravel bottom a few feet below the surface.

Now you step into the river. The water at the edge isn't moving, just lapping cool-tongued at your feet. But as you wade further away from the bank, the current gets gradually quicker and stronger. So that by the time you reach the middle, the bright, clear flow is tugging insistently at your legs. When you move back towards the bank, the flow gradually and smoothly slows, until once again you are standing at the edge in still water.

This is called *lamina flow*.

Lob a ball underarm to someone and this is how the air flows over the ball as it is in flight. The molecules of air touching the ball are carried along with it and travel at the same speed. Then in smoothly progressing 'laminae' further away from the ball (on a near microscopic level), the speed of the air relative to the ball gets quicker and quicker.

Now imagine a different river. This one is identical to the first, except we switch the smooth gravel of the riverbed for a jumble of rocks, boulders and tree branches. As the fast-flowing water hits these obstacles the smooth flow of water becomes turbulent and chaotic. There are waves and white water, swirling eddies are held behind boulders, even flowing back upstream a little, before plunging over and down into rolling stoppers. As with the first river, the water by the bank is entirely still and in the centre it is flowing quickly, but there is no smooth, incremental transition from one to the other: the change happens in a random, disordered fashion. This is called turbulent flow.

Bowl an old ball at high speed (90+ mph) and this is the type of flow that you will see. The rough surface of the ball and the sheer violence of smashing a rough object into still air at that velocity destroys the smooth lamina flow that you see at lower speeds. The air touching the ball is still carried along with it, and the air further from the ball is still untouched by it, but the transition from moving air to still air is turbulent and chaotic rather than smooth and incremental.

These are the two types of airflow you get over a ball in flight, and it is the difference between how the two behave that enables a bowler to get the ball to swing. To understand why, we need to think about how our two rivers cope with a change of direction.

Imagine both rivers come to a bend. The current in the smooth, lamina-flow river carries a lot of momentum: it finds it hard to turn against the weight of its own propelling force, and so as the bend in the river continues, the current swings wide, quickly losing contact with the inside bank.

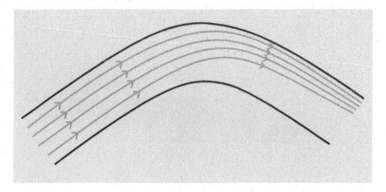

The turbulent river, on the other hand, with its eddies, whirlpools and multiple complex flows, finds it easier to change direction: it follows the arc of the bend for longer. It is capable of making a bigger, sharper change of direction without losing contact with the inside bank.

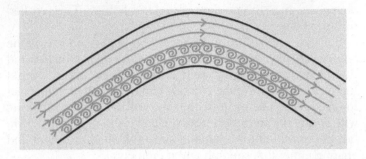

It is this difference in the ability of the two types of flow to follow a curved surface that creates the asymmetry that pushes the cricket ball sideways.

A skilled swing bowler presents the seam so that it is angled slightly to the ball's direction of travel. This means that while on one side of the ball the air flows over a smooth even surface, on the other side it immediately hits the rough seam. This has the effect of 'tripping' the flow into turbulence.

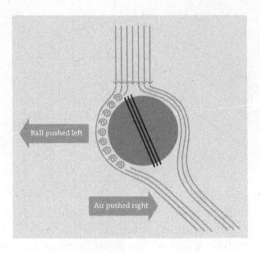

A discrepancy is created between the two sides of the ball. As the air tries to curve around the ball, the smooth lamina flow loses contact with the surface earlier than the 'stickier' turbulent flow, and this means that the airflow coming off the back of the ball is at an angle to the ball's direction of travel. The ball has effectively pushed the air sideways (to the right in our diagram). And as every schoolchild knows, 'every action has an equal and opposite reaction' (Newton's Third Law of Motion). If the air is pushed one way by the ball, then the ball is pushed the other way by the air.

If a bowler can create lamina flow on one side of the ball and turbulent flow on the other, then the ball will swing.

With a new ball the turbulent flow is created by the seam. In an older ball, the fielding side will endeavour to keep one side shiny and smooth, while allowing the other side to deteriorate naturally and become rougher. Done well, this makes it easier to generate the contrasting flows on the two sides of the ball, and so makes it easier to swing the ball.

WHAT EFFECT DOES THIS HAVE?

There is a very good reason that bowling teams go to such extraordinary lengths to get the ball to swing. Top-order batsmen in Test cricket average 38.3 against balls that don't swing and just 27.6 against balls that swing significantly (2.25 to 3 degrees). Getting the ball to swing is a huge factor in allowing quick bowlers to take wickets.

Most balls bowled by fast bowlers in Test matches do not deviate much in the air. Roughly 35 per cent go straight (to within half a degree of movement), and 41 per cent shape slightly (1 degree) in one direction or the other (as you can see in the chart 'Degrees of Swing').

We will look in some detail at the effects of different amounts of swing so it is worth giving you some context for the measures we are using. One degree of swing translates to between 15 and 20 centimetres of movement by the time the ball reaches the batsman. A ball that changes direction by 1 degree during its flight will arrive somewhere between 15 and 20 centimetres to the side of where you would expect given the release point.

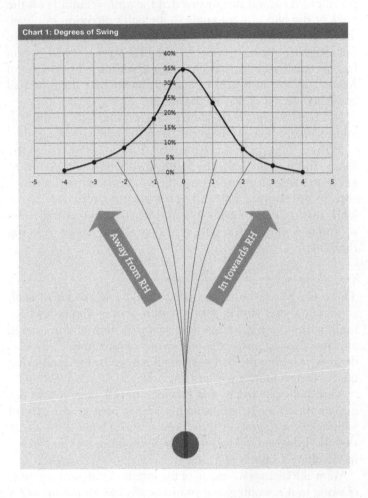

Now let's look at the effect that the direction and amount of swing have on the balance between bat and ball. Swing from right to left causes batting averages to fall sharply.

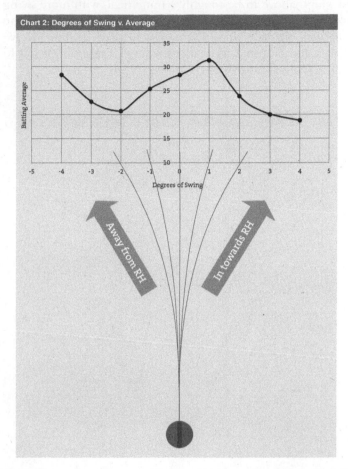

Chart 2: Degrees of Swing v. Average

The ball that goes straight averages 29 against all batsmen in our sample. The ball that swings from right to left (as the bowler looks at it) averages 25 with 1 degree of swing, 21 with 2 degrees of swing, before rising a little with more swing. In contrast, the ball that swings a little from left to right averages 31.4, slightly more than a straight ball, then falls to 24 with 2 degrees of swing.

So here we have an interesting surprise. We would expect the graph above to be roughly symmetrical, with more swing making the batsman's life harder in both directions, and the non-swinging ball being the easiest to play. So how do we explain the fact that the ball swinging 1 degree from left to right actually has the highest average of all?

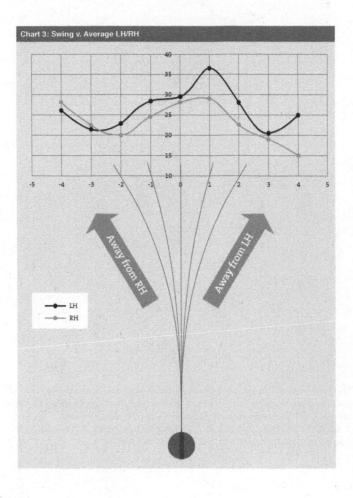

Chart 3: Swing v. Average LH/RH

Well, a traditional viewpoint might explain it like this. The ball swinging away from the bat is more dangerous than the ball swinging into the bat because the batsman's pads offer a second line of defence to being caught or bowled when the ball takes or beats the inside edge. Most batsmen are right-handed, hence the shape of the graph.

But if that was the case, we would expect to see different shapes to the graph when we separate out right- and left-handed batsmen. And as you can see in the chart 'Swing v. Average', we don't. We see roughly similar patterns for both types of batsmen. The ball swinging in to the right-handed batsman and away from the left-handed batsman is less dangerous.

So if it is not the handedness of the batsman, what is it that is causing the difference?

The answer is simple geometry, and the fact that most balls are delivered from the left of the umpire and stumps at the bowler's end (left as the bowler looks at them).

As you can see in the diagram, Ball B, swinging away from the right-hander or into the left-hander, is far more likely to pitch in line and hit the batsman's pads in line with the stumps. Whereas Ball A, swinging the other way, pitches outside the left-hander's leg stump and will be likely to hit the right-hander's pads outside the line of the stumps, taking LBW out of the equation.

You can see therefore that Ball A offers far less threat to the batsman than Ball B, regardless of whether he is right-handed or left-handed.

Because most balls (76 per cent) bowled by pace bowlers are delivered from left of the stumps, this is the dominant effect that creates the shape we saw in the chart 'Degrees of Swing v. Average'.

Indeed, if we separate out balls bowled from the left of the stumps from those bowled from the right, and look at the effect that swing has on batting average, we find that the graphs are near mirror images of each other.

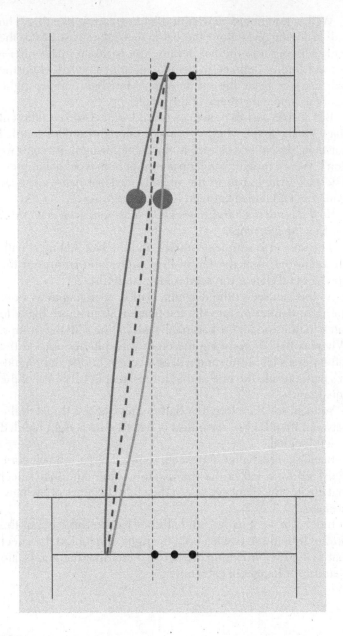

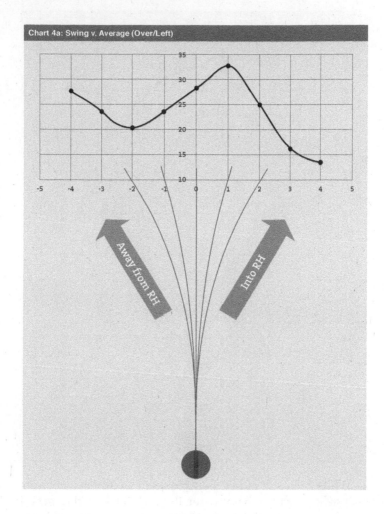

Chart 4a: Swing v. Average (Over/Left)

If we wanted further evidence of what is happening, then the change in dismissal types among left-handers when the ball swings strongly supports our hypothesis. We saw in Chapter 4 what an advantage top-order left-handers gain from the LBW law and it appears that right-to-left swing negates that advantage.

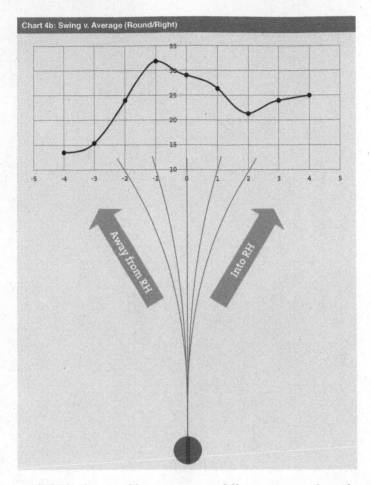

Chart 4b: Swing v. Average (Round/Right)

While both sets of batsmen see a fall in average when the ball swings, left-handers also see the way in which they get out change substantially. Left-handers are more than twice as likely to be out LBW when the ball swings than when it does not, their defence undone by the shape back into them from the right-arm seamer from over the wicket.

Top-Order v. Pace		LBW	Bowled	Caught
RHB	Substantial Swing	19%	17%	63%
	Small Swing	16%	17%	66%
LHB	Substantial Swing	30%	15%	55%
	Small Swing	14%	17%	70%

Top-Order Batting in Tests v. Pace	v. Substantial in-swing	v. Substantial away-swing
RHB	26.68	26.82
LHB	27.62	36.10

SO WHY DID THE BALL GO STRAIGHT?

With swing being such a pivotal and transformative part of the game, it is worth considering what prevents the ball from swinging.

If you have been around cricket for any length of time you will know that there are any number of theories and beliefs about the conditions needed for the bowlers to create swing.

There is a hackneyed old adage that before you toss up at Lord's you should look up not down, because the overhead conditions have more effect on play than the condition of the pitch, and there is no reason to doubt that there are days when that is the case.

There are, though, some factors that we know prevent the ball from swinging.

The first and most obvious thing is damage to the ball. If neither side of the ball is smooth enough to allow lamina flow at the speed that the bowler is bowling at, then the ball will not swing. And this damage can be caused by any number of things:

- An abrasive pitch – many pitches, particularly on the subcontinent, are abrasive enough that it is impossible to maintain a shine on the ball for more than a few overs.
- Spinners – some spinners, particularly wrist-spinners, bowl with a scrambled seam some or all of the time, so the ball lands repeatedly on the shiny side when they are bowling. (When a swing bowler bowls, the majority of balls should land on the seam, thus protecting the smooth leather either side.)
- General wear and tear – sometimes, one boundary, where the ball hits a concrete portion of the stand on the shiny side, can cause enough damage to stop the ball swinging. Some grounds have LED advertising screens on the boundary boards that seem designed to shred the ball, with the same effect.

The other thing that we know stops the ball swinging is a lack of non-turbulent air. If the air is sufficiently disturbed already, before the ball passes through it, then there is no chance of the necessary lamina flow over one side of the ball that is needed to create swing. One thing that we know creates this type of micro-turbulence is the action of the sun heating the pitch.

On a sunny day, the sun's rays heat the pitch, which in turn warms the layer of air next to it. Because hot air rises, this warm air then bubbles up through the colder air above it, creating a block of micro-turbulence – little swirls, eddies and currents in the air – above the pitch. This air is not tranquil enough to allow lamina flow over an object moving through it. So regardless of the condition of the ball and the skill of the bowler, the ball will have turbulent flow around both sides, and won't swing.

How do we know this micro-turbulence exists above cricket pitches? Well, because we can see it. If you have ever seen a heat haze rising off the road on a hot day, then you have seen the sort of micro-turbulence that we are talking about. And photos across a cricket pitch show the same type of heat haze rising off the ground. Once that turbulence is there, you can't get lamina flow, and without lamina flow, the ball can't swing.

This then is why you will often hear cloud cover and twilight mentioned as the types of conditions that encourage swing. Both prevent the sun from heating the pitch and destroying the lamina flow necessary for swing.

On a damp morning, the veteran swing bowler places a hand on the wicket before the start of play, feels that it is cold to the touch, and smiles to himself. This should be his day.

BUT WILL IT REVERSE?

So far, everything we have discussed has involved what is known as 'conventional' swing. But fast bowlers do have another mechanism in their armoury for getting the ball to move sideways in the air, and that is 'reverse' swing. When the seam is tilted to the left and the rough side is on the left, you would expect a ball swinging conventionally to swing to the left; a ball that is reversing, though, will swing to the right when released in that manner.

We will not go into the details of reverse swing, but suffice to say that the aerodynamic mechanism that produces reverse is entirely different from that which produces conventional swing, and it occurs with turbulent flow on both sides of the ball. This means that reverse swing can occur in conditions when conventional swing cannot.

This is one reason that it is such a boon for bowlers, and why teams strive so unrelentingly to get the ball into the right condition for it to happen. Because on a baking hot day in the subcontinent, with a ragged old ball half-shredded by the pitch and outfield, when swing seems less likely than a successfully negotiated Brexit, the bowlers can suddenly get the ball hooping round corners and turn a batting paradise into one of the sternest tests the game has to offer.

Swing in both its forms in cricket seems to be unique in the world of sport. As far as we are aware, there is no other ballgame where the mechanism that produces swing is used to make a ball deviate from its normal ballistic trajectory. There is, though, another way that bowlers bend the ball in the air, and this is far more common in almost all ball sports.

THEY CALLED IT THE 'BALL OF THE CENTURY'

Old Trafford, 4 June 1993. It is day two of the first Ashes Test. Mike Gatting is on strike and England are 80 for 1 in reply to Australia's 289, when Allan Border tosses the ball to his young leg-spinner.

As the youngster tells it later to Australia's Channel 7, he is nervous, it's his first ball in an Ashes contest, with all the pressure and focus that entails, and to start with he does nothing more than try to land his stock ball, try to get into his spell and find a bit of rhythm.

'I'm standing at the top of my mark, it's my first ball, I'm a bit nervous, because I haven't played against England before, and it means so much, Australia versus England. I come on to bowl, and I want to start a normal spell, just bowl a few leg-breaks, get myself into a bit of rhythm, get into the feel of the game.

'So I've run in to bowl, let go of the delivery, it feels pretty good out of the hand . . .'

The ball floats up towards the waiting Gatting, full and straight. Gatting, an excellent player of spin, comes forward to block it or possibly tuck it away for a single. We'll never know, because at this point the ball dips and swerves sharply towards the legside. You can watch it as many times as you want and the sudden deviation is still mesmeric: it looks like the ball is on a wire. Then it pitches, six inches outside Gatting's leg stump, and spits back past his bat to flick the top of the off stump. It is the *perfect* leg-break, an apotheosis of the art form.

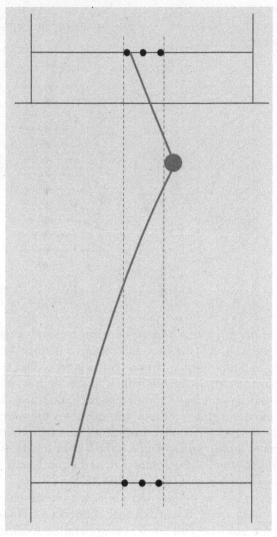

Had Shane Warne never taken another wicket, he would still be famous for that ball. As it is, the Ball of the Century was merely the harbinger of his decade of destructive dominance to come.

SWERVE, DIP AND LIFT

A spinning ball travelling through the air creates something called a magnus force.

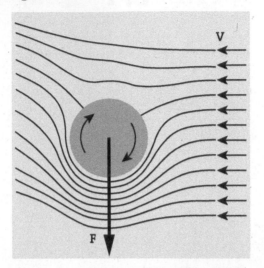

This is the force that a footballer uses to bend a free kick around the wall. It is the force that makes a baseball pitcher's breaking ball dip down and away. It is the force that makes a tennis player's topspin forehand dip into the court and bounce high, and makes his backhand slice seem to float and stay low.

The most recognised form of it in cricket is the swerve and dip that a spinner puts on the ball. (It is his main tool for beating the batsman in the flight, and we will examine its effects in detail in Chapter 9.) That, more so than the prodigious turn, is what so defeated Mike Gatting at Old Trafford.

The other way in which swerve affects a cricket ball is one that is almost never discussed, and it occurs when the fast bowlers are bowling. Fast bowlers in general, and swing bowlers in particular, pull their fingers down the back of the ball as they release it, imparting considerable backspin to the ball. We know that for some fast bowlers this can be of the order of 1000 to 1500 rpm. This is not far off the rates imparted by high-class finger-spinners, but of course where the spinner imparts topspin to get the ball to dip, the fast bowler imparts backspin, and so this has the opposite effect.

Computer models show that the effect of this backspin changes the length of the ball by as much as 3 metres. This is the difference between a good-length ball (7 metres) and a floaty half-volley (4 metres).

Spinners aren't the most extreme examples of bowlers producing dip. That honour goes to the pace bowlers who bowl back-of-the-hand slower balls. Their combination of fast arm action and the release of the ball over the top of the fingers produces huge rates of spin on the ball, and therefore sharp dip into the pitch.

A bowler such as Tom Curran, one of the increasing number of seam bowlers who feel confident delivering these variations, has the same weapon as Rashid Khan or any top-class leg-spinner. Curran's back of the hand slower ball dips at accelerations as high as 12 ms^{-2}, significantly more dip than even a typical Rashid Khan delivery, and with many of the same consequences as we see for leg-spinners. The ball dips wickedly into the turf and then pops off the pitch. It is as much this change of trajectory that defeats the batsman as it is the change in pace. For this reason, the term 'slower ball' seems a poor description of this type of delivery. The baseball term 'change-up' seems to better represent the most important ingredient for success, the fact that the ball behaves differently, either in the air or off the pitch, than the bowler's stock ball. It is a different *kind* of delivery, not just a slower version of the same one.

Imagine if a fast bowler could bowl a ball with no spin on it, land it on a good length and bounce it over the top of the stumps (like the ball in the diagram).

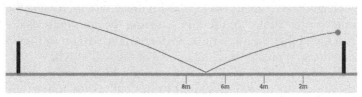

Then if he released an identical ball at the same angle and speed but with his usual backspin on it, that ball would land considerably closer to the stumps and not bounce as high.

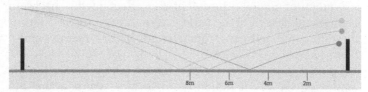

8m   6m   4m   2m

If he could then produce a third identical ball but this time with heavy topspin on it, then this ball would land much shorter and bounce far higher.

We can also see the effect of rotation on the ball after the ball has pitched. Quick pitches, where the ball skids through, allow the ball to retain some of the backspin imparted by pace bowlers. Watch close-up footage of the ball coming off the pitch in Perth, for example, and you will see it still rotating backwards. This means that there is still some up-force on the ball as it travels through to the wicketkeeper, and this magnifies the higher bounce from this type of pitch to produce much greater carry. This is why Perth is the spiritual home of slip-catching. There the slips can stand 10 metres further back than they do on low-bouncing pitches and still have the ball carry through to them comfortably.

In contrast, on abrasive pitches, the ball is grabbed and spun by the pitch, imparting topspin. Again, watch close-up, slow-motion footage of the ball coming off the pitch in Abu Dhabi and you will see it rotating forward. This topspin makes the ball dip, and therefore further reduces the already low bounce and carry on this type of pitch.

In both golf and baseball, the ball is intentionally struck in such a way as to create backspin with the aim of increasing the range of the shot. Even though creating the spin reduces the ball speed slightly, this is more than compensated for by the lift that the spin creates over the course of the ball's flight.

Fundamentally, whether it is created by the seam and a shiny side, or by spin imparted to the ball, or by the arcane secrets of reverse, what swing does is change things. And it changes things in favour of the bowlers. On a good pitch, if the ball goes gun-barrel straight in the air then the batsmen will rule the day – what the great England batsman and coach Graham Gooch called a red-dot day. When the ball left red marks on the pitch where it had landed, he knew it was a great opportunity to score runs.

Swing changes the way the ball moves through the air, and as a result changes the balance of power in the match. The most elusive element of the game, it is also arguably the most important. Without swing, cricket would be a totally different game.

Hitting Against the Spin
– England in India

The sand and the desert winter sun had turned the sky into an arc of blazing white. The air, dry on your skin, felt cooler than the 30 °C that the thermometer showed. In the Abu Dhabi stadium in 2012, as was so often the case, players were in danger of outnumbering the fans. At least at first.

It was the moment when the number-one ranked team in the world were due to surge back into the series. After a shock loss in the first Test, they had enjoyed by far the better of the second match, and now were going out to bat in the last innings to knock off a small total and level the series. It wasn't a foregone conclusion, but the fourth day wicket was no minefield, and they looked like they would be going into the last match of the series 1–1.

They needed 145 to win. They didn't get halfway. As a Pakistani victory moved from possible to probable to a certainty, their supporters streamed into the ground to see the English humbled.

Three years previously, when Andy Flower was appointed Head Coach of the England team in the spring of 2009, English cricket had been at one of its most dismal points. Ranked seventh in the world, they had just lost three Test series in a row plus their previous coach and captain to a falling out that cost them both their jobs.

What followed was a remarkable and rapid transformation and an unbeaten sequence that lasted nine series, including home and away wins against the mighty Australians, and culminated in a 4-0 win against India which took them to the top of the Test team rankings for the first and only time in their history.

It was a team, then, that was on top of the world in every sense that travelled to the UAE in January 2012. After defeat in the first Test, they seemed to regather themselves and were ahead throughout the second Test until that disastrous fourth innings chase. In the third Test they suffered the ignominy of becoming only the second team in Test history to bowl the opposition out for under a hundred and go on to lose.

Then they went to Sri Lanka and lost. Again, it was the batting that failed. Since going to number one in the world they had lost four consecutive Tests and their batting had dropped off a cliff. Against spin in particular they had been taken apart, averaging just 15.8 in those four matches.

It was a staggering collapse in form from a team that had plundered a mountain of runs in the previous two years. And it was now a matter of some urgency, because although they then won the second Test in Sri Lanka, meaning they clung on to their number-one ranking, looming on the horizon was one of the greatest challenges of all.

Fortress India. The spiritual home of spin bowling, and the hardest place on the planet to win away from home.

In the autumn of 2012, they would fly out to India to play a four-Test series against an Indian team captained by M. S. Dhoni that was determined to avenge their 4–0 humbling in England. An Indian team, moreover, who were the proud possessors of the best home record in Test cricket. They had lost only one series at home this century.

Other than that 2012 tour, England have won just four Tests in India in the last 40 years. It is a graveyard for English Test teams. Only in the Caribbean have English cricketers toured so frequently while winning so rarely. The challenge ahead of them was immense.

But Strauss and Flower's England team was nothing if not methodical. And so, six months prior to boarding the plane to India the planning started in earnest. Players, coaches and analysts set to work examining their shortcomings, identifying the changes that needed to be made and modelling the methods of those who had already been successful.

Throughout the summer, as they played home Test series against West Indies and South Africa, coaches and players also found time to work away steadily on those aspects of their method that they would need come the winter.

In November 2011, the England One Day team had toured India and lost 5–0. Out-thought, outplayed and beaten up in subcontinental conditions, it had been a fore warning of the loss in the UAE.

But this time would be different.

To understand what happened next, how England went from zeroes to heroes in such dramatic fashion and stormed the most impregnable fortress in Test history, we will need to spend some time unpicking the intricacies of batting against spin. We will also have to do something the English are coached from birth not to do, *Hit Against the Spin*.

INTERCEPTORS

As we have seen, when a cricket ball bounces it doesn't always continue in a straight line, but changes direction slightly. This can be caused by imperfections in the pitch, the ball landing on its seam, or because of spin that the bowler has imparted to the ball. Whatever the cause of the deviation, it means that the ball doesn't arrive in exactly the position that the batsman expects. Because most shots played by the batsman are played with a vertical bat, horizontal deviation is more likely to cause the batsman to miss or edge the ball than vertical inconsistencies in the bounce. This is the case in all forms of cricket, but it is most important in Test cricket where sideways movement, especially sideways movement off the pitch, is usually the proximate cause of wickets.

If we consider the path of the ball after it has pitched,

we find that there are two relatively safe areas for the batsman to try to intercept it. Shortly after the ball has bounced there has not been time for any sideways deviation to have much effect. Even if the ball deviates it will probably still hit the face of the bat. Then, once the ball has travelled far enough for the batsman to be able to react to any movement and adjust his shot, he enters another relatively safe zone.

In between, though, is a region where the ball has travelled far enough for any deviation to cause it to miss the face of the bat, but not so far that the batsman then has time to see and adjust to that deviation.

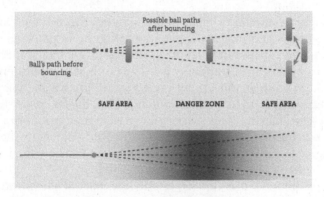

And this is not just a geometry-based hypothesis. We can clearly see, when we look at the statistics, that it is far safer to play the ball within 1.5 metres of where it pitches, or to play it over 3.5 metres away from that point. Those areas both average over 80 for top-order players, whereas the most dangerous zone between 2 and 3 metres has an average of just 14.

When the quick bowlers are bowling, there is only so much that the batsman can do to mitigate this movement. The distance between where the ball bounces and where the batsman tries to intercept it is largely dictated by the length the bowler bowls. If the bowler nails his length, then the relative speeds and distances mean that the batsman is forced to intercept the ball at a dangerous distance after it bounces.

At the speeds that spinners bowl, however, there is more time for the batsman to move (forward or back), and the distances involved are smaller. This means that through judgement of length and quick footwork, batsmen *are* able to change the intercept distance to stay in the safe zones and avoid the danger area.

Batsmen who are consistently able to use their judgement of length and footwork to minimise the number of balls they play in that zone can drastically reduce the risks they take when playing spin.

There is one other factor that multiplies the risk the batsman incurs and that is his intent: whether he is attacking or defending. A batsman defending with classic 'soft hands' meets the ball with a near stationary bat. As a result, late adjustments made to counter movement are far easier than if the bat is being swung hard in an attacking shot. Plus, the far greater bat speed of attacking shots reduces the player's margin for error if he has misjudged the position of the ball. Attacking shots require an earlier decision and commitment to where the ball is expected to be.

For spinners, it is not necessarily the *amount* of turn that defeats the batsman, it is the inconsistency in the amount of turn. It is the fact that the batsman doesn't know exactly how much the ball will deviate when it pitches.

LEARNING FROM THE BEST

Fortunately, England had been given two object lessons in how to bat against spin. In 2011, when India toured England, their most successful batsman was Rahul Dravid, who scored 461 runs in the four-match series. The following year, South Africa toured, and Jacques Kallis scored 262 runs in their three matches. At that time, Kallis and Dravid were the two players who had faced the most balls of spin in the history of Test cricket. In those two series, they scored

223 runs between them against spin, for the loss of just one wicket.

Most Balls of Spin Faced in Tests up to 2012			
Player	BF	Ave	DR
J. H. Kallis	8944	90.4	182.5
R. S. Dravid	8336	75.8	151.5
D. P. M. D. Jayawardene	8211	66.3	126.3
S. Chanderpaul	7551	56.3	127.9
K. C. Sangakkara	7351	64.8	124.5

Dravid in particular had already started to influence the England players and coaches' thinking around the best method against spin. And in their preparations for the tour of India, this focus was redoubled.

All batsmen know that footwork is key when playing against spin. But in analysing a master craftsman such as Dravid, it became clear just how much difference this aspect of the art of batting could make.

In the 2011 series against England, when he averaged 158 against spin, Dravid played a mere 9 per cent of deliveries in the danger zone, and attacked less than 1 per cent of them. Compare that to the English batsmen in the same series who played 27 per cent of their deliveries from spin in that area and attacked 15 per cent, 20 times as many as Dravid.

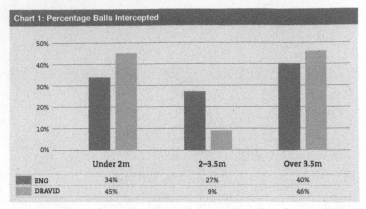

Chart 1: Percentage Balls Intercepted

	Under 2m	2–3.5m	Over 3.5m
ENG	34%	27%	40%
DRAVID	45%	9%	46%

It was very clear that Dravid was using his footwork and judgement of length to massively reduce the risk he took against spin in a way that England were not doing.

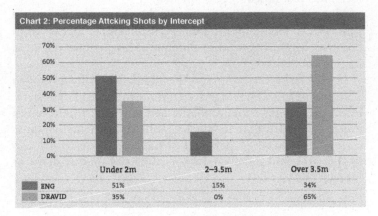

Chart 2: Percentage Attcking Shots by Intercept

	Under 2m	2–3.5m	Over 3.5m
ENG	51%	15%	34%
DRAVID	35%	0%	65%

It was not that the idea was new. It wasn't: getting forward to smother the spin and back to play it off the pitch are accepted parts of batting against spin. It was seeing just how good the best were, and how far behind England were, that was the revelation.

It is worth, at this point, giving some background on the effect of spin in Test cricket. About 4 per cent of balls bowled by spinners in Test cricket don't turn at all. These balls collectively average 59 and have an economy rate of 4.9 runs per over. The 42 per cent of balls that turn in to the bat average 41.9 and go at 3.3 runs per over. The majority of deliveries bowled turn away from the bat, and they average 31.5 and go at 2.71. You can see from this brief summary why spinners try to turn the ball, and why in particular it is valuable to turn the ball away from the bat.

The average amount of turn is just under 4 degrees. That sounds very small, but in reality it is far from insignificant. If you are 3 metres away from where the ball pitches, 4 degrees of turn means a 21-centimetre difference in where the ball arrives. Given that a bat is just 11.8 centimetres wide, you can see that 4 degrees of turn is more than enough to make the batsman miss.

In fact, at 2.5 metres just 2 degrees of turn would move the ball from the middle of the bat to a thin edge. At the speed that the ball comes off the turf when the spinners are bowling, it covers that 2.5 metres in around 0.13 seconds. As we saw in Chapter 3 when looking at fast bowlers' lengths, this is not long enough to allow the batsman to adjust his shot.

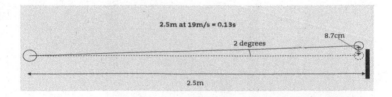

So, at this distance (2 to 3 metres) from where the ball pitches, quite a small misjudgement by the batsman in how much the ball will turn is enough for him to miss or edge it. Yet he does not have time to react to how much the ball has deviated. The geometry and the reaction time are backed up by the performance stats. As with a good length for the fast bowlers, an interception distance of 2 to 3 metres *is the distance that gives the ball the most time to deviate without giving the batsman time to react and adjust his shot.*

The interception distance is therefore one of the most critical aspects that determine how much danger a ball presents to the batsman. Balls intercepted between 2 and 3 metres after they bounce average around 13 (scoring just 13 runs for every wicket that falls). Balls in the range just outside this are not much better. From 1.5 to 2 metres the average is 23; from 3 to 3.5 metres, it is 17.

Intercept Distance All Batsmen v. Spin		
Intercept	Average	Economy Rate
Under 1.5m	60.1	4.59
1.5–2.0m	23.2	2.12
2.0–2.5m	13.8	1.40
2.5–3.0m	11.8	1.28
3.0–3.5m	17.4	1.64
Over 3.5m	62.3	4.22

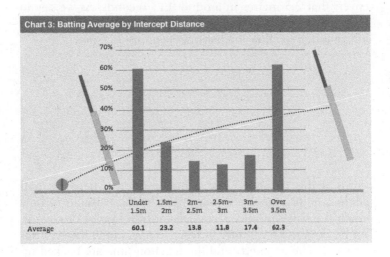

Chart 3: Batting Average by Intercept Distance

	Under 1.5m	1.5m–2m	2m–2.5m	2.5m–3m	3m–3.5m	Over 3.5m
Average	60.1	23.2	13.8	11.8	17.4	62.3

One interesting aspect of playing balls in this danger zone is that it is almost equally dangerous whether the ball is turning in to the bat or away.

Average by Intercept and Direction of Turn			
Ball Turning Away		**Ball Turning In**	
Intercept	*Average*	*Intercept*	*Average*
0–0.5	300	0–0.5	76
0.5–1	45	0.5–1	79
1–1.5	58	1–1.5	59
1.5–2	25	1.5–2	33
2–2.5	16	2–2.5	16
2.5–3	9	2.5–3	12
3–3.5	12	3–3.5	25
3.5–4	31	3.5–4	35
4–4.5	38	4–4.5	51
4.5–5	56	4.5–5	69
5+	32	5+	55
ALL	**32**	**ALL**	**40**

For top-order players, less likely to make unforced errors against safe deliveries, the differences are even more stark.

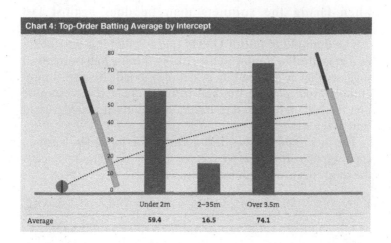

Chart 4: Top-Order Batting Average by Intercept

	Under 2m	2–35m	Over 3.5m
Average	**59.4**	**16.5**	**74.1**

If defending balls in this zone is risky enough, attacking them is even more dangerous. The relative risk of dismissal more than doubles for top-order batsmen when they attack balls in the most dangerous region (2 to 3.5 metres).

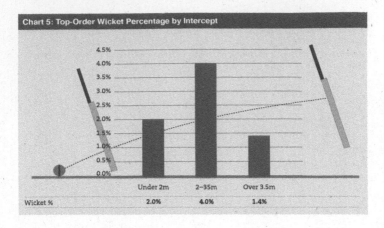

Chart 5: Top-Order Wicket Percentage by Intercept

	Under 2m	2–35m	Over 3.5m
Wicket %	2.0%	4.0%	1.4%

TO WHAT EXTENT CAN THE BATSMAN MINIMISE THESE RISKS?

We have already touched on the fact that the batsman has much more control over where he intercepts the ball when facing the spinners than he does against fast bowlers.

The example of Rahul Dravid suggests that it is possible to do a great deal to minimise the risk the turning ball presents. It suggests that if a batsman is skilful enough, he can almost entirely avoid playing the ball in those areas. If we examine how the ball's length and its intercept distance interact, we can start to see why.

The next table shows the averages for top-order batsmen against spin in Tests, and we can see that 4 to 5 metres is typically the most effective length for a spinner.

Top-Order Batsmen v. Spin		Average	Economy Rate
Full	Under 1.5m	54.4	3.4
Good	4–5m	26.1	2.3
Short	Over 5m	61.9	4.2

The next chart is worth considering at this point. It shows the breakdown of where balls of each length are intercepted. So, for example, 100 per cent of balls of length under 1 metre are intercepted either before they bounce or within 0.5 metre of bouncing. For balls of length 2 to 2.5 metres this figure is 71 per cent, and then 25 per cent are intercepted 0.5 to 1 metre after they bounce, etc.

You can see that the only lengths from which a significant number of balls are intercepted in the 2- to 3-metre danger zone are the lengths between 4 metres and 5 metres from the stumps. This is the reason that this is by far the most effective length for spinners to bowl.

Intercept Distance v Length

	0–05m	0.5–1m	1–1.5m	1.5–2m	2–2.5m	2.5–3m	3–3.5m	3.5–4m	4–4.5m	4.5–5m	5+m
Under 1m	100%										
1–1.5m	98%	2%									
1.5–2m	92%	7%	1%	1%							
2–2.5m	71%	25%	2%	0%	1%						
2.5–3m	28%	61%	7%	3%	0%	1%					
3–3.5m	6%	46%	39%	4%	3%	0%	1%				
3.5–4m	1%	11%	52%	25%	4%	4%	1%	2%			
4–4.5m	0%	2%	13%	44%	20%	7%	8%	2%	3%		
4.5–5m		0%	4%	11%	30%	17%	17%	15%	3%	4%	
5–5.5m			1%	4%	6%	17%	16%	29%	22%	4%	3%
5.5–6m				1%	2%	4%	10%	16%	39%	23%	5%
6–6.5m					0%	2%	2%	6%	18%	43%	28%
6.5–7m						1%	1%	2%	4%	27%	65%
7–7.5m								2%	1%	8%	89%
7.5–8m									1%	3%	96%
TOTAL	5%	10%	15%	15%	11%	8%	8%	9%	8%	5%	4%

Length (metres from stump)

Intercept Distance

But why should that be the case? That region is only 1 metre wide.

Typically 90 per cent of a batsman's shots will be played between 1 metre and 2.7 metres from the stumps. This is a reasonably comfortable range for most batsmen to achieve, from playing right back, to playing right forward without leaving the crease.

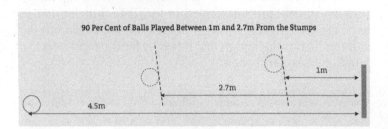

But if the batsman has 1.7 metres of movement at his disposal, and the most dangerous region to intercept the ball measures only a metre, then a batsman who judges length well and uses his feet to counter it should be able to avoid playing any deliveries in the most dangerous (2- to 3-metre) region. And, more so, he should only need to play a small number of deliveries at the edge of the 1.5- to 3.5-metre region.

Indeed, when we look at many of the best technicians, this is what they do. The likes of Dravid and, in more recent times, Virat Kohli, Joe Root and Kane Williamson play a very low percentage of balls in the danger zone. And it is this footwork and judgement of length that is the foundation of their outstanding records against spin.

Top Batsmen v. Spin				
	Danger Zone %	Average	E/R	Wicket %
V. Kohli	11.8%	70.1	3.61	0.86%
J. E. Root	12.2%	61.8	3.61	0.96%
K. S. Williamson	12.6%	58.4	3.61	0.85%

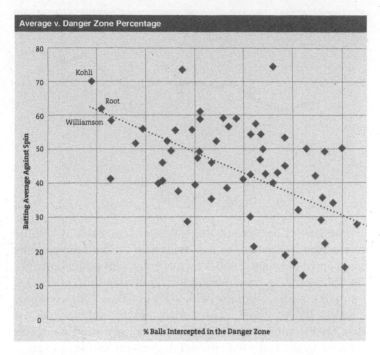

So, if the batsman has enough range of movement to avoid playing in the danger zone, every time he does end up intercepting the ball in that range he has been deceived by the bowler. The bowler has 'done him in the flight', pulled him forward to a ball he should have gone back to, or induced him to play on the back foot when he should have been forward.

He might do this by subtle changes of pace or by second-guessing what the batsman is expecting. Or, as we saw in the last chapter, he might do this by getting the ball to dip in the air. Aided by topspin, the ball lands earlier and shorter than it otherwise would and then bounces more steeply.

Through measuring drop as the acceleration relative to the ball's natural flight we can see that the greater the amount of dip (the more negative the number on the graph 'Drop v. Batting Average'), the lower the batting average for the delivery.

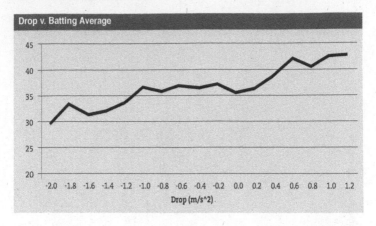

The greater the dip on the ball, the more likely it is to be intercepted in the danger area. Balls with the least dip are only intercepted between 2 and 3 metres 4 per cent of the time. For the balls that drop most sharply, this figure rises to 16 per cent, a fourfold increase. (It might be thought that the falling average is caused solely by more spin on the ball and therefore more deviation off the pitch. The fact that the danger zone intercepts increase so markedly with greater drop seems to rule this out.)

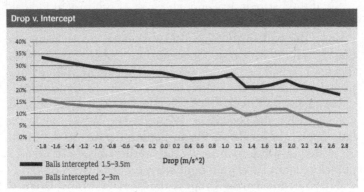

Without the aerodynamic effects of that topspin, spinners would have a much harder time deceiving batsmen into playing the ball in dangerous areas. And they would therefore have a much harder job getting them out. Unlike the backspin and lift that fast bowlers impart to the ball through the mechanism of their bowling action, which are largely unintended and incidental, the topspin and drop that spinners generate are crucial to their method.

As the old adage goes, 'You have to beat the batsman in the air before you can beat him off the pitch', i.e. you must deceive him into playing the ball in the danger zone if you are going to then turn the ball past his bat.

FRONT-FOOT BIAS

There is another interesting thing to be discovered by looking at the breakdown of intercept distances from different lengths.

The optimal length for a bowler to land the ball is 4 to 5 metres from the stumps. This is the in-between length, the length where the batsman finds it hard to get right forward and smother the spin, and difficult to get on to the back foot and have enough time to play the ball off the pitch. You would expect him to play everything fuller than 4 metres off the front foot. If he gets right forward (to an impact point 2.7 metres

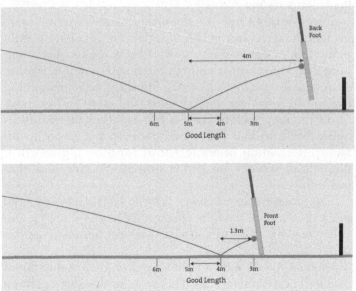

from the stumps) then he will be intercepting the ball 1.3 metres after it pitches with relative safety. Likewise, you would expect the batsman to play anything shorter than 5 metres off the back foot, around 1 metre from the stumps. This would give him at least 4 metres of flight to see the ball off the pitch, and again we know that would afford him relative safety.

One would imagine that between 4 and 5 metres there is a mixture of front- and back-foot shots, those closer to 4 metres being played off the front foot and those closer to 5 metres off the back foot. But this isn't the case. What happens in reality is that almost all those balls (around 83 per cent) are played off the front foot. Indeed, roughly 70 per cent of balls short of a good length, in the 5- to 5.5-metre region, are still being played off the front foot.

This is incidentally the same when the fast bowlers are bowling. The in-between length (for the fast bowlers this is 6 to 8 metres) at which you would expect to see a shift being made from front foot to back foot is actually played almost entirely off the front foot. No collective movement back is made until the lengths are much shorter.

This front-foot bias has been replicated experimentally in temporal occlusion studies (which involve showing players video footage of a bowler bowling and then stopping the video at some point in the bowler's delivery action or during the flight of the ball). Show the batsmen enough footage to know the ball is short and they will go back. Show them enough to see it is full and they move forward on to the front foot. But when batsmen are given insufficient information accurately to determine the length of the ball, they don't stay still or split 50–50, they almost all move forward.

This prompts two questions. Why do batsmen have a front-foot bias? And is it the most effective strategy?

For now we will just consider these two questions as they pertain to spin bowling.

I don't think we have a clear answer to the first question. It may well be a Tethered Cat. There was for decades a policy in cricket of giving the benefit of the doubt to the batsman in umpiring decisions. This meant that with LBW appeals the batsman would rarely be given out if he had got well forward. It was felt that the distance the ball still had to travel introduced enough doubt to make 'Not out' the default decision in those circumstances. This clearly gave batsmen an incentive to be on the front foot, as it removed one mode of dismissal. It may be that the front-foot bias was a perfectly effective policy in years gone by, and still is at the lower levels of the game where future international batsmen learn and refine their methods.

We can fairly easily ascertain the effectiveness of the technique by looking at the returns that batsmen get from each foot.

Batsmen collectively in Test cricket play only 21 per cent of the balls they receive off the back foot, and yet their average to those balls is almost double what it is to the 66 per cent of balls that they play off the front foot.

Batting Average by Foot Movement		
Front foot	29.3	(66%)
Back foot	56.2	(21%)

And this is still the case if we look at balls on the spinners' perfect length of 4 to 5 metres from the stumps. Balls of this length played off the front foot average 16.6, whereas off the back foot they average over 50 per cent more (25.4). These are sweeping observations, containing as they do every different quality of batsman, type of spinner, line of ball and state of pitch. But the statistics do seem to suggest that, whatever the reason for the front-foot bias, it may be counter-productive to a batsman's success.

The most common place for a batsman to make contact with the ball is 2.2 to 2.4 metres from the stumps. (This is a bit short of a full stride forward for most batsmen.) This is also the contact point that has the lowest batting average, so the most common contact point is the least successful one.

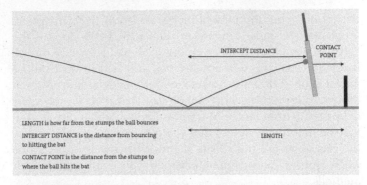

LENGTH is how far from the stumps the ball bounces

INTERCEPT DISTANCE is the distance from bouncing to hitting the bat

CONTACT POINT is the distance from the stumps to where the ball hits the bat

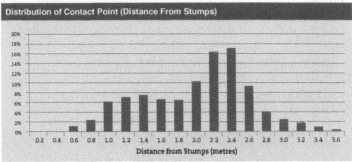

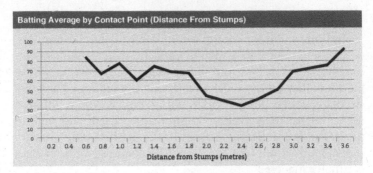

The top five players of spin who are still playing Test cricket are Pujara, Root, Kohli, Steve Smith and Williamson. Kohli, Williamson and Root are excellent examples of players who use the back foot to a far greater degree than most players. All are in the top ten of current players for their back-foot percentage.

Top Current Players of Spin	
	Average
C. A. Pujara	74.9
V. Kohli	69.8
K. S. Williamson	62.5
J. E. Root	61.8
S. P. D. Smith	58.9

Pujara has an alternative approach, one that uses footwork in a different way. He leaves his crease and goes down the wicket on a regular basis: 18 per cent of the time compared to 6 per cent for batsmen in general. It is a method that Michael Clarke (25 per cent) and Steve Smith (15 per cent) among others have also used to reduce the percentage of balls they play pushing half-forward. Indeed, those are the three players who have used their feet most often this century.

THE SWEEP

There is another way for batsmen to combat the vagaries of the turning ball, and that is by sweeping. The sweep shot, with its horizontal, cross-bat swing and its contact point well in front of the batsman's body, allows the batsman to attack closer to the pitch of the ball without leaving the crease. By doing so he can attack a good-length ball with a degree of safety. It also means that if the player has misjudged how much the ball will turn, he still has an excellent chance of making contact.

Traditionally, the sweep shot has been a means by which players who have not been brought up on turning pitches can counter the turning ball. Interestingly the Indians, possibly the finest players of spin in the world, employ the sweep shot less than other nations. They rely on their footwork and judgement of length, as described above.

Unfortunately for England, the sweep shot had for years been a real Achilles heel of theirs. On the previous winter's tours, they had averaged just 17 playing the sweep shot, and had a horrific dismissal rate, losing a wicket every 12 balls when they played it.

Luckily though, they played the last two Tests of that winter in Sri Lanka, one of the best countries in the world for playing the sweep shot, and so they were able to closely observe some masters of the shot in action.

The relative safety and effectiveness of the sweep shot are dependent on conditions. Generally speaking, if the ball is not turning much, then the sweep with its inherent cross-batted risks is an inferior option to playing with a straight bat. It comes into its own on surfaces that are offering a good deal of assistance to the spinners, where attacking with a straight bat can be fraught with danger.

Sweeping is also a lot easier to do safely on pitches with low bounce. Bouncier tracks carry the risk of top edges or gloved attempts going to hand in the field.

Sri Lanka then, with its plethora of low turners, is a place where the sweep shot comes into its own.

Sweep Percentage Played by Venue Country	
	Sweep %
Sri Lanka	5.4%
UAE	5.2%
Pakistan	4.8%
Bangladesh	4.0%
England	3.9%
South Africa	3.6%
India	3.5%
Australia	3.3%
West Indies	3.1%
New Zealand	3.0%

The great Mahela Jayawardene, for example, was a master of the sweep shot. When England played against him in 2012 he had an average of 83.6 when sweeping. As such, he was worthy of close attention for a team for whom the sweep had become such a liability. What England learned from Jayawardene was how to use the bowler's natural angles of attack to minimise the risk of being LBW.

One of the benefits of the sweep shot is that the batsman can use his front pad as a second line of defence. This is why, although the shot results in far more misses than straight-bat shots, there is no proportionate rise in the risk of being bowled. Sweeps result in almost ten times as many play and misses as drives, for example, but only twice as many bowled dismissals.

Top-Order Shot Outcome		
	Miss %	Bowled %
Drive	2.1%	0.2%
Sweep	19.7%	0.4%

But using the pad as a second line of defence brings LBW into the picture, and with the advent of Hawk-Eye and the Decision Review System, umpires became far more willing to trigger batsmen hit on the pad when sweeping.

This was indeed what had happened to England in the winter of 2011–12: 70 per cent of their dismissals when sweeping had been LBW. Contrast that with Jayawardene, who at that point had only been out sweeping *once* in all his Test matches for which we have data.

It became apparent that the key to taking LBW out of the picture was all about angles. The first thing to notice is that there are specific combinations of batsmen and bowlers that have far higher rates of LBWs when sweeping.

When a right-handed batsman sweeps an off-spinner he averages 45.8 and 26 per cent of his dismissals are LBW. When sweeping a left-arm spinner, 45 per cent of his dismissals are LBW, and almost entirely as a result of that his average drops to 40.1.

The same thing is true in reverse for left-handed batsmen. When they sweep left-arm spinners they average 51 and just 27 per cent of their dismissals are LBW. When they sweep off-spinners they average 35.2 with 53 per cent LBWs.

Batting Average		Sweeping v. Finger-Spinners	
		Left-Arm	Right-Arm
Batsman	LH	51.0	35.2
	RH	40.1	45.8

% LBW		Sweeping v. Finger-Spinners	
		Left-Arm	Right-Arm
Batsman	LH	27%	53%
	RH	45%	26%

So why do goofy combinations – right-arm spinners bowling to left-handers, and left-arm spinners bowling to right-handers – create so many LBWs when the batsman sweeps?

Well, consider two balls from an off-spinner bowling over the wicket to a right-hander on a turning pitch. The first ball pitches 50 centimetres outside off stump, turns in to the batsman and is going on to hit middle and leg. The batsman sweeps, misses the ball and it hits him on the pad. The point of impact will be comfortably outside off stump, the batsman is playing a shot, and so despite the appeal from the fielding team, the umpire will correctly give the batsman not out.

The second ball similarly pitches outside the batsman's off stump and turns in to him, but this time strikes him in line with the stumps. The angle of the ball means that it is almost inevitable that this ball will be missing the stumps and going down the legside, so again the umpire will be uninterested in the appeal.

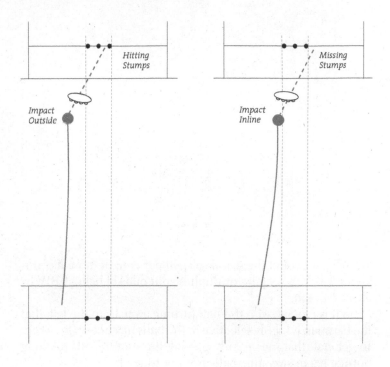

Now consider a ball to our right-handed batsman from a left-arm spinner bowling round the wicket. On a turning pitch it is easy for the slow left-armer to get the ball to pitch on or near the stumps and straighten. If the batsman sweeps this ball and misses it, then there is a very high risk of being LBW.

Sweeping the ball turning away from the bat is fraught with risk. The sweep shot accounts for 4 per cent of the shots played

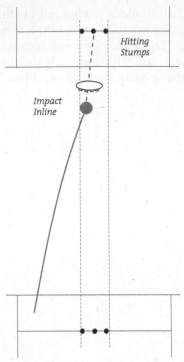

and 19 per cent of the dismissals; 40 per cent of those dismissals are LBW. Sweeping multiplies your odds of being LBW by a factor of ten.

So it is crucial, with the ball turning away from the bat, that the batsman is highly selective in the balls he chooses to sweep. In general, that means only playing the shot to balls pitching outside leg or sweeping balls from outside off.

To summarise all the above, we find:

- sweeping is easier when the bounce is low;
- it is better to play straight when the ball isn't turning and use the sweep when it is;
- it is better to sweep on the line of the ball so as to eliminate LBW; sweep from outside off stump, or when the ball has pitched outside leg stump, for example.

England also discovered something else in their study of the best players of spin and it was in some respects by far the most controversial.

HITTING AGAINST THE SPIN
One of the first things you are taught about playing spin as a young English player is to 'hit with the spin' (i.e. to hit the ball in the direction it is turning). It is axiomatic throughout most of English cricket that hitting against the spin – so hitting an off-spinner into the offside, or a slow left-arm spinner into the legside – is more dangerous.

It was a surprise, then, that when Rahul Dravid was interviewed towards the end of his career and asked what advice he would give to himself as a young player he said, 'learn to play against the spin'. There aren't many less controversial ideas than playing with the spin. So, to hear this from one of the greatest exponents of the art was genuinely eye opening. But there had always been clues that maybe things weren't as simple as was commonly believed.

One of these clues comes from looking at players of other high-speed sports and how they are taught to counter late deviation. In tennis, for example, it is axiomatic that the safest way to hit the ball is to aim it back in the direction from which it is coming. With shorter or slower balls that are easier to hit, a player can safely swing across the line and change the direction of play. But when dealing with stronger shots, struck harder and deeper, the safest way to ensure a solid contact is to hit back in the direction from which the ball is coming.

There is a sport, though, that makes the speeds of cricket and tennis balls look like slow motion.

'IT'S LIKE PLAYING GOLF IN A BATHROOM'
Rackets as a sport originated in the prisons of nineteenth-century England. It then grew in popularity, particularly among the well-to-do, to such an extent that there were reputedly two rackets courts on the *Titanic*.

These days rackets is a fairly niche sport, played largely in the

English public school system, a handful of clubs in the south of England and some of the older cities of the United States. Which is a real shame because it is an extraordinary sport.

It is one of the fastest ball sports, if not *the* fastest, in the world. The small, hard rackets ball can travel upwards of 160 mph when struck by an expert player. Almost impossibly difficult for the beginner, it is nevertheless a thrilling sight to see played well. The court and rules are almost identical to squash, except that the dimensions of the court are twice as big in all directions. (Squash was actually invented as a way of warming up to play rackets, which is why it is played with identical rules on a smaller court with a much, much slower ball.)

One of the most difficult racket shots to master is hitting the ball as it comes off the side wall of the court. Having angled off the front wall, the ball has slowed down considerably but is still travelling at high speed and spinning, so it is difficult to judge exactly where it will glance off the wall and at what angle. All players as they are learning the game are coached to hit the ball back into the side wall. If you swing parallel to the wall you are in effect hitting across the line of the ball, removing any margin for error and making a successful contact unlikely. Plus, a mishit from trying to play in that way can easily ricochet into your face. So players aim their shot back into the wall, thus presenting the full face of their racket to the line of the ball's flight and giving themselves the largest possible margin for error in their attempted contact.

If we use this as an analogy for hitting a cricket ball after it turns off the pitch, then the recommended technique in rackets seems directly to contradict the received cricketing wisdom. And looking a little further at the geometry of both shots, we seem to find that the evidence supports the rackets player's approach rather than the batsman's.

Imagine you are playing an attacking shot to the ball in the diagram below that has pitched outside your off stump, and you are trying to hit it through the offside. Now compare what happens when the ball turns away from the bat, and when it turns in to it.

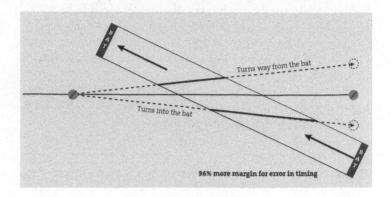

You can see that the path of the bat overlaps with the path of the ball for much longer if the ball turns in to the bat (36 per cent longer than when it turns away for an average degree of turn), giving you a far greater margin for error if you have misjudged the timing of the shot.

Another analogous situation, where an accepted technique for hitting the ball contradicts the idea of playing *with* the spin, comes from cricket itself. When fast bowlers get the ball to reverse swing, they present one of the greatest and most exhilarating threats to the batsman that the game has to offer. One of the reasons that reverse swing is quite so destructive is that the ball swings sharply and late, giving the batsman very little time to adjust.

As a result, one accepted method for counteracting the ball reversing into the right-hander is to stay legside and hit back into the swing. That is, to avoid the risk of being trapped LBW by the late in-swing with the bat coming across the line of the ball, the batsman tries to stay legside of the delivery so as to allow a straight swing of the bat back in the direction from which the ball is coming, targeting the mid-off or extra-cover region.

So, if Rahul Dravid suggests it, and geometry, rackets and methods to counter reverse swing all corroborate the hypothesis, is there any mileage in hitting against the spin?

Well, as you might expect, yes, there does seem to be.

When we look at the relative effectiveness of each type of shot, we find that every straight-bat shot is more successful when it is played against the spin than when it is played with the spin.

When the ball is turning in to the bat, the offside drives have higher averages than the onside drives. When the ball is turning away from the bat the reverse is true.

Batting Average by Shot Type and Direction of Turn			
Ball Turning In	Average	Ball Turning Away	Average
Off Side Drive – Back foot	558	On Side Drive – Back foot	196
On Side Drive – Back foot	151	Leg Glance	176
Leg Glance	129	Off Side Drive – Back foot	115
Pull	77	On Side Drive – Front foot	82
Cut	76	Cut	74
Off Side Drive – Front	72	Pull	70
Average (attacking shots)	65	Average (attacking shots)	56
On Side Drive – Front	54	Off Side Drive – Front	47
Reverse Sweep	41	Reverse Sweep	29
Sweep	36	Sweep	23
Defensive shots		*Defensive shots*	
Back Defence	9	Forward Defence	6
Forward Defence	7	Back Defence	5
Padded Away	1	Padded Away	1
No Shot	0	No Shot	0

You might imagine that this is largely due to the fact that there are fewer fielders protecting that side of the field. Most spinners in Test matches bowl to fields that have more defensive fielders on the side they are turning the ball towards.

But while that is certainly part of the reason, there is also more to it than that. It is not just that shots against the spin average more, but they are also less dangerous: they have higher balls per dismissal rates.

When we compare the dismissal rates, measured in balls per wicket by shot type, we find once again that each straight-bat shot is safer when played against the spin than when played with it.

Dismissal Rate by Shot Type and Direction of Turn			
Ball Turning In	D/R	Ball Turning Away	D/R
Off Side Drive – Back	553	On Side Drive – Back	222
On Side Drive – Back	237	Leg Glance	211
Leg Glance	170	Off Side Drive – Back	184
Average	75	Cut	71
Off Side Drive – Front	68	Off Side Drive – Front	63
On Side Drive – Front	59	Average	61
Cut	50	On Side Drive – Front	56
Pull	38	Pull	28
Sweep	23	Reverse Sweep	21
Reverse Sweep	22	Sweep	15

Once again, we see that when the ball is turning in to the bat, the offside drives are safer than their onside counterparts. But when the ball is turning away from the bat, the reverse is true.

SO WHAT ABOUT THE GREAT MAN HIMSELF?

Let's take the example of Rahul Dravid playing off-spin. In the matches for which we have data, he scored 56 per cent of his runs on the offside, and 69 per cent of the runs he scored from attacking shots came on the offside.

Virat Kohli is similarly offside biased when it comes to attacking off-spinners. He scores more runs on the legside when rotating the strike, but when playing attacking shots he scores the majority of his runs on the offside.

Likewise, when the left-arm spinners are bowling Root, Pujara and Williamson all score the majority of their runs on the legside.

If we restrict our analysis to straight-bat drives, then the pattern of scoring for top-class players of spin becomes even clearer.

Drives v. Off Spin		
	Off-side %	On-side %
J. H. Kallis	65.1	32.5
R. S. Dravid	69.2	30.1
C. A. Pujara	71.8	27.5
K. S. Williamson	76.8	21.2
V. Kohli	78.6	21.3
J. E. Root	80.2	19.7

These players collectively average 192 and score at 10.1 runs per over when they play an off-drive to the off-spinners, compared to an average of 99 and a scoring rate of 6.5 runs per over when they drive on the onside. *They score twice as fast and twice as safely when hitting against the spin.*

INDIA V. ENGLAND 2012
Back to 2012 and England's assault on Fortress India.

Andrew Strauss retired at the end of the 2012 summer. And so England travelled to India under new captain Alastair Cook in their attempt to became the only England team in the last 30 years to conquer the ultimate prize.

The Test series did not start well for England. Attempting to follow the pattern of the other teams who had enjoyed success in India, they picked three fast bowlers plus Graeme Swann for the first Test in Ahmedabad. India won the toss and plundered a toothless-looking English attack for over 521/8 declared on a typically flat Indian Test pitch.

When Ravi Ashwin took the new ball on the evening of day two and started to extract sharp turn and bounce, it was clear that England would need to bat very well to save the match. They didn't and lost by ten wickets. It was only some extraordinary heroics from Alastair Cook that forced the Indians to bat again.

One–nil down having been comprehensively outplayed, and with the Indian captain M. S. Dhoni calling for more spin-friendly surfaces in the press, there were few people in the cricketing world who would have bet against India gaining revenge for their 4–0 humbling in England with a similar scoreline in this series.

And none who would have given England a price to come back and win the series.

When the teams arrived in Mumbai, England coach Andy Flower took one look at the used pitch and said, 'Well you can make plans for days four and five, because this match isn't going three days.' It was clear that the series would be won or lost by the two teams' spinners.

Again, India won the toss and batted first. James Anderson removed Gautam Gambhir in the first over of the match, and that was the only wicket to fall to a fast bowler in the whole match. Spinners bowled 83 per cent of the overs, and the game finished, a session later than Flower had predicted, on the fourth morning. Swann and fellow spinner Monty Panesar bowled beautifully, Cook got another hundred, and Kevin Pietersen played the sort of innings of which only he is capable to give England a ten-wicket win.

The third Test went the same way, with England winning on a spinner's pitch.

The fourth Test pitch looked likely to be similar, with most pundits predicting a short, low-scoring contest. But halfway through the game the pitch lost all life, and with neither side's bowlers able to extract any threat from the surface, England were able to bat the game to a draw and seal a historic series win.

In doing so, England did something that was unprecedented. They went to India and won a series by winning the spin battle. Very few sides have won in India. No other side since the very first Test tour to the subcontinent in 1933 has ever won a series there by bowling and playing spin better than the home team. The rare recent triumphs by overseas teams, by Australia in 2004 and South Africa in 2000, had relied on dominant pace attacks.

The English spinners' total of 39 wickets in the series was the most taken by visiting spinners in a series since the 1960s.

Swann averaged 24.8 with the ball, Panesar 26.8. No Indian spinner in the same series averaged under 30. Harbhajan Singh and the peerless Ravichandran Ashwin, now with 800 Test wickets between them, took their wickets at 42 and 52.6 respectively.

Spinners in 2012 IND–ENG Series			
	Team	Average	SR
G. P. Swann	England	24.8	56
M. S. Panesar	England	26.8	65
P. P. Ojha	India	30.9	76
P. P. Chawla	India	33.3	72
R. A. Jadeja	India	39.0	140
Harbhajan Singh	India	42.0	69
R. Ashwin	India	52.6	102

SO HOW DID ENGLAND DO IT?

How did they manage to do what no other visiting team had got close to doing in the previous 15 years? And do so from 1–0 down.

Well, first of all, Swann and Panesar had the series of their lives. Both bowled magnificently and together they produced the most effective spin-bowling performance ever by an overseas team in India.

But if Swann and Panesar out-bowled the Indians, then the English batsmen outplayed their counterparts too. How did they do it, given their long history of struggling in subcontinental conditions? What was the key to the transformation in their playing of spin?

From the winter of 2011–12 to the winter of 2012–13, two areas of their game improved beyond all recognition.

Firstly, they improved their footwork and reading of length to the extent that they were better than the Indians. Not only did they improve collectively, but every single England batsman who played in both series improved, significantly reducing the number of balls they played in the danger zone, and the number of balls they attacked there. Where they had been significantly inferior to their Indian counterparts in the One Day International series of November 2011, they were superior to them in the Test series of November 2012.

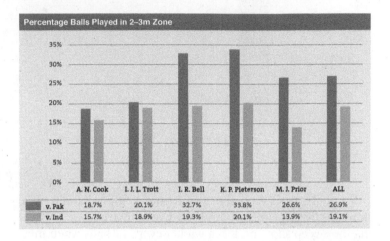

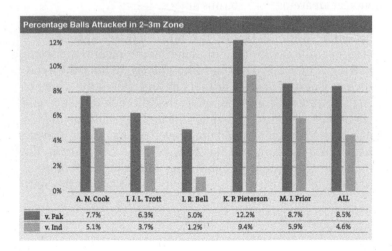

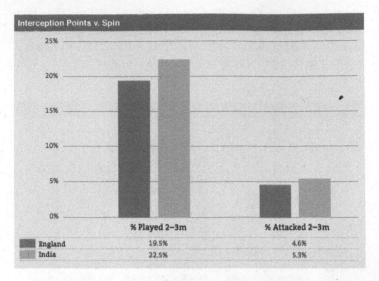

Interception Points v. Spin	% Played 2–3m	% Attacked 2–3m
England	19.5%	4.6%
India	22.5%	5.3%

Secondly, the sweep shot went from being a liability to a strength. In the winter of 2011–12 England averaged 17 playing the sweep shot and lost a wicket every 12 balls when they played it. In India they lost just two top-order wickets to the shot, at an average of 116 runs apiece.

In an era when home advantage feels, at times, like it is becoming insurmountable, the rare successes against high-class opposition with armour-plated home records are worth looking at in detail. The sides who manage to buck the trend, such as England in 2012 or India in Australia in the winter of 2018–19, are welcome reminders that through diligence and attention to detail it is possible to learn the skills required to play and win in alien conditions, even against those who are native to those surfaces and styles of play. Overcoming the innate structures in your upbringing and cricketing culture is possible, to overturn what is expected – to Hit Against the Spin.

Part Two

T20 – Changing the Game

Shortening the Game
·····························

TIMED CRICKET

Professional cricket was, for well over a hundred years, a contest that had innings of unlimited length. Each team could bat for as long as they wanted, or for as long as they could last without being bowled out, until the time that was allocated for the match to be played ran out. This meant that there were four results possible, a win, a loss, a draw and (very rarely) a tie. The draw acted as a counterweight to allowing the teams to bat for as long as they wanted, because it meant that to win the match a dominant batting side needed to leave enough time to bowl the opposition out, usually by declaring their innings closed.

The ultimate expression of this was a Timeless Test – a match played with no limit to its length, and therefore theoretically no chance of a draw. In Durban in 1935, England played South Africa in a match that lasted nine days and yet still ended in a draw. The England team, needing just 42 runs for victory, had to leave to catch the boat home.

Time-limited games were, and still are, a clever solution to creating a fair and interesting contest between sides who may or may not be well matched, on a pitch that may or may not tilt the contest in favour of bat or ball. Unlimited overs per innings, but a time limit on the match itself, create a self-regulating dynamic that gives both teams something to play for throughout the contest.

The dynamics of timed cricket are simple and elegant. The batsman is trying to score as many runs as he can before he gets out. He will optimise his scoring rate to do this. In the modern era this generally means that he will score at approximately 50 runs per 100 balls, or about three runs per over. But he will also be happy to defend and score slowly or not at all for periods when scoring at three runs per over is difficult or dangerous, for example early in his innings.

Likewise, the bowlers are optimising their approach so as to dismiss the batsman as cheaply as possible. Scoring rates may have some influence on their tactics, but overwhelmingly they will prioritise runs per wicket ahead of everything else. (There are instances when this isn't the case, when teams are about to declare, or when they are batting for the draw, but 90+ per cent of Test cricket is played with a fairly constant exchange rate between runs and a batsman's wicket.) It is only the final total that matters.

LIMITED OVERS

Much of modern cricket is now played with a limit to the number of overs in an innings. What happens to the internal dynamics of the game if we limit the length of the innings, to 50 overs, say? The two most obvious things that change are:

1. scoring rates now matter;
2. taking wickets is still important, but no longer vital.

If we think about it from a team perspective, the team's collective scoring rate is now far more important than their batting average – so long as their average is not so low that they get bowled out on a regular basis and therefore waste overs.

This also shifts the balance of power between batsmen and bowlers. In a Test team, the players who have the biggest effect on winning matches are the bowlers, and in particular the most potent wicket-taking bowlers. Replace an average bowler with an exceptional bowler and you increase your chances of winning by far more than if you replace an average batsman with an exceptional batsman. To simplify, bowlers win matches for you, batsmen stop you losing.

To put it another way, when the innings is unlimited, the batting team has one limited resource to use to score runs, and that is their wickets left in hand. Those wickets have a fairly fixed value. If a player's expected average on this pitch against these bowlers is 45, then his wicket is worth 45 runs. Drop a simple catch off him, and it will cost you, on average, 45 runs. Wickets are limited, overs are not.

In limited overs contests, the batting team has two limited resources in their attempt to score maximum runs: wickets in hand and overs remaining. This changes the value of a wicket. If an opening batsman is out in the first over, then his team's expected total is reduced, but not by the full amount of his batting average as it would be in red-ball cricket. That early wicket is worth more like 20 to 25 runs. This is because, although the player has scored far less than expected, his remaining teammates now have more time to bat than they would otherwise expect to have. So if his average is 45, as above, he has scored 45 runs less than you would expect, but his teammates will score 20 to 25 runs more as a result of having longer to bat, reducing the cost of the wicket to the team.

The other thing that changes is the value of a wicket as the game goes on. A wicket that falls in the first over is worth 20 to 25 runs, and the run value of subsequent wickets then varies as the match situation evolves, but follows a general trend of decreasing in value until you get to the last over of the innings, when if a wicket falls off the last ball of the innings it is exactly equivalent to a dot ball, worth, at that stage, slightly less than two runs.

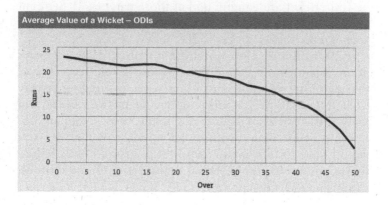

Average Value of a Wicket – ODIs

In limited overs cricket there is no stable equivalence between wickets and runs as there is in red-ball cricket: the value of a wicket is entirely dependent on the stage of the match. This means that a simple metric such as a batting or bowling average, so elegantly powerful in red-ball cricket, becomes a far less accurate measure of a player's effectiveness in limited overs cricket.

A bowler who takes the majority of his wickets with the new ball, early in the innings, will find he is undervalued by his bowling average, especially compared to a different bowler with the same average who takes most of his wickets late in the innings. Wickets at the death *are* important, and in tight contests can swing matches, but they are nevertheless less valuable on average than wickets earlier in the innings.

FIELDING

As the value of wickets changes, so does the value and importance of different types of fielding.

In Test cricket, fielding essentially equates to catching. The consistently high value of wickets in run terms means that any piece of fielding that takes (or helps take) a wicket is incredibly valuable. So the quality of a Test team's fielding comes down almost entirely to the quality of its catching, and in particular its close catching: 61 per cent of dismissals in Test cricket are caught, and of those catches 71 per cent of them are close to the wicket – slips, short leg, wicket-keeper, etc.

In Test cricket, close catching is critical to the success of any team, in any conditions. And the relative value of that catching compared to other types of fielding is very high. For example, a full-length dive in the covers that saves four runs is of almost negligible value compared to the slip catch that dismisses an opposition opener. You would have to fumble an awful lot of ground balls before their combined effect is equal to the value of one difficult catch successfully caught.

Sports analytics company CricViz measure the value of each piece of fielding, and they are able to show that catching currently accounts for 74 per cent of the value of fielding actions in Test cricket.

Compare this to T20 cricket. Here, the average value of a wicket is around eight runs (a little higher or lower depending on which method you use to calculate it). Obviously, wickets are worth more than eight runs towards the start of the innings, and less towards the end. But on average, we can take the effect of a wicket on a team's eventual total to be approximately eight runs.

This means that the relative value and importance of different T20 fielding events is radically different to Test cricket, where the importance of catching dwarfs everything else. Now, the full-length diving stop that saves four is almost on a par with the diving catch. Indeed, in the last over of the innings, the diving stop has a greater impact on the match than the catch.

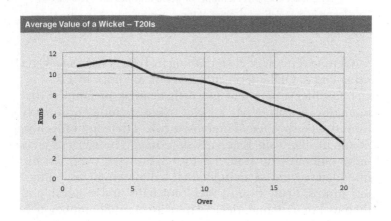

Average Value of a Wicket – T20Is

In T20s, the overall proportion of dismissals that are catches is 60 per cent, almost exactly the same as in Test cricket. But in Tests, a large majority of those catches are taken close to the bat. In T20 cricket, only 19 per cent of catches are taken by close catchers (and half of those are by the wicketkeeper).

Overall, when looking at the value of each fielding action, CricViz estimate that catching accounts for just 28 per cent of the total value of a T20 team's fielding. There will be days when that is higher, and days when it is lower. But it is clear that when you compare the different types of fielding in the different formats, the relative importance of ground fielding and throwing at the stumps varies enormously from one form of the game to another. And the type of fielding and catching that players are required to perform is equally varied.

SCORING RATES

If we were to summarise, these are the principal qualities of each format that define tactics, and the relative value of different types of player to a team:

- Test cricket puts the highest value on a wicket.
- T20 cricket puts the highest premium on scoring rate.
- ODI cricket contains elements of both, and has the greatest variation in the relative priorities of those metrics over the course of an innings.

'Getting yourself in' costs nothing in Tests. It has a small and rising cost in ODI cricket, and a significant price in T20s.

The other aspect that is worth bearing in mind is that increases in scoring rate are not made smoothly or linearly from the perspective of increased risk. There are inflection points on the 'Run Rate v. Risk' curve. The run rate may move smoothly up from 4.2 to 4.5 runs per over, but the intended scoring off an individual ball moves in discontinuous jumps, firstly from 0 to 1 (dot balls and singles), and then to 4 or 6 (boundaries). (There are a small number of 2s in limited overs cricket and a tiny number of 3s, but they rarely account for a noticeable proportion of the total run rate so we can ignore them for now.) So once the run rate has moved to a level where it is difficult to match it by scoring more singles, any further increase must come in an increased boundary rate.

This is particularly the case in T20 cricket, where an average score off 20 overs is around 160. This means that, under most circumstances, a single is a win for the bowler. A run a ball will only get the batting team to 120. There are on average only four 2s in a T20 innings and slightly less than one 3. This means that the result of a T20 match is decided largely by boundary hitting. Indeed, only 6 per cent of T20 International matches are won by teams who lose the boundary count by more than two boundaries.

If we look at a chart of 'Run Rate v. Risk %' in ODI cricket we can see that there is an inflection point at around 3.5 to 4 runs per over. This is the 'natural' rate of scoring for the average batsman in ODI cricket. It equates to a batsman who is taking the available singles (about 2.2 per over) and picking up the odd boundary either through good fortune or from bad balls that can be put away without undue risk.

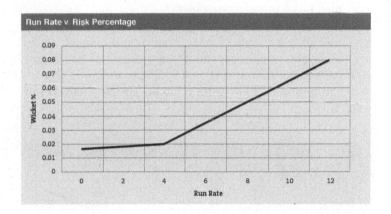

The key insight here is that there is an optimal cruising rate, where maximal scoring is achieved at the lowest level of relative risk. You can score slower than this and it will reduce the risk, but not to a proportionate degree. This is akin to teams batting out for the draw in Test matches: they score more slowly and as a result there is a reduction in their risk of dismissal, but it is not proportionate. Halving your scoring rate increases the length of your innings, but it doesn't double it, in fact, far from it.

Likewise, you can choose to score faster than this optimal rate, but it comes with an increased risk, and this risk is proportionate to the rate at which you score additional runs. So doubling your run rate more than doubles your risk.

Think of it as buying runs with risk. The most efficient way to compile the maximum number of runs is to buy at the lowest price, which is at the inflection point, about 3.5 to 4 runs per over for most batsmen in white-ball cricket.

We use the analogy of a discount warehouse. Imagine you are a business and you need to buy widgets from a wholesaler to produce your product. The wholesaler charges you a monthly fee of $250, but then allows you to buy your widgets at a discounted price of $1 per widget for the first 200 widgets. After that, he charges $6 per widget.

You can see, I'm sure, that the cheapest way to buy widgets is to buy 200 per month: 1 widget per month costs you $251 per widget, 200 widgets per month costs you $2.25 per widget, 1000 widgets per month costs you $5.25 per widget. This then is straightforward. There is an optimal rate at which to buy widgets.

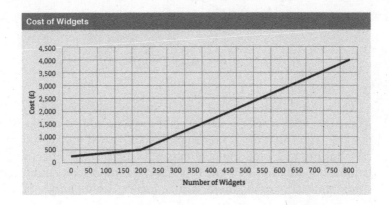

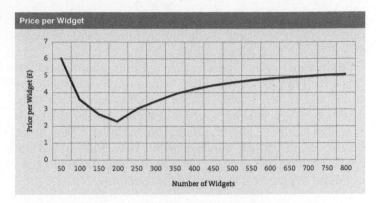

Price per Widget

But there is also a corollary. Namely, that if you have a slight excess in either funding or demand, then the optimal rate to buy is to distribute that excess demand evenly across months. If you need to buy 3000 widgets per year then you should buy 250 per month. Distributing your excess risk evenly across a number of months makes sense.

Likewise, the most efficient way to distribute risk across an innings is evenly. This was the insight that led England to their seemingly gung-ho ODI batting approach.

In ODI cricket, this equation of risk and reward is not constant. It varies according to the strengths of the batsman and the fielding restrictions in that phase of the game.

For example, in the first ten overs of the innings only two fielders are allowed outside the 30-metre circle. This severely restricts the batsman's ability to score in singles but makes hitting boundaries far easier.

It is also the case that the natural tempo and means of scoring varies from batsman to batsman. Some (Type A in the following 'Run Rate v. Risk %' graph) have a higher cruising speed at which they can score relatively safely. These players rotate the strike well, they are skilful manipulators of the ball, particularly against spin, and are characterised by having a high ODI batting average (often 50+) and a low dot-ball percentage. Jonathan Trott and Joe Root would be prime examples of this type. They are perfectly suited to compiling low-risk runs in the middle overs and building a strong position in the game from which the boundary hitters can launch the assault on the final overs.

At the other end of the scale are the pure boundary hitters (Type B). They find it difficult to deal in singles and rotate the strike, and so rely largely on fire power to score their runs. They have a low cruising speed, but then a shallow risk curve from that point on. They deal largely in boundaries, and so are best suited to causing damage in the PowerPlay and at the death. Players such as Chris Gayle and Babar Azam are good examples of players at this end of the spectrum.

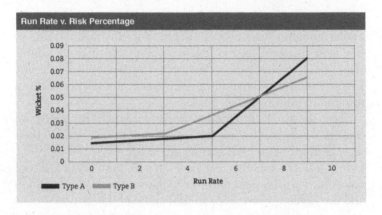

You can see from the graph that there are run rates where one type of player buys their runs at a cheaper price, and run rates where the other type of player is more efficient. ODI teams trying to assemble their batting resources in such a way as to score as many runs as possible for the minimum level of risk choose a variety of batsmen and compile their batting order so that the likely fall of wickets puts the appropriate type of batsman at the crease for each phase of the game.

This creates roughly three specialisms within the batting line-up – PowerPlay batsmen to open the innings, skilful rotators to bat in the middle overs, and boundary hitters who can take down the final overs with five fielders out on the boundary.

The point here is that as you shorten the game, you don't just accentuate the same skills more acutely. Nor do you cause the same players to shift into different but similar modes. You fundamentally change the balance between and importance of different skillsets in interesting and unexpected ways.

Shorten the game again, from 50 overs down to 20 overs per team, and the relative importance of different types of players shifts again.

Leg-spin and the Right
to Feel Good

······························

In late 2009, England travelled to South Africa to play a four-match Test series. Graeme Swann was in his pomp and in many ways the cornerstone of the four-man England attack. For South Africa, the great Jacques Kallis was about to prove the perfect counterfoil to Swann's brilliance.

In the first innings of the first Test the two came up against each other with Kallis on 16, and he immediately went on the offensive. The fourth ball that Swann bowled to him he launched over long-on for six. England captain Andrew Strauss pushed mid-on back to the boundary. Two balls later Kallis dropped to one knee and slog swept for a one bounce four. Once again Strauss pushed a fielder back to the boundary to protect his off-spinner on a first-day pitch offering him little assistance.

Kallis went on to get 120, Swann collected five wickets in the innings and the Man of the Match award. But in terms of their personal duel the pattern for the series was established.

Reviewing the scoring patterns of South Africa's top batsman after the final match of the series, England noticed that Kallis had scored 100 runs off the 184 balls he faced from Swann but had hit only those two boundaries in normal play (though Kallis did hit a couple of fours late in the third innings of the third Test when South Africa were in full-blown attack to set up the declaration). Having pushed long-on and deep midwicket back in the first half-dozen balls he faced, he had then been happy to score in singles and twos for the next four tests.

It is an interesting insight into the method of a great player of spin. But it also points towards a fundamental aspect of spin bowlers. Namely that while they find it easier than fast bowlers to prevent boundaries, they tend to concede more singles. (It is hard to imagine a fast bowler pushing midwicket and long-on back to the boundary and bowling with that field for most of a Test series.)

And just as importantly, while spinners are better at preventing boundaries, they are dependent on their fielders to do so.

It is a truth that becomes important as you shorten the game, and the relative importance of preventing singles and boundaries changes.

When English cricket first introduced the Twenty20 Cup in the summer of 2003, very few involved realised the revolution they were kickstarting. Seventeen years later, and T20 is the most-watched form of cricket, filling stadiums and airwaves in every corner of the cricketing world. It has been praised for widening the appeal of the game and encouraging a much larger range of demographics and communities to engage with the sport.

While few could have anticipated the ensuing revolution, which still divides cricket along the lines of those in favour of the form and those against it, even fewer could have accurately predicted the way this new format would look on the field.

For a start, although much was uncertain about the new competition, one thing seemed clear in the minds of those tasked with playing in the initial T20 matches. As Adam Hollioake, Surrey captain in that 2003 season, put it: 'Straight away, we thought "spin bowlers are going to get hit out the ground" ... we thought they'd be hopeless.' (*Cricket 2.0* by Freddie Wilde and Tim Wigmore).

He was certainly not alone in his view. As Australian coach Tom Moody put it: 'One thing that was being echoed through the corridors of our game was a concern for spin bowlers.' (*Cricket 2.0*). The prevailing view was that the advent of T20 would be the death of spin bowling; this delicate, fragile art would not survive in a world of small boundaries and big hitting.

Those early fears about spin bowling drove selection during T20's infancy. In T20 Internationals, where teams were free to pick the players most suitable for the format, not just from squads already assembled for the longer forms, there was a clear reluctance to give spinners a chance.

In the first ten T20Is, just 18 per cent of deliveries were bowled by spinners. While it is fair to say that these early matches were not overburdened by seriousness (pranks, costumes and a general atmosphere of fun were the default), it underlines the point. Pace was the instinctive choice when faced with a new, shorter format.

But as those involved became more familiar with the nuances of 20-over cricket, and the unique challenges it posed, the attitude towards spin bowling gradually changed. Far from seeing the demise of spin, those early years saw a steady rise in its use and importance; against the odds, spin flourished. The number of overs sent down by the spinners rose year on year for the best part of a decade.

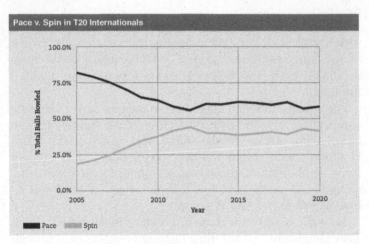

Pace v. Spin in T20 Internationals

The captains and coaches making these choices weren't acting on a whim, of course. It was a reaction to the fact that spinners were, fundamentally, doing a better job in this format than the seamers were. As the West Indian spinner Samuel

Badree put it in an interview with Nagraj Gollapudi in *The Cricket Monthly*: 'All of us spinners who have come through the T20 circuit know that spin bowling is more effective than fast bowling in this format . . . If you look at T20 cricket around the world, the most successful teams are the ones with quality spin bowlers who are dynamic and versatile, who can bowl through any stage of the game.'

While Badree might be personally inclined to push the case for spin, he is not wrong. Since that first T20I, spinners have had a better bowling average and a better economy rate than seamers in almost every calendar year. Slow bowlers bowl their overs more cheaply than fast bowlers, and their wickets cost less too.

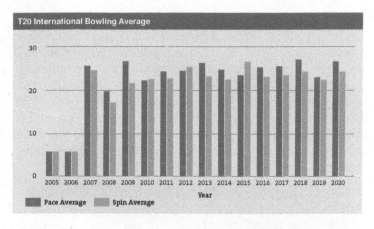

To understand why this is the case, let's think back to Swann v. Kallis in 2009 and look at how spin bowlers and fast bowlers compare across the formats. As you will see from the graphs showing wickets, singles and boundaries per 100 balls, there are some clear and consistent patterns. Compared to pace bowlers, in all forms of the game, spinners:

- take wickets at a marginally slower rate;
- concede more singles;
- concede fewer boundaries.

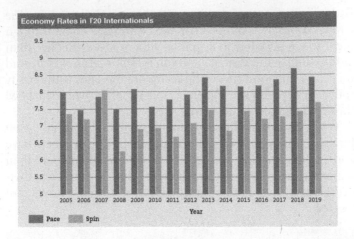

The net effect of those differences is that spin bowlers have a better economy rate than pace bowlers in all formats, and pace bowlers tend to have a better bowling average (although this is not the case in T20Is).

This determines the balance of power as you move from format to format. In Tests, where batting and bowling averages are the most important statistic, fast bowlers tend to dominate (although this is very dependent on conditions). Almost all the top-ranked Test bowlers bowl fast.

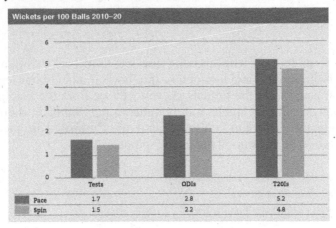

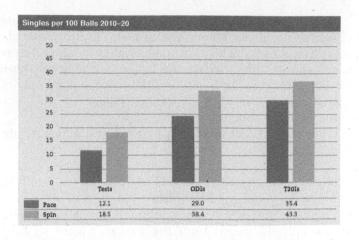

Singles per 100 Balls 2010–20

	Tests	ODIs	T20Is
Pace	12.1	29.0	35.4
Spin	18.5	38.4	43.3

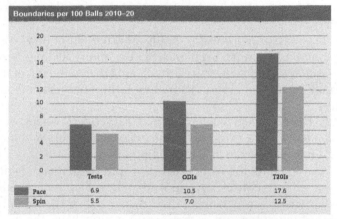

Boundaries per 100 Balls 2010–20

	Tests	ODIs	T20Is
Pace	6.9	10.5	17.6
Spin	5.5	7.0	12.5

In T20s, on the other hand, where economy rate is the more important measure of quality, almost all the top-ranked bowlers are spinners.

Primarily, this is because of their ability to control the rate of boundary scoring. T20 cricket is fundamentally a boundary-hitting contest.

And as we have already touched on in Chapter 1, while discussing England's World Cup-winning team, when the run rate is above six an over, a single is a win to the bowler.

In Tests and most periods of an ODI, spinners' greater rate of conceding singles counts against them. In T20s, though, conceding a run a ball is a winning strategy in almost every match you will play. So whereas fast bowlers generally have the upper hand in Tests, and in ODIs pace and spin are of equivalent value, in T20s the spinners outperform the quick bowlers in most conditions.

It is a point worth considering in detail, and we will return to it later.

While all spinners were doubted in the early years of T20, one type was neglected and distrusted most of all. At the embryonic stage of T20's development, leg-spinners were almost entirely absent from the format, trusted to bowl only a tiny fraction of the overs sent down in the first few years.

This was, in many ways, simply an extension of how wrist-spinners had always been treated. Leg-spin had long been considered a little different, distinct and other to the rest of the game. An art that even in its highest form is distinctly hit and miss.

In the new, high-octane world of T20 cricket, where every loose ball is likely to disappear into the stands, how could such a fallible, vulnerable style of bowling survive?

And so, amid the early distrust of spin in general, leggies were almost entirely overlooked. They had traditionally been viewed as attacking luxuries, used predominantly against tailenders and in the second innings once the pitch was turning. What use were they going to be in a format where bowling was almost entirely defensive, where the tail rarely batted, and there was no second innings? In 2007, just 5 per cent of all balls bowled in T20 cricket were from leg-spin bowlers.

But by 2018, leg-spinners had reached parity with off-spinners in terms of how often they were bowled, and had long outstripped them in terms of reputation and performance. Despite their near total exclusion when the format first began,

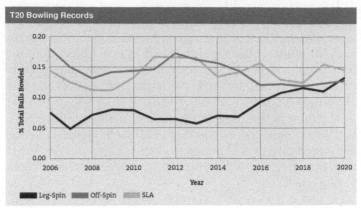

it is unequivocally the case that leg-spinners are the kings of T20 cricket. They have proven themselves to be the only bowlers who can *consistently* achieve the dual goals of taking wickets and limiting runs.

They take wickets more regularly than finger-spinners and concede fewer runs than seamers. Pioneers such as Shahid Afridi and Samuel Badree laid the template for the next generation; veterans such as Imran Tahir have torn up league after league after league; Rashid Khan is arguably the finest bowler the format has ever seen.

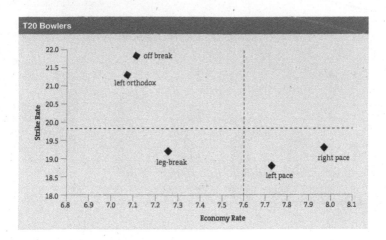

The years since 2015, in particular, have seen the prevalence of leg-spin bowling increase dramatically as the unique value of these bowlers is recognised more and more. In many ways, throughout the rapid development of T20 cricket, the triumph of leg-spin has reflected the ever-increasing sophistication of the format and the clear and distinct tactical challenges it poses.

The irony of this rise to pre-eminence in the shortest form is that it has coincided with a steady decline in the effectiveness and prevalence of leg-spin in red-ball cricket. And the key to understanding one of those trends is to understand the reasons for the other.

TEST TRAVAILS

Since 1990, only 27 leg-spinners have lasted long enough in Test cricket to deliver 1000+ balls, and only three of them have averaged less than 30: Anil Kumble, Shane Warne and Stuart MacGill. (For comparison, there are 265 pace bowlers who have bowled 1000 balls in that period and 83 of them average under 30.)

Leg-spinners have the worst average of any type of bowler in Test cricket, their wickets in the past ten years coming at the cost of 39 runs apiece.

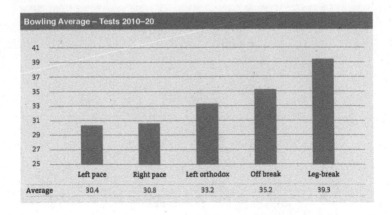

Bowling Average – Tests 2010–20

	Left pace	Right pace	Left orthodox	Off break	Leg-break
Average	30.4	30.8	33.2	35.2	39.3

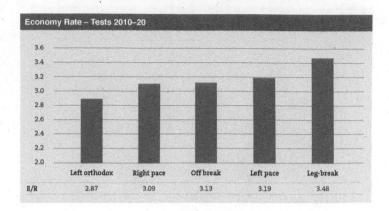

Economy Rate – Tests 2010–20

	Left orthodox	Right pace	Off break	Left pace	Leg-break
E/R	2.87	3.09	3.13	3.19	3.48

This is because, although they take wickets at a similar rate to finger-spinners, they concede runs far faster. And compared to fast bowlers, they are both more expensive and slower at taking wickets. Rattling along at nearly 3.5 runs per over, they are by far the most expensive bowling type in this form of the game.

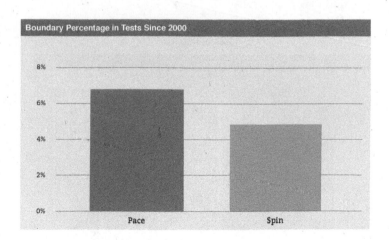

Boundary Percentage in Tests Since 2000

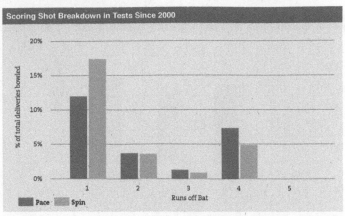

Scoring Shot Breakdown in Tests Since 2000

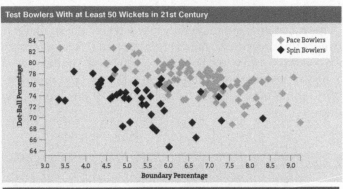

Test Bowlers With at Least 50 Wickets in 21st Century

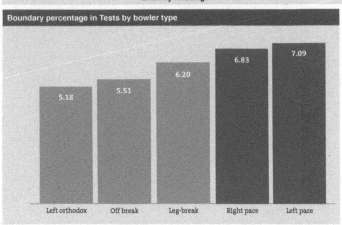

Boundary percentage in Tests by bowler type

GOOD SCENES, BAD SCENES

The American film director Howard Hawks had a formula for what constituted a good movie. A successful picture was, in his words, 'three good scenes, and no bad ones', i.e. a basic level of competency throughout punctuated by moments of higher quality. The theory applies equally well to constructing an over in Test cricket.

The foundation of red-ball bowling is the principle of 'no bad scenes'. Build pressure, control the run scoring, while waiting for the moment when the batsman makes a mistake or you produce a ball good enough to get through his defences. A high-quality over of Test match bowling is three good balls, and no bad ones.

We can start to understand the leg-spinner's travails if we consider what those good and bad balls look like. If we simplify for a moment and consider just the lengths bowled, the reasons for their issues in Test cricket become clearer.

Because of the pace they bowl, the area of the pitch where a spinner can safely land the ball and keep control of scoring is pretty small. There is, in the entirety of the cut strip, a 3-metre length where the bowling average of spin deliveries falls to acceptable levels, and within that there is a 1-metre length where it reaches a desirable one. A Safety Zone, and a Hot Zone.

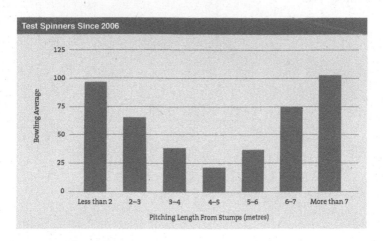

One of the most important keys to success for a Test match spinner is to bowl as few 'Bad Balls' outside of that 3- to 6-metre Safety Zone, and to bowl as many 'Good Balls' as possible in that 4- to 5-metre Hot Zone.

The issue for leg-spinners is that they struggle on both fronts. They stray from the Safety Zone far more regularly than finger-spinners, and they find the Hot Zone more rarely. They bowl more bad balls, and fewer good ones.

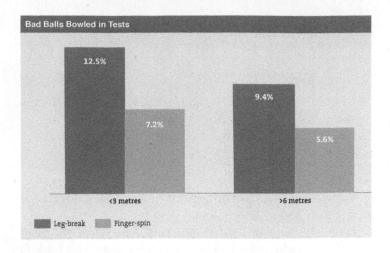

Bad Balls Bowled in Tests

12.5%
7.2%
9.4%
5.6%

<3 metres
>6 metres

Leg-break   Finger-spin

All that contortion of the body, the effort and strain of putting all those revolutions on the ball, the inherently high-risk nature of projecting a ball out of the back of your hand, take their toll. This is the classic image of the wrist-spinner, unable to build pressure with any consistency. They err from the Safety Zone too often, leaking runs, and although their best balls are more potent than those of other spinners, there are not enough of them to make them more dangerous overall.

There are too many bad scenes, and not enough good ones.

And yet, those good scenes sure are worth the wait.

When they land those good balls, when they find that Hot Zone, leg-spinners are more dangerous than anyone else. All that strain, all those revolutions and contortions, this is where they show their true worth, where they make the most impact on the game. Of all the deliveries in the game, from all bowling types, the lowest averaging delivery is a ball from a leg-spinner pitching between 4 and 5 metres from the stumps. A delivery from a leg-spinner on a good length may be one of the rarer deliveries in Test cricket, but it is also the most potent.

279

Test Bowling Average by Length									
	<1	1–2	2–3	3–4	4–5	5–6	6–7	7–8	8–9	9+
right pace	35.7	32.0	52.6	44.9	31.3	21.0	22.7	39.1	36.9
left pace	26.6	19.2	33.6	38.9	28.9	22.7	24.1	43.1	34.8
off break	105.3	71.9	40.6	22.3	35.5	80.9	106.		
leg-break	100.89	69.1	34.8	19.1	49.9	67.4	92.5		
left arm	84.37	60.9	40.4	22.6	36.2	80.9	165.5		

Leg-spinners have two things in their favour, and this is what makes their best balls so potent.

Firstly, because of their extravagant wrist action they can impart more spin to the ball than finger-spinners. This leads to more dip and swerve in the air, and more turn off the pitch. Both of which make it harder for the batsman to play the ball safely.

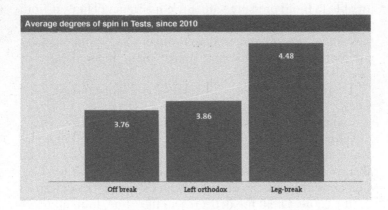

Secondly, most leg-spinners have a googly, and so can turn the ball in both directions. This means that they can deceive the batsman as to which way the ball will turn off the pitch, or at least add a layer of decision-making to his shot selection – he must first 'pick' the delivery before he can play it.

In Test cricket, picking a leg-spinner is one big compromise, accepting an inability to defend with an unparalleled ability to attack. In essence, you are picking them for those good balls, knowing the bad ones will make up a significant minority of their work. You are picking them for the ability they have to conjure the magic delivery, to access a level of threat and incision that is not often available to your other bowlers. But you have to take the downsides too, the passages where runs will flow and good balls will be few and far between. Like watching a cult classic, you sit through the bad scenes to get to the good ones.

Only the best leggies, the ones who transcend their art, are able to play a holding role in the first innings of a Test match when the pitch isn't turning. For the rest of them, you pick them knowing there will be long periods of the game where you don't want to bowl them, when you have to lean entirely on the rest of your bowling attack. That's why, other than the greats, you rarely see a leg-spinner playing as the only spinner in a Test attack.

THE GREATS

If you took a glance at the all-time leading Test wicket-taking chart, you would be forgiven for thinking wrist-spin ruled supreme. Behind the great Muttiah Muralitharan (in some ways an honorary wrist-spinner), the two most prolific bowlers in the history of the game have been leg-spinners; Shane Warne with 708 wickets, and Anil Kumble with 619. They are without doubt two of the finest bowlers to grace the game.

Leading Test Wicket-Takers		
Player	Bowling Style	Wickets
Muttiah Muralitharan	off break	800
Shane Warne	leg-break	708
Anil Kumble	leg-break	619
James Anderson	right pace	584
Glenn McGrath	right pace	563
Courtney Walsh	right pace	519
Stuart Broad	right pace	485
Dale Steyn	right pace	439
Kapil Dev	right pace	434
Rangana Herath	left orthodox	433

As a man, Warne was a showman, a larger-than-life presence who perfectly encapsulated the Australian sporting ideal; outrageous natural talent, an almost unrelenting commitment to entertainment and a remarkably competitive core. As a bowler, Warne was a far more subtle presence. The most important element of his game was the hard-spinning leg-break, slow and drifting, the revolutions imparted on the ball giving it that trademark hum through the air, that 'flit, flit, flit'. His approach to the crease was slow, like a lion stalking its prey, his head staying level and still throughout, never taking his eyes away from the man at the other end. A childhood injury had forced him to wheel himself around for a year, an event that has both added to his considerable folklore and left him with extremely muscular, overdeveloped shoulders. This allowed Warne's arm to sling lower and quicker than many leg-spinners, ripping the ball from side to side and providing almost unparalleled amounts of turn. Quicker variations came into his bowling later in his career, when shoulder operations had limited his ability to bowl the classical googly, but the base of Warne's game was always the slower leg-break that spun big, spun hard.

In action on the field, Kumble could not have been more different. Bouncing to the crease with everything on the move, head rocking and arms flailing wide and high, Kumble's approach looked chaotic alongside the Australian, but it all served a precise purpose. This run up, quicker and longer than Warne's, was in part a relic of his early days as a seamer, an occupation he sometimes returned to on days where pitches were particularly unforgiving. Normally, however, it all served to gather momentum in the approach to the crease so that, at the moment of delivery when Kumble's head dipped for the final time, that pace through the final stride was extreme. The wrist appeared loose and straight as the fingers came over the top, the high arm allowing Kumble to get substantial topspin on the ball; the ball turned less from right to left, but the dip and bounce were lethal. The final ball was quick, really quick, and the complete package was devastating.

Test Bowling Styles		
	Speed	Spin
Shane Warne	78.9 kph	5.7°
Anil Kumble	88.3 kph	2.1°

Kumble is only 2 centimetres taller than Warne, but released the ball from almost 20 centimetres higher into the air, the most pronounced physical difference between their actions and the cause of their differing styles: '[Warne's] naturally lower arm was the source of his sidespin.' (*On Warne* by Gideon Haigh). Kumble's action gave him a weapon Warne could not emulate easily, and vice versa. In different ways, these two giants of the game showcased what was possible for leg-spinners in Test cricket, and made clear the extreme and outrageous gifts that bowlers of this type could possess, the impact they could have. Through their unique and opposing actions, Warne and Kumble demonstrated the fact that leg-spinners had at their fingertips – and in their wrists – the ability to produce dip and turn that was simply not available to other bowlers.

And yet, ironically, the sheer extent of their dominance highlights the limitations of bowlers like them. Warne and Kumble have taken 20 per cent of all wickets ever taken by leg-spinners in Test cricket; if we included Muralitharan as a de facto wrist-spinner, it rises to 27 per cent. By comparison, Glenn McGrath and James Anderson – the two leading right-arm seamers – have taken 3 per cent of all wickets from right-arm seamers. The two leading leg-spinners in Test history are, in the most literal sense, exceptional.

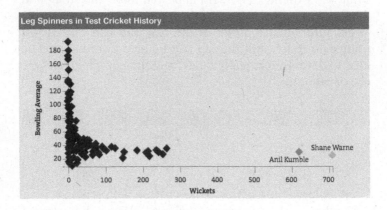

While leg-spin dominates the very top of the wicket-takers chart, it lacks representation as you look further down – *severely* lacks representation. Warne and Kumble may sit proudly among that top 3, but they are also the only leg-spinners in the top 40.

GOOD BALLS BETTER, BAD BALLS NOT AS BAD

A common theme when examining leg-spin and why it has done so well in T20 cricket has been to look at how the shorter format forgives leg-spinners their flaws more readily than Test cricket. For 'inconsistency' in red-ball cricket, see 'unpredict-ability' in T20.

'The key to spin in Twenty20 is never bowl the same ball twice. You might bowl six leggies per over but they would all be delivered from different parts of the crease and at different paces. It is about not being predictable,' Shane Warne wrote in the *Telegraph* in 2014.

This seems to be true when looking at bowling patterns in T20. For all bowling types, only around 25 per cent of deliveries in T20 are on a good line and length; in essence, while those areas are still largely the best place to be bowling, if a batsman can set themselves and know where the ball will be delivered, they have a big advantage. It is not hard to see why bowlers avoid bowling the same ball too often, wary of allowing the batsman to 'line them up'. Finger-spinners find themselves trying to create the inconsistency/unpredictability that leg-spinners have always had, now rebadged as a virtue.

We can see this if we look at the return spinners get from different lengths in T20 cricket and compare it to what happens in Tests.

Leg-spinners in Tests struggled to bowl the 'three good balls and no bad ones' that typified a high-class over. In the 'Leg Spinners' graphs here, you can see that the penalty for missing length is much smaller in T20 cricket.

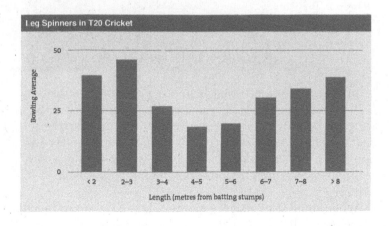

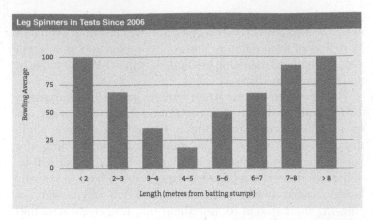

At the same time, as they are being forgiven for their bad balls, leg-spinners are getting more credit for their good ones. Leg-spinners not only still bowl the most potent ball in the game, they now have a larger margin for error in bowling it.

	<1	1–2	2–3	3–4	4–5	5–6	6–7	7–8	8–9	9+
right pace	33.1	21.4	27.6	33.8	27.8	23.4	22.1	26.3	30.0	27.8
left pace	31.5	21.4	26.1	28.2	23.0	21.5	21.5	24.7	29.7	27.7
off break	40.1		36.5	35.9	26.0	20.4	29.8	35.8	37.5	
leg-break	38.7		45.8	25.9	18.8	19.6	29.9	33.3	38.2	
SLA	37.3		39.0	33.5	25.9	23.2	27.6	37.5	46.0	

T20 Bowling Average by Length

In general, spinners struggle to bring about false strokes in T20 cricket, compared to seamers. When they are bowling, an edge or miss comes 14 per cent of the time, while for seamers it is 25 per cent. That 4- to 6-metre zone for leg-spinners is the only place on the pitch where spinners – any spinners – consistently bring about false strokes in T20 cricket.

Why should it be that leg-spinners' best balls are so much more potent than each of the other bowler types?

False Shot Percentage in T20s, by length								
	<2	2–3	3–4	4–5	5–6	6–7	7–8	8+
Off-Spin	10%	10%	11%	17%	14%	13%	10%	10%
Leg-Spin	12%	9%	14%	22%	22%	14%	11%	9%
SLA	10%	9%	9%	14%	12%	11%	10%	8%

Well, white-ball cricket is a very batsman-friendly game. And one of the main reasons for that is that the modern white ball itself is a very batsman-friendly object. It is primarily designed and manufactured to go straight. It has a small seam and an almost unpolishable finish.

Compared to all the various red balls used around the world, it offers less movement off the pitch and less swing in the air. It is designed to be relatively easy for the batsman to hit, with very little deviation in the air or off the pitch, which would make a clean contact less likely.

So, leg-spinners, because of the prodigious spin they impart to the ball, are the only type of bowler who can reliably get the ball to deviate.

In Test cricket this is less of an advantage to them. There, most bowlers can get the ball to deviate, and when the leggie does land their best ball, the batsman only needs to defend it.

In T20 cricket, that movement off the straight sets the leg-spinner apart to a much greater degree. Batsmen play very few defensive shots in T20. They have to attack the leg-spinners' best balls, and they have to try to hit them for boundaries. Doing so is difficult and dangerous.

THE WRONG 'UN

Another advantage leg-spinners have in T20 is that most of them have, as part of their armoury, the ability to spin the ball both ways. The nature of wrist-spin, and the action required to bowl it, makes it far easier legally to bowl a delivery that turns the other way – a googly, or wrong 'un.

This gives the bowler two advantages. The first runs in parallel to the advantage that left-arm pace bowlers have in T20 cricket.

Left-arm seamers have an advantage over their right-arm colleagues because batsmen find them 'harder to read'. They find it harder to predict from the bowler's action where the ball will land. This comparative advantage grows from Tests to ODIs to T20Is as the batsmen become more attacking. Attacking shots require an earlier decision, an earlier commitment to the shot, and therefore place more reliance on anticipation. The more attacking the format, the more of an advantage left-armers have.

The same is true for leg-spinners and their ability to turn the ball both ways. Because the batsman has to 'pick the ball' (predict which way it will turn) and then play it, his decision-making is slower. This gives him an advantage in Test cricket, but as we move to 50-over and then 20-over cricket, that comparative advantage grows.

In the same way that batsmen find it harder to 'line up' left-armers, they find it harder to do the same for mystery spinners who can turn the ball in either direction.

The second advantage is tactical. As in other formats, the ball turning away from the bat has a much better record in T20 cricket than the ball turning in to the bat.

Leg-spinners (and other 'mystery spinners'), because they can turn the ball both ways, can choose to bowl more balls that turn away from the batsman regardless of whether he is right- or left-handed.

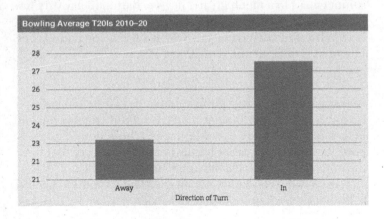

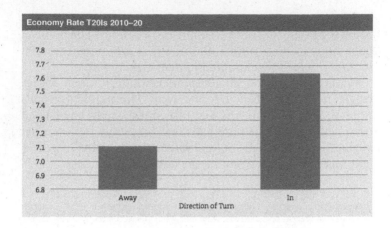

Take a look at the graph of 'T20 Bowling Records'. Why would we see that sudden rise in T20 leg-spin that started in 2014–15?

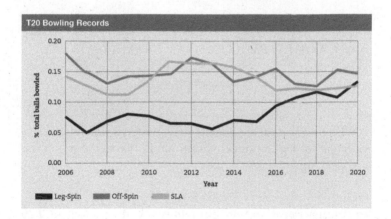

Well, in 2014 the ICC started to crack down on what they deemed to be suspect bowling actions. Many finger-spinners who could turn the ball both ways, the likes of Saeed Ajmal, Mohammad Hafeez and Sachithra Senanayake, had their 'doosra' – the off-spinner's ball that spins 'the other way' – banned and were forced to remodel their actions. The dubious bent arms, to which the authorities had previously turned a blind eye, were forced out of international cricket.

From that point on, finger-spinners found it much harder legally to turn the ball the other way. The number of balls from off-spinners in T20Is that turned the wrong way halved overnight. (The remaining balls that turn away from the bat are mostly 'carrom balls', a legal variant that is harder to deliver and generally less potent than the doosra.)

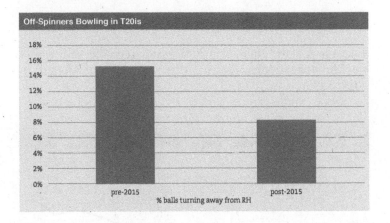

With the removal of so many rival mystery spinners, the way was clear for leg-spinners to continue to rise to the top of the T20 pecking order.

THE BEST OF BOTH WORLDS

To summarise, what leg-spinners succeed in doing in T20 cricket is not only to combine the best aspects of fast bowlers and finger-spinners, but outdo both of them in those regards.

They take more wickets than fast bowlers, and they concede fewer boundaries than the finger-spinners.

Currently in the ICC's T20 rankings, nine of the top-ten ranked bowlers are mystery spinners, seven of them leg-spinners. That has been the pattern for the last few years and looks set to continue.

The world is still catching up with the full extent of their potency, so the only question really is, how much further can they rise?

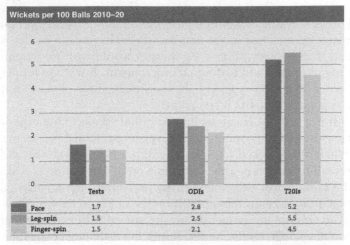

Wickets per 100 Balls 2010–20	Tests	ODIs	T20Is
Pace	1.7	2.8	5.2
Leg-spin	1.5	2.5	5.5
Finger-spin	1.5	2.1	4.5

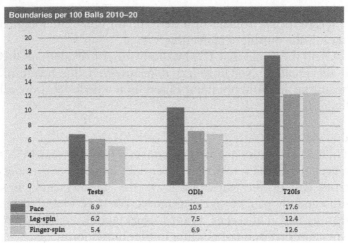

Boundaries per 100 Balls 2010–20	Tests	ODIs	T20Is
Pace	6.9	10.5	17.6
Leg-spin	6.2	7.5	12.4
Finger-spin	5.4	6.9	12.6

There is a reason that so many deliveries dubbed the 'Ball of the Century' have come from a leg-spinner's hand. A crisp away swinger that takes the top off is a thing of joy; a cover drive that reaches the fence seemingly a split-second later is a thing of beauty; but they exist more obviously as a part of a grander plan, as a coda to the bars that preceded it.

There is a short aside in Haigh's *On Warne*, where Terry Jenner – Warne's long-time coach and mentor – goes over an exchange they had in the nets one day: 'His protégé bowled a ball that did everything a leg-spinner would wish for – spinning, dropping and tearing off at a tangent. But when Jenner opined that it was a good ball, Warne asked plaintively: "If it was good, why didn't it feel good?"'

It is a story, as Haigh well knows, that speaks to the experience of being a leg-spinner on a level deeper than it first seems. When Warne asked Jenner, 'why didn't it *feel* good?' he was revealing something inherent in the craft. The nature of it all, the endless bad balls followed by perfection, the knowledge that more than any other player on the field you have the ability to conjure this particular magic, cursed with knowing that this magic is as elusive as it is destructive – that invites a different mindset.

It calls for a personality obsessed with the chase and inclined towards the pursuit of perfection.

Of all the things that T20 has done for cricket, perhaps this is the greatest. Not only has it resurrected this beautiful, beguiling art form, but it has raised it on a pedestal above all the rest.

CODA: WHY DON'T THEY BOWL MORE SPIN?

There is one more question to answer when it comes to this aspect of T20 cricket. We have seen spin initially being underestimated in the early years of the format, and then subsequently rising to pre-eminence. We have looked at the reasons why it succeeds, against expectations, and how and why it outperforms fast bowling in the shorter form.

But that seems to raise the obvious question, why don't teams bowl more of it? A vast amount of money is invested each year in T20 bowling attacks around the world. If the best bowlers in the world are spinners, spinners outperform pace bowlers in all phases of the game, and this fact is widely known, then why don't teams pick more spinners? Why is the proportion of spin stuck at about 40 per cent?

Either teams are getting this wrong and wasting money – and there are plenty of people who will make that argument. Or they are intuiting something about the game that is missing from the raw stats. We have sympathy for both points of view but tend towards the latter.

To explain the reason why we think teams are broadly correct in their approach we need to again go back to Swann v. Kallis.

If we look at the proportion of spin bowled throughout the innings in T20Is, we can clearly see three distinct phases to the innings.

- The PowerPlay Overs 1–6: Pace dominated.
- The Middle Overs 7–14: Spin dominated.
- The Death Overs 15–20: Pace dominated.

This split (12:8) fits well with the overall proportion of spin bowled, which tends to hover around 40 per cent, and the fact that the default five-man bowling attack for most teams is three fast bowlers and two spinners.

But why the distinct phases?

Well, the demarcation between overs six and seven is clearly a reflection of the change in the fielding restrictions at that point. And the sharp change there in the proportion of spin bowled points us towards those fielding restrictions as the biggest determining factor in the effectiveness of spin at that point in the game.

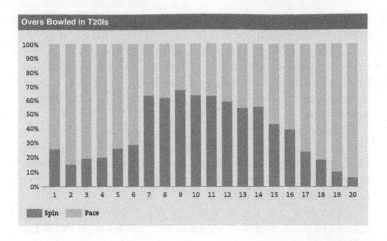

Over	Spin	Pace
1	26%	74%
2	15%	85%
3	19%	81%
4	20%	80%
5	26%	74%
6	29%	71%
7	63%	37%
8	61%	39%
9	67%	33%
10	63%	37%
11	63%	37%
12	59%	41%
13	55%	45%
14	55%	45%
15	43%	57%
16	40%	60%
17	24%	76%
18	18%	82%
19	10%	90%
20	6%	94%

In the sixth over, with only two fielders outside the circle, most captains opt to bowl a seamer. The very next over, with a potential five fielders on the boundary, the overwhelming consensus is that a spinner should bowl.

The reason is simple, and a reflection of the Swann v. Kallis duel. Spinners are better at preventing boundaries, but they rely on their fielders to do so.

Pace bowlers prevent boundaries in large part by getting the ball past the bat (more leaves, more plays and misses), or by inducing a poor contact that will not travel to the boundary. But with pace on the ball, they are vulnerable throughout the full 360 degrees of the boundary.

Spinners prevent boundaries differently. With less pace on the ball, the batsman makes a clean contact far more often. But because of their slower speed and greater control, spinners find it easier to direct where the batsman hits the ball. In particular, it is harder for the batsman to hit the ball behind square (with any pace). With less boundary to protect, the spinners' fielders are far more effective at doing so.

All of this is dependent on ground dimensions and pitch conditions, but we can speak in general. In the PowerPlay, where most of the scoring comes in the form of boundaries, the fast bowlers' method of defending tends to be more reliable. In the seventh over, with the field back, it suits the spinners more.

Why then do the pace bowlers come back into favour towards the end of the innings? The fielders, after all, are still out on the boundary. But captains shift more and more towards their seamers, to the point where there is less spin bowled in overs 19 and 20 than in any other periods of the match, PowerPlay included. This is a harder answer to find, but one to which we think we have discovered some clues.

Although spinners leak fewer boundaries than seamers in all three forms of the game, they are hit for more sixes. Five times as many in Tests, for example.

In the PowerPlay of T20 cricket, when boundary fielders are largely out of the equation, spinners concede fewer fours than pace bowlers, but 34 per cent more sixes.

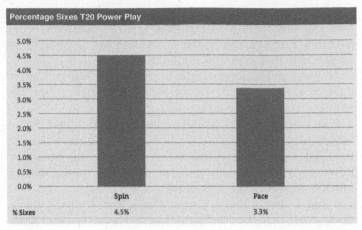

As the innings goes on, a greater and greater proportion of the run scoring comes in sixes. Wickets become less valuable and batsmen become willing to take greater risks hitting over fielders on the boundary. As this happens, the relative advantage spinners have is eroded. As the deterrent effect of their boundary fielders disappears, the balance of power swings back towards the quicker bowlers.

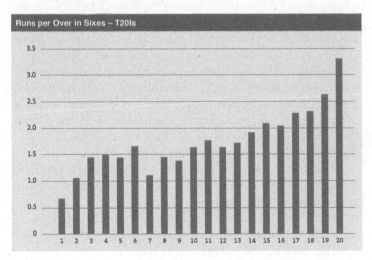

The final point to make here is that the amount of spin you bowl as a team is not a smooth, sliding scale. Rather it moves in large, discrete jumps. It might be the case that in most matches the optimal amount of high-quality spin to bowl is higher than 40 per cent, but this is hard to achieve with most teams fielding five specialist bowlers/all-rounders. Forty per cent might be too low, but 60 per cent is usually too high.

The most dangerous periods of the innings for the fielding captain are the PowerPlay and the death overs. So, given a choice between being a couple of overs short of spin bowling, and a couple of overs short of pace, most captains opt for the former. They don't want to leave themselves exposed at the beginning or the end of the innings.

And that leads us to the final advantage of having a genuine high-class mystery spinner. The likes of Rashid Khan, Imran Tahir and Sunil Narine can bowl in all three phases of the innings. On top of their overall quality, they give the captain tactical flexibility, and the selectors the strategic ability to balance the side in ways they otherwise couldn't.

That is why they are the kings of T20 cricket. And that is why we love them.

Technicolour Cricket

Throughout his writing, Homer describes the sea rather oddly. Of all the phrases at his disposal, the one he turns to when painting a picture of the water is 'wine-dark'. It is a phrase that appears almost 20 times across the *Iliad* and the *Odyssey*, his two most famous works.

Critics have long wrestled with the phrase, and there have been many theories to explain his use of it. Some have suggested that the blind poet of the *Odyssey*, Demodokos, is Homer inserting himself into the narrative, and that he himself was blind, relying on others to describe the world. In which case seeing the sea as one great mass of Merlot doesn't feel like too great a leap. Other critics invoke the intention of the image, arguing that a depiction of the sea as stumbling and intoxicated is the more likely. The former British prime minister, William Gladstone, contended that the ancient Greeks' eyes were different and, in some way, unable to see colour in the way modern eyes do.

Since then a more sober explanation has taken hold as the orthodoxy. Analysis of the way in which languages produce words for different colours has revealed that the process is surprisingly consistent, throughout the world and throughout history.

In 1969, linguist Paul Kay and anthropologist Brent Berlin published *Basic Color Terms: Their Universality and Evolution*. It offered, among others, one pertinent hypothesis. If a language had only three basic colour categories, they were almost always words for black/dark, white/light and red. If it had four or five categories, then the additional words tended to refer to green or yellow. Only once a language had six or more basic colour categories did you begin to see more complex colours given their own word. Among those was the colour that we would call blue.

In the view of Kay and Berlin, Homer's Greek didn't *have* a word for blue.

Colour exists on a spectrum; what isn't obvious is how you break that spectrum down into different categories. Where does one colour stop, if you don't have words to describe the two colours either side of the barrier?

And if you have no word for blue, how can you see it?

Bill James is the doyen of sports data analysis. An amateur statistician who published numerous influential findings over decades, he eventually became a figure of influence and success with the Boston Red Sox from 2003. For many a dabbler in the art of analysis, James is the dream, the template. His methods, and profile, have been hugely influential in making baseball the sport it is today; every other sport in the world, perhaps with the exception of motorsport, looks at baseball's sophisticated relationship with analytics with envy. A large part of that is down to the work of – and cult surrounding – Bill James.

While clearly very skilled with numbers and in manipulating data, James was not beholden to statistics in his life more broadly. 'I didn't care about the statistics in anything else,' he wrote in his 1985 *Baseball Abstract*.

> I didn't, and don't pay attention to statistics on the stock market, the weather, the crime rate, the gross national product, the circulation of magazines, the ebb and flow of literacy among football fans and how many people are going to starve to death before the year 2050 if I don't start adopting them for $3.69 a month; just baseball. Now why is that? It is because baseball statistics, unlike the statistics in any other area, have acquired the powers of language.

As Michael Lewis put it in *Moneyball* (2003), '[For James] baseball was theatre. But it could not be artful unless its performances could be properly understood.' James held degrees in both English and Economics, and the ability to articulate the world of one with the words of the other was key.

There are some statistics in cricket that have the quality of language, and express in perfect shorthand fundamental aspects of a player's game. Even if you had never seen them bat, you could deduce that Alastair Cook is a very different sort of opener to David Warner without watching him – the numbers alone would tell you. They communicate more than just quality or ability.

Test Batting Records			
	Average	Scoring Rate	Dismissal Rate
Alastair Cook	45.35	2.81	96.5
David Warner	48.94	4.37	67.1

Because there has always been an emphasis on the individual, the language of cricket is very good at describing what an individual does on the field. Be it about a batting stroke or a bowling action, the sport is blessed with a very deep, specific vocabulary for describing *technique*, and that vocabulary has achieved a level of objectivity. The data collection company Opta records huge swathes of information from numerous sports all over the world. Their analysts watch the action and record it straight into a centralised system. But while their football analysts do not record the type of finish that a striker makes, in cricket every shot is described and logged using one of a set list of terms: cut, drive, pull, hook, sweep, forward defence, etc.

In contrast to many sports, cricket terms are a lingua franca within the game. Ask a football fan to picture a 'chip' in their mind's eye, and the results will vary. Some will picture David Beckham knocking the ball over the goalkeeper's head from the halfway line; some will picture Lionel Messi lifting the ball into the net from 5 metres out. There is an imprecision to the technical language of football. Ask a cricket fan to picture a 'cut', and they are largely going to picture the same stroke.

What that allows people watching the game to notice readily is the difference in the way certain players execute different strokes. Brian Lara's pull shot, right leg up in the air, is just as much a pull shot as Kevin Pietersen's long-armed heave, and it's the fact we know they are both pull shots that allows the contrast to be interesting.

And yet, when it comes to a language of style and tactics, the inverse is true. Football has a rich, varied and vivid terminology; cricket's is meagre and drab.

At the outset of *Inverting the Pyramid* (2008), Jonathan Wilson's seminal work on the history of football strategy, the author tells an anecdote about a group of journalists discussing an England match from the 2004 European Championship. England's formation had moved to an old-fashioned 4–4–2, and several of the press pack were discussing what had driven the decision. 'The formation is the only thing that's important,' she [an English colleague] said. 'It's not worth writing about anything else.'

There is the key point. Football is aware – in more enlightened cultures – of the primacy of tactics and strategy. The average footballer has the ball for about three minutes in any given match. The importance of any one individual – or rather, the extent to which they can influence the game – is less than in other sports such as cricket. So the overall team structure has more scope to draw the eye.

Defensive lines can be deep and narrow, or high and wide, or in between. Formations can be asymmetric, Christmas trees, diamonds, WMs. Teams play it short or go direct. In the words of Johan Cruyff: 'Choose the best player for every position, and you'll end up not with a strong XI, but with 11 strong 1s.' Football has, in the intellectual sphere at least, understood this.

There are reasons for this. Of late, the amount of money involved in top-level football means that taking it seriously, speaking in a heightened almost scientific register about its tactical construction, is accepted more than in other sports. When hundreds of millions of pounds are in play every time Manchester United step out onto the field, discussing their style of play in forensic detail feels proportionate.

There are other reasons, though. A football score tells you very little about the game. The average match finishes 1–1, so the mere fact of a goal in and of itself changes nothing. The majority of a football match is spent watching people *not* score goals.

In cricket, scorecards have always told much of the story of the match. Built into a Test match scorecard is the game's narrative; the order of events, and a level of descriptive information about them; the progression of time. As the eye moves down the batting order, the hands on the clock are turning, the story unfolding.

For a Test match, the scorecard is a précis of the novel in full. But this is much less the case for a T20 match.

AN OPPORTUNITY FOR CHANGE

T20 is in the same family as Test cricket, but they are siblings with different interests. And there are one or two profound differences between them, ones that extend beyond the aesthetics of the spectacle. The relative value of runs and wickets changes throughout a T20 match; in a Test match, they largely do not.

As a brand-new sub-sport, T20 cricket inherited the players, tactics and techniques of the longer forms of the game that had evolved over the previous several decades. Since then, it has changed rapidly and unpredictably in its strategies, tactics and techniques. And the torch has been passed to a new generation of players. Players who have evolved 'for' T20 cricket, who have played it throughout their evolution as players and been shaped by it. The game has grown up, and now knows its own mind.

But along with the players, tactics and techniques, it also inherited the language of the longer forms. And if that language is just about serviceable to describe the shots and techniques of individual players in T20 cricket, it is woefully inadequate when it comes to describing the larger macro-patterns of selection and team strategy.

If there was already a paucity of terminology to describe

strategic themes in Test cricket, then T20 with its richer and more varied set of interconnecting strategic choices would always have found it wanting. It is further complicated by the fact that Test cricket lacks one of the dimensions in which T20 is played – namely the limited over count – and T20 lacks one of the results that Test cricket has – the draw. As a result, the terminology to describe what we need to say about T20 teams simply doesn't exist.

Nor is it possible to ship in strategic terminology wholesale from other sports.

In football, as in most sports, tactical choices largely exist on a spectrum between attack and defence; cricket, being asymmetrical, is different. One team bats, one team bowls, then they swap. If football (or any other invasion game) was played with the same principle, where for 45 minutes Manchester United were allowed to score and Liverpool to defend, then vice versa, the game would naturally look rather different, and the terms attacking and defending would cease to mean what they do.

Test cricket strategy plays out differently. You can *attack* with the bat but *defend* with the ball. It's not just a spectrum of attack and defence; it's attack and defence *for bat and for ball*. You can be two different teams in one, broadly without compromising either strategy.

The T20 compromise

In Sheffield Shield and County Championship cricket since 1950, 1611 teams (Surrey in 2011 and Surrey in 2012 being two different teams, etc.) have taken part. Of those sides, more than a quarter registered higher batting averages and lower bowling averages than the competition average and vice versa. There is an inverse correlation between batting average and bowling average (when compared to the competition average) in First Class cricket. This pattern holds when you just consider the performance of top-order batsmen; it also holds in Test cricket since 1950 (minimum five matches). In red-ball cricket, if you are a good batting side, you are likely to be a good bowling side.

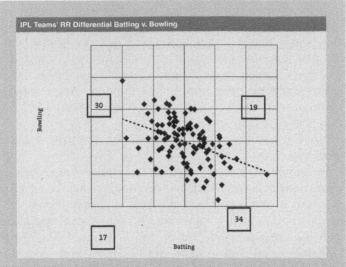

In T20, this is not the case, for a number of reasons. The fact that bowlers can only deliver a maximum of four overs dictates that at least five players in the side, but more likely six, and sometimes seven, must be able to bowl. It's also a consequence of how recruitment plays out. In T20 leagues with auctions or salary caps, batting and bowling strengths have inverse correlations. In the Indian Premier League (IPL) – the longest-running league with such a structure – this pattern is clear. In T20 cricket, if you are a good bowling side, you are more likely to be a poor batting side.

Think of it this way. You're trying to cover yourself with a duvet in bed, but it's too small. In T20 leagues, you have to put up with it, and accept that covering your chest leaves your feet cold, and vice versa. In First Class cricket, if you can afford to, you just buy another blanket.

In Tim Wigmore and Freddie Wilde's *Cricket 2.0: Inside the T20 Revolution,* Kane Williamson offers his belief that 'T20 cricket is, out of all the formats, the most "team" format of cricket.' Test cricket is not a team sport, per se, but an individual sport played in a team environment. You play as a group, but almost every action is conducted in isolation. The XI stands together as a group of soloists. But not so in T20.

The difference between these two formats is leading to a junction. The rapid rise and development of T20 cricket as the most popular form of the game is leading to – and demanding – a switch in the way we talk about cricket.

In part, this difference has been recognised. White-ball teams, and T20 teams in particular, are often described as being in one of two camps: batting sides and bowling sides. This is a logical first step, but needs to be taken much further.

A bowling side who hunt wickets, and a bowling side who seek to preserve runs above all else, are very different beasts; a batting side built on security and control bears little comparison to one that focuses on explosiveness. Within these areas of strength, which is largely what 'batting side' or 'bowling side' indicates, there are different possible approaches.

Batting and bowling scatter graphics

For the purposes of describing different team styles in T20 cricket, we'll be using these scatter graphics. One displays the position of a team's batting (scoring rate and dismissal rate) in comparison with the other teams in the same league, and the other displays the team's bowling (economy and strike rate). These are two of a great number of measures we could have chosen to sum up team styles, but for now the fundamentals of runs and wickets are enough to show what we are discussing.

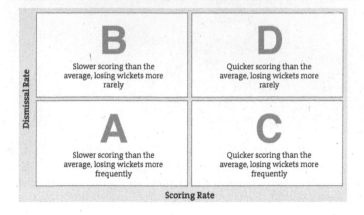

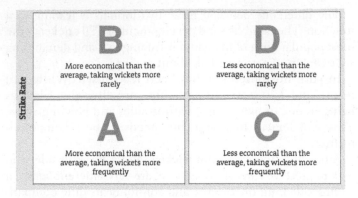

Every team in every T20 league can now be classified with a batting style and a bowling style. A team who scored more quickly than the average side, with a higher than average dismissal rate, would be a 'D' batting side; a team who took wickets more regularly than the average side, with a lower economy rate, would be an 'A' bowling side. If a side exhibited both of those traits, then they would be a 'DA' side – though such a team is extremely rare.

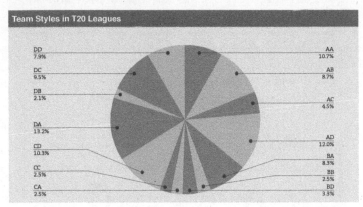

Some teams *stretch* the game. They want the number of runs in any given match to be as high as possible, content with 200 v. 201, knowing that they are going to outhit the opposition. Sides with 'D' and 'C' styles for both batting and bowling are pedal to the metal from the get-go with bat and with ball: England's 2016 World T20 side; Andre Russell and Chris Gayle-fuelled Jamaica Tallawahs; Brisbane Heat, every year.

Some teams *shrink* the game. More than content with low-scoring arm-wrestles in every match they play, they want to keep the total run count as small as possible. 'B' and 'A' style, they want to keep things tight, and back themselves in a match where runs are highly valued: the Sunrisers Hyderabad side who won the IPL in 2016; the 2019 Big Bash League (BBL)-winning Melbourne Renegades; the Barbados Tridents team that won the 2019 Caribbean Premier League (CPL).

There's not only a descriptive benefit to be had here, but an analytical one; the benefit of understanding more precisely how teams play is that you understand better how to beat them.

Bowling distinctions

Of course within these groups we can divide teams further into *what* each of them bowl more of: pace or spin. It's a basic distinction, but simply the proportion of overs bowled by the two types can give a clearer indication of style. The Trinbago Knight Riders side who won the CPL in 2015 were a 'BA' side, but they differed hugely from the Perth Scorchers, and other BA sides, because of the volume of spin bowled.

T20 LEAGUE WINNERS – 'BA' STYLE	
Team	% overs from spin
2017 Peshawar Zalmi	21.1%
2019–2020 Sydney Sixers	21.3%
2016–2017 Perth Scorchers	29.9%
2012 Kolkata Knight Riders	32.6%
2014–2015 Perth Scorchers	36.7%
2016 Islamabad United	39.8%
2015 Trinbago Knight Riders	52.0%

This leaves you with a short and sweet description for every team. For example, a spin-heavy 'BA' side – one that shrank the play and bowled plenty of spin.

THE FURNACE AND THE ROAD

Coached by Justin Langer, the Perth Scorchers sides of 2013–17 had remarkable success in the Australian Big Bash League. Winning a single title is one thing; building a dynasty is quite another. Langer's side managed the latter, with three trophies in four years making them the first side to dominate Australian domestic T20 cricket. Across the four seasons where the Scorchers won their three BBL titles, Scorchers played 39 matches, won 25, lost 13 and tied 1.

The Scorchers' success was forged in The Furnace. To previous generations of fans, the iconic ground with its flood-lights rising above the Perth skyline was the WACA (Western Australian Cricket Association). But with the rebrand and re-focus that came with the Big Bash, a generation latched on to the new, snappier title.

Yet a rebrand cannot change the soil in Western Australia. The pitch at The Furnace was as hard and quick and bouncy as those seen in Perth Tests down the years, and it made batting tough. Scorchers shrank the game. The Furnace was the second slowest scoring venue in the BBL during this period, the 'Spotless' Showground in Sydney the only venue to see batsmen struggle more. The two grounds couldn't have been more different, though. Spotless was not a cricket-specific venue, and the pitches were slow and sticky; The Furnace was, well, the WACA. The value of a run at The Furnace, in a Scorchers game, was higher than a run elsewhere against other teams.

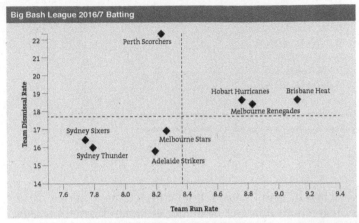

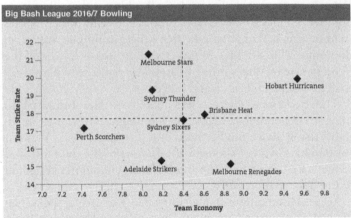

The most distinctive feature of that Scorchers side – certainly of their batting – was their approach to the PowerPlay. In each of those four seasons, they began their innings with caution. They scored at less than the average run rate; they preserved their wickets far more than the average side. Several players opened for those four seasons, but a Scorchers opener had a clear profile. Initially Langer favoured strong First Class players such as Simon Katich and Shaun Marsh, players used to facing fast bowling on hard tracks and focused on survival. It was on Boxing Day 2014 that Langer pushed Michael 'Maxi' Klinger up to open. For the next two-and-a-half seasons, nobody would score more BBL runs than Klinger.

In these four seasons, Scorchers had a better economy rate in the PowerPlay than the average every time, and a better strike rate three times. Their overall style was cautious, secure batting, low-frequency batting, with few boundaries and few wickets – and incisive, economical bowling. In their latter two titles, Perth Scorchers were a 'BA' side, lean and efficient and always in control, who shrank the game down.

How do you beat a side like that?

'Match-ups' are a very fashionable idea in T20 cricket. At its core it's a very simple idea – that it's better to target a batsman with a type of bowler they have historically struggled against – and one that has taken hold in many T20 dressing rooms. Spin the ball away from Player A, high-pace quicks for Player B, variation seamers for Player C. While the analysis that goes on behind the scenes to sort these recommendations can be as advanced as you like, a large part of why the match-up has caught on is its essential simplicity. This batsman likes to face these bowlers; whereas they don't like to face these bowlers.

The logic may have started in player v. player contests, but it's unlikely that it will stop there. Looking at how a side has performed, over a period of time, against different sorts of teams and attacks is clearly worthwhile.

If teams play in a certain style and have particular attributes, then they will have specific weaknesses. If so, then surely there are other teams who are well-suited to exploiting those weaknesses? Teams who might not be of the same 'quality', but with a better chance of winning this particular match?

There are varying samples here; some styles have played each other only a handful of times, and little can be read into them. The more frequent contests, however, offer insight. There have been 33 occasions when sides who stretch the play more than any others, 'DD' teams, have come up against sides who really shrink the play more than any others, 'AA'. In those matches, between two equal and opposite teams, we've seen 16 wins each and 1 tie. There is balance here, an equilibrium, in the way acid and alkaline neutralise.

Elsewhere, there is plenty of *imbalance*. Which is where we return to The Furnace.

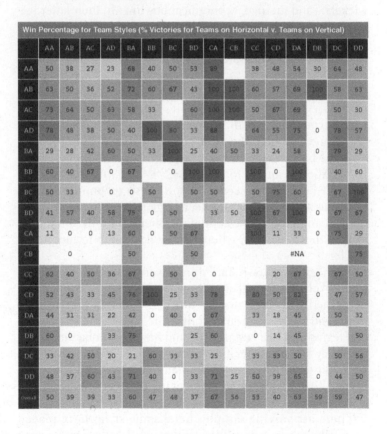

Win Percentage for Team Styles (% Victories for Teams on Horizontal v. Teams on Vertical)																
	AA	AB	AC	AD	BA	BB	BC	BD	CA	CB	CC	CD	DA	DB	DC	DD
AA	50	38	27	23	68	40	50	53	89		38	48	54	30	64	48
AB	63	50	36	52	72	60	67	43	100	100	60	57	69	100	58	63
AC	73	64	50	63	58	33		60	100	100	50	67	69		50	30
AD	78	48	38	50	40	100	80	33	88		64	55	75	0	78	57
BA	29	28	42	60	50	33	100	25	40	50	33	24	58	0	79	29
BB	60	40	67	0	67		0	100	100		100	0	100		40	60
BC	50	33		0	0	50		50	50		50	75	60		67	100
BD	41	57	40	58	75	0	50		33	50	100	67	100	0	67	67
CA	11	0	0	13	60	0	50	67			100	11	33	0	75	29
CB		0			50			50			#NA					75
CC	62	40	50	36	67	0	50	0	0			20	67	0	67	50
CD	52	43	33	45	76	100	25	33	78		80	50	82	0	47	57
DA	44	31	31	22	42	0	40	0	67		33	18	45	0	50	32
DB	60	0		33	75			25	60			0	14	45		50
DC	33	42	50	20	21	60	33	33	25		33	53	50		50	56
DD	48	37	60	43	71	40	0	33	71	25	50	39	65	0	44	50
Overall	50	39	39	33	60	47	48	37	67	56	53	40	63	59	59	47

Royal Challengers Bangalore (RCB) are one of the few original

Indian Premier League sides never to win the competition. They have been a side filled with stars down the years, from A. B. de Villiers to Chris Gayle to Virat Kohli, a champagne side heavily weighted towards batting, largely but not entirely because of their home venue. The Chinnaswamy Stadium, in Bangalore, is tiny by the standards of Indian grounds; fours and sixes come more easily, through a combination of a helpful surface and much smaller boundaries. It's long been one of the best batting venues in the world; only five grounds in the history of T20 have seen a higher run rate. Mishits from fast bowlers can fly over the ropes and into the crowd, and 200 chases carry no fear.

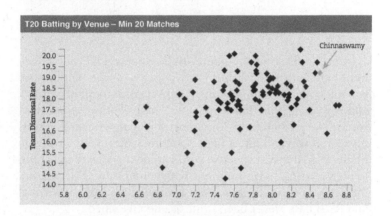

While RCB's home may have shrunk the playing area, it also stretched the game. That strategy reached its zenith in 2016. That year, RCB were the fastest scorers in the Indian Premier League, but that phrase barely does justice to what they did. One infamous contest saw de Villiers and Kohli put on a mammoth 229-run partnership, still the highest in domestic T20 cricket, as RCB charged to a remarkable total of 248 for 3 against Gujarat Lions. That season was the peak of Kohli as a T20 batsman, swaggering his way around in full captain-leader-legend mode, smashing his way to 973 runs over 16 matches. No batsman has ever surpassed that total in an IPL season.

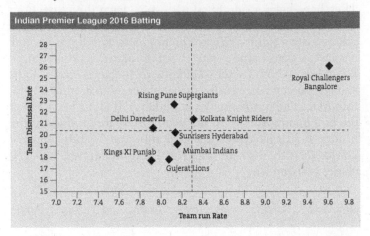

Indian Premier League 2016 Batting

In every phase of the game, RCB were a 'DC' side. They went hard with the bat, but lost wickets; with the ball they let you hit, but went after wickets. There is an element of chicken and egg about this. If you play at a high-scoring venue then you will be pushed in the direction of playing cricket that suits there, and you will, most likely, end the season with a run rate higher than the average. You could argue this makes style hard to divorce from home venues. At the end of the 2016 season, the pitch at the Chinnaswamy was relaid. It lost something, and RCB have never been quite as effective since.

The way they played in that final season, however, took them to the final. They eventually lost to Sunrisers Hyderabad, who, despite playing a very controlled, conservative brand of cricket throughout the competition, found a way to set RCB 209 to win, a target beyond even a top order of Chris Gayle, Kohli, de Villiers, K. L. Rahul and Shane Watson.

These two sides had wildly differing levels of success. RCB trophyless; Scorchers trophy-laden.

And yet, when their two styles have come up against each other, it's gone almost entirely one way. In the history of the Big Bash League, Caribbean Premier League, Indian Premier

League and Pakistan Super League, there have been 14 matches between sides like RCB and sides like Perth Scorchers; the RCB-style side has won 11 of them. No other style has a better record against Scorchers-type sides.

This is an extremely simple, first iteration of this topic. More sophisticated analysis would group these teams into more subtly representative categories, ones that more accurately reflect the styles involved. It is an illustration of how you might start to illuminate the macro-patterns and attributes of T20 teams, not just the individual styles of their players.

Understanding of T20 itself is in its infancy; it is only natural that the language and strategy associated with it are at a similar stage of development. But we can break the game up with even with basic categories and vocabulary, and establish the obvious point that certain styles of play are more effective against other styles, regardless of any base-level, inherent quality.

If there are no words for the way that T20 cricket is played, then the game will only ever be viewed through simplistic lenses. If data analysis can be used correctly, to help aid the growth of the language around the game, that will be a contribution to the sport far greater than it has made to any single bowling attack or batting order.

If we can succeed in identifying and giving name to the macro-patterns and strategies that already exist and shape T20 teams, then we can start to understand and describe them. More importantly, we will be able to 'see' them. We will know that blue is blue, and know it when we see it.

We will no longer be forced to talk about the 'wine-dark sea'.

Moneyball 2.0
....

In 2018, the Rajasthan Royals re-joined the IPL after a two-year absence. This meant they had to rebuild an entire playing roster of 25 players in just one auction, then compete against franchises who had spent years building their teams.

Not only were they able to secure all their main targets in the auction, but they also managed to capture Jos Buttler, one of the finest white-ball batsmen in the world, and for the knockdown price of $690,000. This is the story of how they did it . . .

BILLION-DOLLAR BILLY

Brad Pitt is explaining the difference in wealth between Oakland Athletics and the other Major League Baseball franchises. He holds his hand up at head height. 'There are rich teams . . .' he says, then he moves his hand a little lower, 'and there are poor teams. Then there's fifty feet of s**t . . .' he slowly drops his hand all the way down to near floor level, 'and then there's us.'

He is playing the part of Billy Beane, general manager of the Oakland A's, in the film *Moneyball* (2011, directed by Bennett Miller and produced by Michael de Luca, Rachael Horovitz and Brad Pitt). Not many general managers get to be played by matinee idols, but Beane is worthy of the honour. In the early 2000s he revolutionised baseball, and indirectly all professional sport.

In 2003, Michael Lewis wrote *Moneyball: The Art of Winning*, a book about the data revolution in baseball that Beane had begun at the Oakland A's. It is one of the most influential books ever written about sport, and sparked a wave of change that has left very few sports in the world untouched.

When Billy Beane became general manager of the Oakland A's he was already something of an oddity because he was an ex-player. Major League Baseball pros might go on to become coaches at the end of their career, or commentators, or scouts even, but they didn't go into the front office. But a desire to be a GM was only the start of Beane's non-traditional thinking.

Faced with the frustrating reality of running a poor club in a rich league, he started searching for ways to allow his Oakland teams to compete with the likes of the Yankees and the Red Sox, who had spending power many times greater than the A's. The method he chose was one that consisted of abandoning baseball's orthodoxies and making use of one of the richest data sets in any field in the world.

RIGHT TIME, RIGHT PLACE, RIGHT SPORT

There is a continuum of sports when it comes to the application of data-based thinking. The internal structure and workings of each sport dictate how easy it is to analyse statistically in a way that allows you to add value to subjective judgements and received wisdom. At one end of the scale you have football, a set of fluid continually changing patterns with no naturally occurring discrete units into which to break it down. Football is about as hard as any sport to analyse statistically. In the middle of the scale you have sports such as cricket, rugby and American football. They can be broken down into discrete units more easily (very easily in the case of cricket), but other factors create complexity.

Way out at the other end of the continuum is baseball. Of all the ball sports, baseball is almost perfectly designed to be analysed using data. For a start there are nice discrete units – pitches, and innings that are highly homogenous. Then there are the different counts of balls and strikes, and the different permutations of runners on bases, sets of interlocking states with connecting probabilities, which weight the likely outcomes in a way that is easy to calculate statistically, but hard to navigate intuitively.

And finally there is the sheer size and richness of the data set. Baseball teams play 160 matches a year, batters will have roughly 550 innings per season. And they have been playing the game largely unchanged for well over a hundred years. For that entire period, every significant action has been dutifully noted and recorded, and is available to analyse. In more recent years, ball-tracking technology records velocity, spin rates and flight path for every pitch thrown and for every shot that leaves the bat.

In cricket, it is having a grass pitch that complicates matters. It nudges us endlessly away from science and towards art. Batting in Chennai and batting in Perth are so different that they are almost different sports. Baseball has none of that stats-defying idiosyncrasy. For someone wanting to apply evidence-based thinking to a team sport, it is close to perfect. So not only is it no wonder that baseball was the first professional sport to be data hacked, it was probably inevitable.

Under Beane, Oakland embraced the use of data in every aspect of their business. They used it to analyse and refine on-field tactics, they used it to identify undervalued players in their recruitment, and they used it to optimise their picks in the draft.

There was a furious backlash, from fans and the media, at some of the seemingly absurd choices to which these methods led. This only intensified after the publication of Michael Lewis's book. *Moneyball* made Beane a hero to many in the sporting world, but it also made him the primary target for the reactionary forces that hated this new direction the sport was taking. The argument raged furiously back and forth, and any potential flaws in Oakland's approach were seized upon gleefully by their critics.

It has often been stated, even by supporters of *Moneyball*, that perhaps the benefits of Oakland's strategies were exaggerated both in the book and subsequently by its fans. It is worth, then, taking a careful look at their performance over the whole period covered by *Moneyball*. The highly respected data website fivethirtyeight.com recently did exactly this with very interesting results.

Looking at the period 2000–14, they concluded that not only had Oakland under Billy Beane hugely outperformed how you would have expected a team with their payroll to perform, but that the value of that difference was well over a billion dollars, in money that they would have had to spend to expect to achieve the same results.

As this period took in a number of different sets of players, and different head coaches, it seems safe to attribute the bulk of this overperformance to Billy Beane and his methods. In which case, he is responsible for a massive 180.2 wins above expectation. Wins above replacement (WAR) is a standard baseball measure of a player's contribution to his team's performance. The highest ever career total was 163 wins above replacement by Babe Ruth, the greatest player in the history of baseball, the game's Don Bradman.

In terms of adding wins to his team, Billy Beane as general manager was more valuable than the greatest player ever to pull on a glove. He was more valuable than having Bradman in your team.

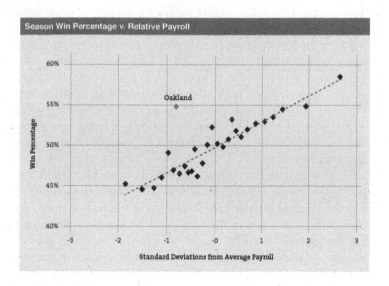

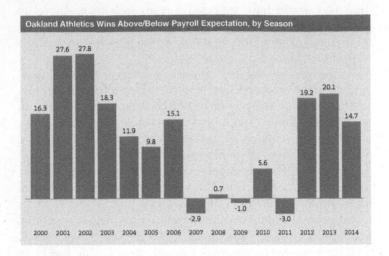

Oakland Athletics Wins Above/Below Payroll Expectation, by Season

MONEYBALL IN CRICKET

There were two distinct parts to the *Moneyball* approach, to the way in which the Oakland A's used data to level the playing field against their wealthier competitors. The first part was in gaining a tactical advantage. They were the first club to take analysis seriously as a way of finding better ways to win baseball games. The analysis itself, thanks to stats fans such as Bill James and his *Baseball Abstract*, had been around for a good while. But clubs hadn't taken it seriously, relying instead on the received wisdom accumulated by generations of players and coaches.

The second part of the approach laid out in *Moneyball* was taking advantage of market inefficiencies. It was the science of identifying and buying bargains when it came to players. As one of the characters in the film says, 'Remember, you aren't buying players, you're buying wins.' One of the things the A's did was to realise that the traditional metrics, such as batting average, that were used to judge the quality of a player were not as good at valuing their contribution to winning matches as people thought. There were other metrics, in particular their on-base percentage, that gave a better idea of the impact a player would have on the results of the matches in which he played.

They also started to take advantage of the fact that unorthodox or odd players were undervalued compared to those who conformed more closely to the scouts' and coaches' view of what a baseball player should look like. Another thing they did was to notice that some aspects of the game, including fielding, were systematically overrated. So they sold their good fielders, pocketing the erroneous premium those players carried, and bought poor fielders at knockdown prices.

If it sounds like the A's would end up with a team of odd-looking players who couldn't field by following this approach, then that's exactly what they did end up with. But to the surprise and annoyance of the traditionalists, this team of misfits and oddballs won baseball games, and consistently outperformed their higher-budget rivals.

So to simplify their approach, the A's did two things. They used data to optimise their on-field tactics, and they used it to find and buy great-value bargains in the marketplace. This is where the comparison with cricket becomes interesting, because at the international level of the game, this second, and arguably more potent, aspect of data use in baseball is not particularly applicable.

International teams do have some scarce resources. For example, the number of caps they can invest in developing a strong squad with international experience is limited. If a new player is struggling to perform, then the selectors have to choose between giving him long enough to prove whether he is good enough or not, and having the opportunity to look at a different potential player. So they still need to make investment decisions of sorts.

In general, however, the dynamics of player recruitment for an international cricket team are very different for those experienced by a baseball franchise. This is partly because there is far more agreement about who the best players are than there is about the relative merits of players who are further down the pecking order.

If you asked ten good judges what they thought England's best squad was for the 2019 Cricket World Cup, then they would be virtually unanimous on 10 to 12 of the 15 names. There would be broad agreement on one or two others and then genuine differences of opinion about the final one or two places. England's squad is strong and settled, but you would get similar agreement on most other countries' squads as well. The very best players are normally clear to everyone.

But if you took those ten good judges, gave them a limited budget, and asked them to compile the strongest IPL squad they could, then it is likely you would get ten completely different squads.

Firstly, there would be disagreement about the relative values of different players. All ten selectors might agree that Batsman A is better than Batsman B, but they are likely to have very different views about exactly how much more he is worth, and therefore which of them is the best value for money.

Secondly, there will be different opinions on the relative values of different types of players.

- Are top bowlers better value than gun batsmen?
- If a batsman can keep wicket, how much does that add to his value?
- Will fast bowlers be more effective than spinners on your home ground?
- If you spend a huge chunk of your budget on two or three star players and fill the rest of your roster with cheaper buys, does that produce the strongest team, or is it better to take a more balanced approach?
- Foreign players are clearly less valuable than their like-for-like Indian counterparts because you are only allowed to play four of them at a time. But how much less valuable are they?

All these added complications mean that the task of valuing players, and in particular assessing their value to *your* team, is bound to throw up a variety of different answers, not all of which can be correct.

It is for this reason that the place in cricket that you find the fullest expression of *Moneyball*-style ideas are at T20 franchises and particularly, because of the bigger budgets and the greater exposure, at the Indian Premier League. And if there is one team that seized on those ideas from the start and pursued them to the fullest extent possible, it was the Rajasthan Royals.

CRICKET LIKE WE'VE NEVER SEEN IT BEFORE

In 2008, the IPL was launched. It is strange, now that it has become such a juggernaut of success, to look back and remember what a leap into the unknown it was at the time. No one knew what to expect, no one knew if the new competition would attract fans, or whether it would be accepted by the top players as anything more than a curiosity.

And for the teams and their owners, no one knew the best way of building a successful team. They didn't know how to put a value on different types of players, they didn't know how to navigate and get the most out of the auction process. The first IPL auction consisted largely of hunches, guesswork and billionaires' egos. And once it was over, and fans and commentators could take a look at the squad lists each franchise had assembled, there was still very little consensus over who had done well and who had done poorly in the process. In fact, there was very little agreement on anything. The only thing that everyone agreed upon was that the Rajasthan Royals were going to finish last.

The Royals had spent considerably less than every other team in the auction, and many of the players they had spent money on were relative unknowns. Whereas every other team in the competition had spent all or most of their $5 million maximum budget in the initial auction, Rajasthan had spent only $2.9 million.

When they were hammered by nine wickets in their opening match, it confirmed everybody's initial thoughts on their chances, and prompted the *Times of India* to print an article saying that this was why foreign owners (the Royals were owned by a mixed Indian and foreign consortium of investors) shouldn't be allowed in the IPL. They clearly weren't interested in winning it, and were just looking to make money, so the argument went.

But the Rajasthan Royals didn't come last. In fact, they went on to win 13 of their next 15 matches including the final, where they became the IPL's inaugural champions. Their record of 13 wins and 3 losses is the most successful season by a team in the IPL ever.

All IPL Results 2008 to 2015	
Team	%W
Chennai Super Kings	59.8
Mumbai Indians	57.9
Rajasthan Royals	51.6
Kolkata Knight Riders	51.2
Royal Challengers Bangalore	48.3
Sunrisers Hyderabad	48.8
Kings XI Punjab	47.5
Kochi Tuskers Kerala	42.8
Delhi Daredevils	41.1
Deccan Chargers	38.6
Pune Warriors India	26.0

In the years that followed, Rajasthan continued to underspend and outperform most of the other franchises in the IPL. Between 2008 and 2015, only Chennai and Mumbai had a higher win percentage in IPL matches, and yet Rajasthan did this while spending less than every other team in the league. To understand exactly how they did this, it is worth taking a while to understand the mechanism at the heart of player recruitment at the IPL, namely, the player auction.

MORE MONOPOLY THAN MONEYBALL

It is loved as a spectacle, transfixes players from around the world, and has been criticised by some as being cruel and unfair. The IPL auction is loved and loathed in equal measure depending on your viewpoint. But most discussions of it miss its genuinely innovative brilliance. The auction is a very elegant solution to a problem that could easily have torpedoed the new league – 'How do you stop a salary cap being circumvented?'

Cricket, even T20 cricket, is a sport in which the better team tends to win. So to produce the maximum interest in each individual match it is important that the teams are close enough in quality that the result is not a foregone conclusion. If you want to produce a competitive league, with well-matched teams, then you need to find a way to limit the spending power of the wealthier clubs. A salary cap is a natural way of levelling the playing field, and one many different sports employ to do so. But it brings with it problems of enforcement; teams are incentivised to find ways to pay players 'off the books' and so circumvent the cap. Trying to implement such a cap in the wild commercial landscape of the newly formed IPL seemed destined to failure.

Which is why turning the recruitment process into an auction was such a neat way of removing any incentive for, or possibility of, that type of cheating. By making teams bid for players, and making the price paid that player's salary, the auction elegantly levels the financial playing field in a way that is next to impossible to subvert. But interestingly for our purposes, the auction creates a particular dynamic when it comes to allocation of funds to players.

One thing it's important to realise about the auction process is that it is not an open marketplace. Considerable ink is wasted commenting on player purchases in a way that misunderstands the basic mechanism of how teams are forced to recruit. The auction is not a stock exchange, where assets can be traded for agreed upon and widely available prices. Nor is it even akin to a transfer market, where offers and counter-offers are made, and a price eventually agreed upon. In both of those situations, overpaying for a player would be poor business, and clubs who did so could be rightly criticised.

The IPL auction is more like a cross between a game of Monopoly and poker. If you own the green properties Oxford Street and Regent Street, then Bond Street, the remaining green property, becomes very valuable to you. It gives you the opportunity to complete a set and so you would likely be willing to pay a high price for it, far higher than if you didn't own the other two green properties. The price printed on the card, or what you might have paid under other circumstances, is immaterial. Context dictates the value of the card to you, and its effects on your chances of winning the game.

In a similar way, the price that a player is sold for is not necessarily a reflection of his quality or even of his utility to a given team, but is largely a function of circumstance. Imagine you are representing a team in the auction and you are keen to recruit a particular overseas fast bowler. The player you are interested in comes up relatively late in the auction, and so you could easily find yourself in one of two situations.

If the only teams who have money left to spend are interested in recruiting a different type of player (a batsman say, or an Indian-based player), and so have a limited interest in your fast bowler, then you could easily pick him up for next to nothing. On the other hand, if he is the last high-quality fast bowler in the auction, and two other teams need a bowler as well, then you could end up paying a very high price for him.

Hopefully, you can see that it is perfectly possible for the same player to be sold at wildly different prices despite everyone in the auction behaving entirely rationally. You may well pay $2 million for a player who would go, on average, for about $1 million. But even though you are paying over the odds it is still a rational decision to make, because if that's the player you need, then his value to you is greater than the value of having unspent money at the end of the auction. On the other hand, under different circumstances you might buy the same player for a tenth of that price.

Clearly, IPL recruitment is far from an exact science. You can only buy the players who are available, and on whom you are not outbid. And it is further complicated by the poker aspect of the whole contest. Every team there has a finite sum of money to spend, and for every team there is a potential competitor for the players that you are interested in. Therefore it makes sense to try to force another team to spend as much money as possible for the players they want to buy. If you can bid them higher on the players they want, then they will have less money left to bid against you when it comes to the players that you are really targeting.

So, many of the bids made by teams in the auction are for players they have no actual interest in buying. They are merely trying to push the price as high as possible for the teams who do want to buy, so as to reduce those teams' spending power later in the auction.

This means that the auction becomes a game in and of itself. When we first started to study how franchises go about valuing and recruiting players we thought that the search for a more accurate valuation, for a more refined measure of a player's value to that particular team, would be the primary objective of each team. As it was for the Oakland A's under Billy Beane. It quickly became apparent, though, that the accuracy with which you value players was secondary to how well you played the auction.

In the early days, there was scope for discovering untapped talent, and for recruiting undervalued players neglected by the other franchises. As the IPL has evolved, though, those opportunities have largely disappeared, and so now the Royals' focus has shifted more and more to the auction, and how they can play it to ensure that they get the maximum possible return on the money they spend.

It is an effort that starts months in advance of the auction. Cricket analytics are important to the process, but game theory is more important. They simulate the upcoming auction endlessly, roleplaying the likely sequence of bids over and over. The parts of the other franchises are played by people who have been studying and attempting to replicate their behaviour for years. Every permutation of outcomes is worked through, even those that they consider highly unlikely, so that whatever happens in the auction they understand its ramifications and can adapt their strategy to take advantage of it.

Manoj Badale is the principal owner of the Royals and has been the driving force behind their analytically sophisticated strategy throughout.

One trend that Badale has noticed is that, as more of the franchises become more structured in their efforts and possibly more rigid in their thinking as a consequence, many of them have become less agile when it comes to responding to unexpected opportunities. Although the increased rigour of their approach has improved the quality of their planning pre-auction, the chaos of the auction inevitably creates situations that haven't been anticipated. Therefore, the key to success is to plan as rigorously and thoroughly as possible, but maintain an approach that is flexible enough to take advantage of unforeseen bargains that appear.

One good illustration of this came from a rival franchise whose whole approach seemed fairly shambolic. They had two co-owners who refused to talk to each other, each wearing a headset through which they were getting advice from different support teams, who at one point were engaged in wrestling over the paddle used to make bids. 'The table was chaos,' says Badale, 'and yet at the end of the day, you looked at the squad they had bought and thought, that's a pretty good side.' Whereas many teams had stuck over-rigidly to their pre-auction plans, the chaotic franchise had been willing to seize unexpected opportunities that presented themselves. The lesson learned was that there had to be a balance, a balance between planning and the ability to react in real time and play the situation in front of them.

The best example of this came when the Royals were trying to rebuild their team after coming back from a two-year ban.

Zubin Bharucha is the Rajasthan head of cricket. One of the most insightful thinkers around when it comes to T20 cricket, Bharucha has been with the Royals since their first season and leads their ongoing efforts to improve every possible aspect of their preparation and planning.

'We start months and months in advance. We start to look at patterns, and it is literally in terms of "Who's going to bowl the first over?" So then you look at who are the best PowerPlay bowlers? and what are the trends emerging at the time? For example, we might see that players aren't used to coming up against off-spin during the PowerPlay and so we would start to look at that type of player . . . and then we slowly work our way into the auction strategy, which is all based around game theory, and you work out how you can manoeuvre your way through a situation to get the outcome you want. So you might be trying to push the price of these players here who you aren't actually interested in, so that it creates an opportunity for you to buy this other player who is actually your target. And you also have to take into account where the different players come out [in the auction]. There are lots of different permutations and combinations that you have to think your way through.

'The best way to do that is through simulation. So we are able to simulate [the auctions]. We have the same team of people in the room each year. For example, the same people who have played the part of Mumbai Indians for the last eight years for us do that every year. So they understand the mentality of that particular franchise, they know how, for example, ad hoc a certain team might be when it comes to auction strategy, that they are a big celebrity-based team who value the big marquee players and like to win those bidding battles. We have trained these guys . . . and they know that they have to follow the patterns and trends of that team's bids over the last few years.

'So in the simulations we're as exact as we can be. Of course, you can't predict someone's mind on the day, and there's always a chance they'll do something different. But we get about 80 to 85 per cent accuracy on that. So we are able to tell not only where a player is going, but at what price.

'As you keep going through it, as rigorously as you can, eventually you get closer and closer to an understanding of the various dynamics at play. And it varies from auction to auction. In the smaller auctions it can be harder to predict. But in the bigger auctions you can get pretty close.

'We've looked at doing these things by algorithm, and maybe one day we will, but for now, you can't beat having the look and feel of the live auction.

'I think in the early days, there was value to be found, by going down a level to your scouting operations and your development level, where you are looking at a player, maybe based on the pitch that you're going to play on. And in the early days, the systems weren't there, the data wasn't available, so you could find value in these players. So Tambe, Sanju Samson, all these guys were available at very low values, even Jadeja. Because the market hadn't evolved. Now there are players who haven't played a single IPL game who go for over a million dollars.'

It is interesting to hear Zubin reference Pravin Tambe, because he is one of the most interesting examples of Rajasthan's willingness to look beyond the obvious.

PRAVIN TAMBE
Having achieved such initial success by thinking differently in that first season in 2008, the Royals were aware that their methods would attract imitators, and so were constantly on the lookout for the next edge that they could find. It was part of those efforts that led Zubin and Rajasthan to examine their home ground in Jaipur and analyse the types of bowlers likely to succeed there. Both its large boundaries, particularly square of the wicket, and the pitch itself meant that it was likely to provide a happy hunting ground for a particular type of bowler. So it was that Zubin started looking for a leg-spinner who could bowl skiddy deliveries into the pitch, bringing those big square boundaries into play. And he found one, though not in any of the places that you might expect.

Pravin Tambe was a 41-year-old leg-spinner playing club cricket in Mumbai who had never played First Class cricket and hadn't even represented his city. When the Royals recruited him, you couldn't even say that he was underrated, because no one had even heard of him. Nevertheless, he went on to win the Champion's Trophy for Rajasthan in 2013, when he averaged just 8.42 with the ball at an economy rate of 4.06. That season the Royals had the youngest and oldest players in the competition.

Results, particularly in a season as short as the IPL, are always going to see a large amount of random variation. Perhaps a better way of judging how good a franchise is at recruiting players is to look at how the value of those players trends after they are bought. And here we see clear evidence that the Royals know what they are doing. If we compare the net increase or decrease in the value of players that each IPL franchise has bought, in subsequent years, then we find that the Royals are top of the pile. The players they have bought have on average gone up in value more than the players bought by any other franchise.

THE INCOMING TIDE

The pattern of how analysis has come into each sport has been remarkably similar across each of them. From baseball, to basketball, to rugby, to cricket, you see the same sequence of events play out in the same order.

First comes the initial wave. Someone reads *Moneyball* and decides to import that style of thinking into the sport in which they are a coach or owner. These early adopters have some success, and there is a wave of publicity and enthusiasm for data and analytics. Due to enthusiasm and only having a partial understanding of its scope, there is considerable over-selling in this early phase. Analysis is presented as the answer to everything, and the only way to succeed going forward.

Then there is the backlash. Whichever team or coach has become synonymous with the new approach inevitably suffers a setback or slump in form at some point. This is seized on by critics and reactionary voices within the sport, who conclude that this data approach was a load of nonsense, and just the latest fad to be discredited. Like the initial wave, the backlash overcorrects and so for a short while, analysis is highly unfashionable.

And then, in the third and final phase, the tide comes in. There is a steady but inexorable rise in the use of data and analysis. Coaches and analysts learn from the early mistakes and, proceeding with less hubris, they refine and improve their methods and find the right way to synthesise the new tools with the sport's traditional wisdoms. In time, all teams and coaches adopt the new methods as part-and-parcel of normal good practice.

THE 2018 AUCTION

Ben Stokes was the Royals' number-one target going into the 2018 auction – a player capable of turning a game with his batting, with his bowling or with his fielding, and whose sheer presence would inspire others to greater heights. The Royals had him earmarked as the cornerstone of the team they wanted to build, someone who covered so many different bases on his own that it gave them much greater flexibility in terms of who they chose to fit around him. If they could secure his services, then it didn't matter whether the off-spinner they were chasing could bat, it was no longer as important whether or not the top-order batsman they liked the look of could bowl a couple of overs when needed.

To them his value lay not just in the roles he could perform, but in the duties from which it freed other players.

They had also earmarked Jofra Archer as a future star. Although he had played neither international nor IPL cricket before, they had identified his remarkable potential and were willing to spend what it took to recruit him.

After Stokes and Archer, they had a target list for each type of player: batsmen they thought might become available, bowlers who would suit the pitch at Jaipur, all painstakingly researched by Zubin Bharucha and his team.

We asked Zubin how long they had spent simulating the auction. 'We would sit for up to four or five hours at a time, and do that maybe twenty times. We did a lot of manual work.

And then you reach a point where you're just not gaining any further insights, you're not learning anything new, and so then you have to just stop.'

Every player in the auction was in one of three categories. Target, push or pass . . .

Going into the auction, Jos Buttler was on their 'push' list. He was a player they would dearly love to buy, and in a free contest they would have targeted him. But in every simulation of the auction that they had run during their prep it had proven impossible to win his services. However they tried to manipulate the flow of the auction, there was no way they could engineer his availability. So they were resigned to bidding his price as high as possible, so that whoever did buy him at least had to pay a suitable premium.

The main reason that he was beyond their reach were the 'Right to Match' cards. This was one of the rules that meant having to rebuild from an empty roster was such a huge handicap. Each team had two such cards, which they could use to retain ownership of any player who had played for them the previous year.

Rajasthan assumed that Mumbai would use one of their Right to Match cards on Buttler, meaning Mumbai could sit out the bidding, and then swoop in at the last moment to take the Englishman at whatever price the auction had finished. That's what common sense told Rajasthan, and that's how each and every one of the simulations they had war-gamed had played out.

But they had misread the Mumbai Indians' priorities.

The first intimation that this was the case came when Mumbai used their Right to Match on Kieron Pollard, buying him early in the first round for 5.4 crore (a crore is 10 million rupees). Unexpected as this was, and as much as it seemed to throw all of their carefully weighted plans awry, it was also good news, because it seemed to put Buttler in play. It did, however, force a series of highly stressed and against-the-clock recalculations at the Royals' table.

In 2018, and in contrast to all previous auctions, Rajasthan had decided to invest the maximum possible amount in that year's auction to try to overcome the disadvantages of their post-ban situation. If you are massively handicapped by having to compete against franchises with an established power base, then the only logical course is to commit all the resources you are allowed into trying to level the playing field. So unusually for them, they were going all in. We will let Zubin explain.

'When we came back, we had a scenario where every other team is sitting on five iconic players, and we're sitting on zero. So if we don't put the money in now, we'll be five years behind everyone else. So that's why you have to go and bid for the Stokes's and you have to pay a high price then, because everyone knows that you need them, and so they're playing game theory too, and trying to push you up. So the strategy going into that auction was very simple – we have to spend ninety per cent of our money on eleven players and then just wing it from there.'

As such, in their planning they had allocated all of their available funds to pursuing other players. This meant that in order to free up funds to bid for Buttler they had to hurriedly reshuffle their priorities against the clock. As the minutes clicked by, they had to decide how much they dared shave off each potential bid, and which players they could forgo buying if it meant having a chance to secure the star keeper-batsman they thought could transform their team.

The tension in these auctions is huge. Million-dollar decisions are being made in real time, and mistakes made then can cost a franchise dear, handicapping them on the field for years to come.

All too soon, Buttler was the next player up, and the Royals had to commit to their new, hurriedly rearranged plan. The fact that Mumbai were bidding competitively confirmed Manoj's supposition that they weren't going to use their remaining Right to Match, and so the contest was on.

As the bidding went on, it became clear that Rajasthan had put themselves in pole position for their new target, and they went on to win the bidding at a price of 4.4 crore. Not only that, but they were able to secure almost every player on their target lists. Even though the auction had taken a huge swerve in an unexpected direction, their weeks and weeks of planning and simulations had served them well. The instinctive feel this had given them for the landscape of the auction had enabled them to navigate its web of interconnected probabilities while improvising in real time around their pre-auction plan.

Unfortunately, the sting in the tail for the Royals was that bad luck turned their Buttler triumph into something of a Pyrrhic victory. At the start of the 2018 season, England appointed Ed Smith as their new chairman of selectors. His first major call was to reverse the previous selection policy and recall Buttler to the England Test team for their May 2018 series against Pakistan. So Buttler, in barnstorming form for the Royals, had to return home along with Stokes before the knockout stages of the IPL. Shorn of two of their star performers, the Royals lost in the semi-finals, ending their hopes of a dream return from exile.

The Sultans of Spin –
Multan Sultans in the PSL
....

Despite having to wind their way patiently through concentric rings of airport-style security, a process that takes up to two hours, the crowd has filled the ground to capacity long before the first ball is bowled. Over 30,000 fans have made the pilgrimage, and once inside the stadium they are determined to make their presence felt. Every home player venturing on to the playing surface is cheered ecstatically.

It is February 2020, and the Multan Sultans for the first time in their history have the opportunity to play a match in their home stadium. All previous editions of the Pakistan Super League (PSL), which began in 2016, have taken place in the UAE because of the security threats that prevented any international cricket from being played in Pakistan. Now, finally, the crowd have the chance to see their heroes up close, and when the team takes to the field the roar is deafening. The shape of the stadium in Multan seems to collect and intensify the crowd noise, then bounce it out into the middle of the pitch in an amplified tsunami of sound.

Of all the players the fans have queued to see, there is one in particular who causes a detonation of cheering whenever he gets near the action. His nickname 'Lala' echoes back and forth all evening. It is impossible to overstate how big a name Shahid Afridi is in Pakistan. If Prime Minister Imran Khan is the most famous person in the country, then Lala is second.

In the very first over, Peshawar Zalmi's opening batsman slashes an uppish drive through the offside, and Afridi, forty-plus years old, dives full-length to grab the catch. Whatever the crowd had hoped to see, as they filed their way through those endless security queues and searches, whatever they had waited for, through four seasons of PSL matches played overseas, this moment is the answer. For the next minute, it is simply impossible to make yourself heard, even to someone standing right next to you. The noise just keeps coming, wave upon wave, like some extraordinary collective catharsis.

Multan go on to win the match, as they do all three of their home matches in PSL 5, each time cheered to the rafters by supporters as enthusiastic as any you will find anywhere in the world. The story of that team, and how they came to that moment, starts 12 months earlier and is one I was lucky enough to be involved in.

WE WANT TO DO THINGS DIFFERENTLY

In early 2019 I got a message from Chris Jordan. He was in Dubai playing in the Pakistan Super League. He wanted to know if I would mind him passing on my contact details to the owners of his franchise team, who wanted to get in touch. Having said I was happy for him to do so, I subsequently got a call from the general manager of the Multan Sultans who arranged for me to meet Ali Khan Tareen, one of the franchise's two owners.

Just prior to the World Cup I met Ali Tareen for lunch in the bar of a London hotel. Whatever expectations I might have had as to what a PSL franchise owner would be like, Ali did not match them. He was younger than I had expected, with a close resemblance to a young Jawaharlal Nehru.

Urbane and charming, there was nevertheless a polite reserve to him as he introduced himself and we navigated the requisite pleasantries of a first-time meeting. That reserve vanished, though, as soon as he started to talk about the Multan Sultans. In its place was an ingenuous enthusiasm for a project that clearly inspired and excited him in equal parts. It seemed like the Sultans were his baby, the thing that got him out of bed in the morning.

Ali and his Uncle Alamgir had become owners of the Sultans after the previous owners defaulted on their payments to the Pakistan Cricket Board (PCB). This had happened between the draft and the tournament the year before. They had inherited coaches, players and backroom staff already in situ, and so had taken the opportunity to sit back, observe and learn how a PSL team operated.

After watching a season of franchise cricket from up close, Multan's new owners were convinced that things could be done differently and better. And so, they were about to embark on an ambitious project that was intended to take their team to the very forefront of modern cricket innovation and beyond. They wanted to embrace everything that evidence-based, analytical thinking had to offer and use it as the central, guiding principle of how they ran their franchise. Turning the usual method of working on its head, analytics would not be an adjunct to a traditional operation but rather the foundation of a new way of working and thinking.

It seemed, at that first meeting, that the usual motives for buying a sporting franchise were not foremost in Ali's mind. He didn't seem motivated by profit, nor by the vicarious glamour and excitement of owning a team that won titles and trophies. Instead, he spoke primarily of doing two things. Firstly, he wanted to do something that had never been done before. He wanted to pursue the idea of data analysis in cricket as far as it was possible to take it, to put analysis truly at the centre of every decision taken, from recruiting coaches and players, to choosing on-field tactics. And secondly, he spoke of creating a transformational hub for young talent, that would enable young cricketers from Multan and from all over Pakistan to lift their cricketing dreams as high as their ability and enthusiasm could take them.

I subsequently met Ali's Uncle Alamgir, the larger than life majority shareholder in the Sultans. Alamgir had had a home in Oakland, California, for many decades. He had been a huge Oakland A's fan since well before Billy Beane took over there. As a result, he had been thinking about cricket and the potential of statistical analysis for decades. Now he had the opportunity to put his ideas to the test.

I have been around professional sport long enough to know that what people say does not always correlate very well with how they then behave. Fortunately, Ali and Alamgir were different. In everything I subsequently saw at Multan they were as good as their word and the vision of Multan's future that they laid out was exactly what came to pass.

The M-word

If you work in the world of sports analysis then the word 'Moneyball' is one that invariably crops up whenever you have to explain what you are doing to people outside that world. It has become a shorthand term for the application of economics-style quantitative analysis to professional sport, but to almost anything involving 'numbers'. Whenever anyone expresses an interest in making use of analysis not only with their team, then they or someone else almost inevitably ends up describing it as 'doing a Moneyball' or some equivalent phrase.

I have nothing at all against *Moneyball*, the book by Michael Lewis. Firstly, it's a great book. If you haven't read it, then do; it is a lovely way to spend a couple of days (and the film is fun too). And secondly, it got me a job. Ultimately, it was Andy Flower reading *Moneyball* that led to him recruiting me to work with the England cricket team and launched a whole new career for me.

It is the term 'Moneyball' I find problematic. Because, like all such zeitgeisty words (think synergy, paradigm shift, etc.), it ends up being used to mean something slightly different by everyone who uses it, and so ends up not meaning anything at all. *Moneyball* was and is a story. It is not a technique, not a well-defined concept, and not a philosophy.

(Yes, I know, we've used it in one of our chapter headings. But that chapter is about Billy Beane and the Oakland A's and their influence over certain IPL teams. So we think that's OK.)

NOT TAKING NO FOR AN ANSWER

Those first conversations and meetings I had with Multan were largely out of politeness and a desire to help someone with what sounded like an interesting project. I was focused on

England and the approaching World Cup. Becoming an analyst at a PSL franchise was not something I had previously considered doing, nor was it something I thought my role with England would allow me the opportunity to do.

Multan, however, were not taking no for an answer, and it turned out that their approach was indeed going to be genuinely different. Some teams are built around a captain or senior player, many are built around and by the head coach. At Multan, the first hire was going to be the person who would oversee their analysis, their director of strategy. Analysis would then be heavily involved in the recruitment of coaches, support staff and players. Ali and Alamgir were fully committed to taking the use of analysis as far as it was possible to do so. I was sold.

Post-World Cup, I asked the ECB the question and they generously gave me permission and a leave of absence to pursue the project with Multan. And so it was that in early December 2019 I found myself on a plane to Lahore for the PSL draft and the start of one of the most enjoyable adventures of my working life. Next to me was Andy Flower, and we had started to assemble the new Multan coaching team and backroom staff.

A few days later, and we had our first Multan Sultans squad.

Although we had considered a range of candidates, the choice of Andy as head coach was in many ways a simple and obvious one. Although he had made his name primarily by taking the England team to the top of the Test rankings, winning series in Australia and India, he had also been in charge of England's first ever success at a global ICC tournament when he won the T20 World Cup in 2010.

He had also always taken a keen interest in analytics and had kickstarted the use of data in cricket during his time with England. If anyone was capable of marrying traditional coaching methods and virtues with the Multan owners' vision of futuristic data-driven methods, then it was Flower. He was also someone with whom I was used to working and with whom I had a long friendship. With Andy on board I felt for the first time that what Ali and Alamgir envisioned would actually come to pass.

Drafts and auctions

It is worth spending a little time exploring the differences between the sort of auction run by the IPL and a draft.

In an auction there is an element of poker. Who will bid for who is uncertain, how high they will go is not clear. There is an overall cap on what each team can spend, so teams will bid for players they don't want so as to push the price up and take money away from a team they think they'll be bidding against for one of their targets later on in the auction. Teams spend weeks game-playing the auction in advance but it is still highly unpredictable. Even things such as the body language of team owners can affect the outcome.

In a draft, the teams take it in turns to select from the pool of players who have made themselves available for the competition. At the PSL draft the order of these picks is generated randomly. The players are grouped into different groups, each of which has a specific salary range associated with it. Teams choose first from Platinum, the highest category, and then progress down through the different levels until they have completed their squad.

So going into a draft, you know the order in which teams will take their picks, and the various categories in which each player can and can't be chosen. So, if you are thorough, you can plan in advance every important decision you might have to make. You still go into the draft not knowing what your final squad will look like, but you could list all the possible squads you might come out with. It is just a decision tree.

Drafts are less complex than auctions, and also in a funny way less competitive. In an auction you are very much playing *against* the other franchises; your strategies are often designed to have a negative impact on their fortunes.

Drafts are almost collaborative. Every team is trying to serve its own interests obviously, but there is no real incentive for blocking or other negative tactics (not that I'm aware, anyway). Such a strategy would only make sense in a very unusual and extreme situation; there are just too many unknowns to make such a ploy work.

SO HOW DID THEY DO IT?

Well, you now understand our methods. What would you do? You are building a franchise venture from the ground up, and you are being given pretty much carte blanche by your dream owners to do it as you see fit. How would you go about it?

Before you start to think about it, let me just outline some of the problems you are facing.

Firstly, you are the newest franchise. This puts you at a significant disadvantage. Two things conspire to make this the case. Every season each franchise is allowed to keep some players on its roster from the previous year. For example, in 2019 each team could retain eight players who had played for them in that year's competition. And the most valuable players, as in any league, are the best of the homegrown cricketers. These are the players that every franchise wants and so they are those least likely to be traded or released back into the draft. All of these players are already attached to franchises, so any new franchise struggles to build a core of homegrown talent.

Secondly, you don't have much of the data that you would like to have. If you were going to go about building a T20 team based entirely on analytical methods you would first use the data to answer three questions.

- What does the cricket look like in this league, i.e. which types of player are effective and which are not?
- What are the conditions like, i.e. what do the pitches and grounds favour in terms of style of play and which type of players do they suit best?
- What is your home ground like, i.e. what is the pitch like and what are the dimensions of the boundaries?

Unfortunately, the tournament is moving from the UAE to Pakistan for the first time in its history. This means that not only is much of the past data on the PSL of no use, but also that there is little relevant data on the tournament, grounds and pitches. Multan's home ground has been renovated ahead of the new competition, changing its dimensions, and the pitch has been relaid, changing its characteristics. All this means that many of the more obvious avenues for tuning a team to the specific requirements of the competition are not open to you.

Thirdly, the move to Pakistan obviously brings security

concerns. This will be the first time that the PSL is played in Pakistan. There had been a ten-year period where no international cricket was played in Pakistan following the terrorist attack on the Sri Lankan team in 2009. All of Pakistan's international cricket and the previous editions of the PSL have been played in the UAE instead.

The move to Pakistan presents two challenges in recruiting a squad. Firstly, many international players are nervous of travelling to Pakistan and some have withdrawn from the draft for that reason. Secondly, those who do travel will be subject to incredibly tight security for the whole duration of the tournament, unable to leave the hotel for several weeks except to travel to the cricket ground.

So those are your limitations. What would you do?

HORSES FOR COURSES

Every T20 league is different. Each has its own rules for recruitment; some are draft based, some have an auction. They allow different numbers of overseas players, and the amount that they are able to pay their players varies hugely. They also have different underlying strengths and weaknesses that they inherit from their host countries. The pitches and grounds in each country are different and suit different types of player. Some nations find it easier to produce certain types of players, and harder to produce others. So the typical overseas recruit looks different at the IPL than he does at the Big Bash or the PSL.

Obviously, the first step in starting to choose a squad is to evaluate the relative quality of all the players available in the draft. These days there is ample data on most well-known players, particularly those who have been on the T20 circuit for a few years. Just by looking at raw figures you can tell what a player's strengths and weaknesses are and roughly how good he is. If you further weight his career record by the standard of cricket he has played and the underlying characteristics of the pitches he played on, you can come up with a very complete picture of that player and his likely performance levels in your tournament.

But the raw quality of a player is only one factor in determining his value and, in particular, his value to you in a team.

Every T20 league has its own characteristics. The value of a player is not constant across leagues. One player might be worth more to a team in the Big Bash than in the Indian Premier League, while for a second player it is the other way round.

Firstly, you have the rules of the competition. There is normally a limit on the number of overseas players that each team is allowed to field. This means that the value of domestic players tends to be higher than that of overseas players because teams are not limited in their selection of them. Glenn Maxwell, for example, is a great player to have at the IPL but he is comparatively even more valuable in the Big Bash because he is Australian and doesn't take up one of the limited overseas spots in that competition.

Secondly, there are the underlying conditions in which the league is played. If most of the pitches in a competition offer spin then that increases the relative value of spinners and decreases that of pace bowlers. Likewise, the size and shape of boundaries can change the balance between pace and spin. Grounds with short, straight boundaries don't tend to favour spinners, for example.

The knock-on effect of the conditions that the tournament is likely to be played in is that it also changes the suitability of different batsmen. A tournament played on turning pitches will suit a batsman who plays spin well more than one who specialises in hitting the quicks.

Thirdly, there are the strengths and weaknesses of the host nation's player pool. Many countries seem to specialise in producing a certain type of player. The quality and depth of pace bowling in Pakistan or Australia, for example, means that in those countries most teams can put together a quality pace attack without having to resort to overseas players. Whereas in Bangladesh or India quality domestic finger-spinners seem relatively easy to find.

And, as above, the strengths and weaknesses of the host nation affect which categories of players will prosper in those leagues. Tournaments that are chock-full of quality spinners will not favour a batsman with a weakness against spin, whereas he is likely to be far more valuable to a team in a tournament where pace bowlers dominate.

All these factors affect the relative value of a player to a given team. You must also consider the other players in the squad. A leg-spinner, for example, will be of little interest to a franchise that already has two high-quality mystery spinners on its books, whereas to a franchise with limited spin options this player could be gold dust.

WHAT ARE THE DIFFERENT CHARACTERISTICS OF EACH OF THE MAJOR T20 LEAGUES?

One way to determine this is to look at the proportion of domestic to overseas players in each category and how those two cohorts compare to each other in terms of performance. To take the IPL as an example, 40 per cent of IPL top-order batsmen are overseas players, and those players outperform the domestic contingent. Overseas players are even more over-represented among the pace bowlers: they bowl nearly half of the overs in the IPL and again outperform their domestic counterparts. For both finger- and wrist-spinners, though, it is a different story. Overseas spinners bowl only 27 per cent of the spin overs bowled at the IPL.

The PSL turns out to be pretty unusual in certain aspects. For a start there are some marked differences in the number and quality of local players in each of the different player categories.

A HOMEGROWN PACE-ATTACK

The first thing you notice when you look at the distribution of overseas players at the PSL is that most of them are batsmen or batting all-rounders. If we look at top-order batsmen (positions one to five), 50 per cent of them are overseas players. That is compared to just 26 per cent of bowlers.

When it comes to overseas players, each T20 league has its preferences. Big Bash teams tend to recruit more spinners, IPL teams recruit relatively few. Caribbean Premier League teams have less use for overseas pace bowlers, and Bangladesh Premier League (BPL) teams are less interested in finger-spinners than in the other player categories. But (as you can see in the graph 'Percentage Overseas by Player Type'), the discrepancy between overseas batsmen and bowlers at the PSL is by far the largest in any of the main T20 leagues.

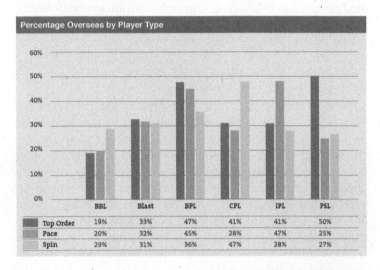

Percentage Overseas by Player Type						
	BBL	Blast	BPL	CPL	IPL	PSL
Top Order	19%	33%	47%	41%	41%	50%
Pace	20%	32%	45%	28%	47%	25%
Spin	29%	31%	36%	47%	28%	27%

PSL veteran Liam Dawson is one interesting example of this. Dawson plays for England as a bowler and he is considered a bowling all-rounder at his county Hampshire, and yet in the PSL Peshawar Zalmi use him more as a batsman who can also bowl some overs. In PSL 5 he bowled roughly one over per match.

The other side of the equation, when assessing the relative value of different player categories, is to look at how they perform compared to domestic players of the same type. Here again, the PSL had a characteristic that was unique in the major T20 leagues.

In any T20 tournament you expect overseas players to outperform domestic players on average. If you have to select seven of each team from a single country and can choose the other four players from anywhere in the world, then the quality of the four is likely to exceed that of the seven. And indeed, this is the case in almost every category of player in every league in the world.

The one major exception to this rule is pace bowlers at the PSL. There, the local pace bowlers perform, on average, 2.7 runs per match better than the foreign imports. This is a remarkable feature of the PSL and testament to the famous ability that Pakistan cricket has for producing high-quality fast bowlers.

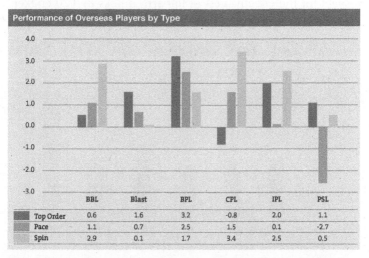

	BBL	Blast	BPL	CPL	IPL	PSL
Top Order	0.6	1.6	3.2	-0.8	2.0	1.1
Pace	1.1	0.7	2.5	1.5	0.1	-2.7
Spin	2.9	0.1	1.7	3.4	2.5	0.5

The graph shows the match impact of each type of player. The match impact is a measure of the overall effectiveness of a player in white-ball cricket and takes into account both average and economy rate. It is measured in runs relative to an average player. So a player who has a +2-run match impact will give his team a +2-run advantage in the game compared to an average player.

It was a feature of the tournament that every team seemed to have a pace attack of international quality, almost all entirely homegrown. From tearaway youngsters such as Naseem Shah, the 16-year-old bowling 90+ mph, to 40-year-old veterans such as 7-foot-tall Mohammad Irfan, still terrifying opposition opening batsmen.

High-quality Pakistan batsmen were in short supply, outstanding pace bowlers were not. So for Multan, the most efficient approach appeared to be the recruitment of a home-grown Pakistan bowling attack, which would enable them to target top-order batsmen for their overseas-player slots.

LEFTIES GALORE

The PSL had other interesting skews to its distribution of players. It was, for example, oversupplied with left-arm fast bowlers compared to the rest of the world. For those of us with a healthy respect for the effectiveness of left-arm quicks in T20 cricket, this made recruiting that type of player easier.

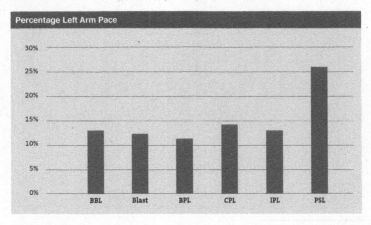

We have discussed the pre-eminence of leg-spin in the shortest format at length. But it is worth saying again that in every T20 league in the world, in almost any way you choose to evaluate performance, the most effective players are leg-spinners. And this was true for the PSL as well.

But it is an interesting feature of T20 recruitment that while the success of leg-spinners is no secret (at any given time, eight or nine of the ten top-ranked T20 bowlers are wrist-spinners),

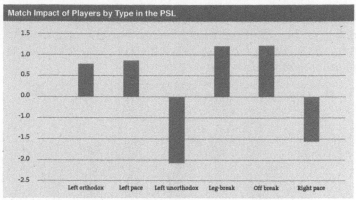

Match Impact of Players by Type in the PSL

| | Left orthodox | Left pace | Left unorthodox | Leg-break | Off break | Right pace |

There can be issues with sample size and classification problems when doing this type of study. For example, Sunil Narine, who is a genuine mystery spinner and one of the best T20 proponents in the world, is classified as an off-spinner. Given that the number of off-spinners in some T20 leagues is very small, the presence of a Narine can skew the figures significantly. He may end up bowling a large proportion of the total off-spin bowled in that league's season. This was actually the case in some of the past seasons at the PSL, and skewed how effective off-spin appeared to be.

it does not always translate into what teams do in practice. For example, only 2 of the first 36 picks in the 2020 PSL draft were leg-spinners.

Multan, though, were keen that their bowling attack in the middle overs would be built primarily on leg-spin and drafted three high-quality bowlers in that category. In addition to the legendary Lala, they were also able to recruit Imran Tahir, one of the all-time great T20 bowlers inexplicably overlooked by the other franchises during the early part of the draft, and Usman Qadir, son of the famous Abdul Qadir and already in the Pakistan T20 squad.

Alongside their leg-spinners they could field three veteran left-arm quick bowlers in Mohammad Irfan, Sohail Tanvir and Junaid Khan, ably supported by one of their emerging players, Mohammad Ilyas, and with Moeen Ali's off-spin and Khushdil Shah's slow left-arm spin for variety.

In a format where left-armers and leggies dominate, in a tournament where homegrown quicks are pre-eminent,

Multan recruited their bowling attack using Occam's razor. In doing so they built the most effective bowling attack of the tournament while leaving most of their overseas slots open to recruit top-order batsmen.

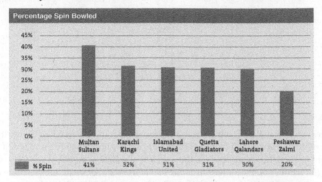

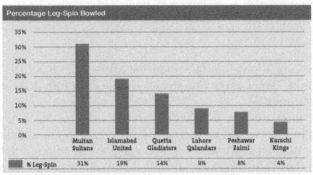

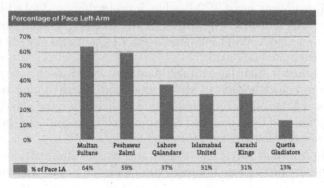

Bowling Economy Rates	
Team	E / R
Multan Sultans	8.30
Karachi Kings	8.36
Lahore Qalandars	8.83
Islamabad United	8.87
Peshawar Zalmi	8.87
Quetta Gladiators	9.06

Team Net Run Rates	
Team	NRR
Multan Sultans	0.44
Islamabad United	0.27
Karachi Kings	0.18
Lahore Qalandars	-0.02
Peshawar Zalmi	-0.10
Quetta Gladiators	-0.76

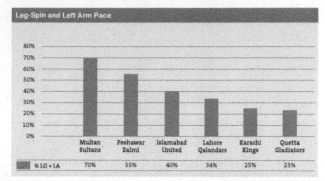

Another quirk of the PSL was how little off-spin was bowled. Although teams in the league bowled roughly the amount of spin that you would expect for a T20 match, very little of that spin turned in to the right-hander and away from the left-hander. In fact, off-spinners and left-arm wrist-spinners had bowled only 6 per cent of the overs in PSL history.

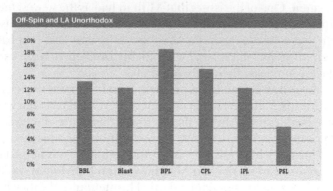

With so few off-spinners in the league, and most of them primarily batsmen who bowled some off-spin rather than specialist spinners, it was clear that left-handed batsmen would have an edge, particularly in the middle overs. Multan intended to capitalise on that fact and ensured via the draft that in their first-choice line-up five of the top six would be left-handers.

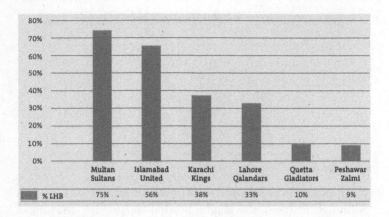

	Multan Sultans	Islamabad United	Karachi Kings	Lahore Qalandars	Quetta Gladiators	Peshawar Zalmi
% LHB	75%	56%	38%	33%	10%	9%

PICK FOR THE FUTURE

As we have mentioned already, the player type that was in shortest supply in the PSL was high-quality homegrown batsmen. One of the issues that Multan had as the newest franchise was a dearth of these highly prized assets. Franchises who were able to retain the services of the best Pakistani batsmen invariably did so, and were highly unlikely to trade such players or release them into the draft.

The only way round this problem for Multan was to pick for the future. If the best of the current crop of local batsmen were unavailable, then Multan had to invest their time, energy and funds in unearthing and acquiring the future best players.

This was where one side of Multan's strategy was helped by the other. Part of Ali's and Alamgir's vision for Multan was for it to be a hub for emerging talent. Throughout 2019 they had been organising training camps for young players, inviting the best foreign coaches they could find to work with the best young Pakistan cricketers. And not just Multan players: they invited cricketers from all the franchises to come and work with the likes of Jonty Rhodes.

Their motives were altruistic, but the by-product was an excellent working knowledge of the best young talent around in Pakistan. And when it came to betting on unheralded local batsmen in the draft, Multan had a clear idea where to place their chips.

The first batsman Multan secured was Shan Masood. The Pakistan Test-match opener had had a modest T20 career up to that point. But Multan thought highly of him as a leader and tactician, and believed the true potential of his T20 batting had not yet been tapped. As a willing convert to the analytical methods Ali and Alamgir espoused, Shan ticked all the boxes for Multan as captain and top-order batsman.

Khushdil Shah, the dynamic middle-order batsman with power to spare, was also on their list, as was Rohail Nazir, the Pakistan Under-19 captain. Multan's early picks in the Silver and Emerging categories enabled them to draft both of those players. There was one other player that the Multan coaching network had identified, and this was the pick that would shock the PSL.

NOW *THAT* IS A WILDCARD

Zeeshan Ashraf was exactly the sort of player Multan wanted to acquire. A dynamic wicketkeeper-batsman who had made run-a-ball hundreds in First Class cricket. He was a vital piece of Multan's vision.

Before the draft you don't know what team you will end up selecting. Indeed, planning for a draft is a fascinating exercise in managing uncertainty. Other franchises are picking ahead of you, so all of your picks are contingent on what they do. This means you enter the draft with an array of possible teams, and the exact one you end up selecting is decided by the opposition team's choices.

Zeeshan was in every different version of the team Multan's management wrote out before the draft.

If he had known it at the time, this would probably have surprised Zeeshan himself. Just months earlier, he had been batting with a borrowed bat and, at 27, considering abandoning his cricketing dreams.

With no top-level T20 pedigree he was the sort of player who might get picked up in the PSL draft but could easily be overlooked. But Multan knew that other franchises were interested in him, and because of the draft order Multan would not get the first chance to recruit him.

Interviewed before the draft, Zeeshan was asked what he would do if he got a PSL contract. Although he was in the Silver draft category, the lowest and least well paid, he was very clear that for him and his family a PSL contract would be nothing short of life changing.

The rules of the PSL draft are complex and sometimes slightly whimsical. It can feel at times like playing a board game that one of your children has invented in their bedroom. There are various minimum and maximum numbers of local and overseas players that must be taken in each round of the draft. And players can only be selected in the categories in which they have been placed (or a lower category if they have consented to it).

Because of the vagaries of the draft structure there was only one way that Multan could be sure of securing Zeeshan plus all the other players they wanted, and that was to make him a Wildcard pick, and select him in the Diamond round (the second highest category). (A Wildcard pick is very rare in the PSL draft, and can only be done once, but it enables a team to pick a player in a *higher* category than they are listed.)

The Sultans did exactly that, creating by far the biggest shock of the entire draft. Not only was a virtual unknown being drafted in the Diamond category, surrounded by cricketing royalty, but he was being picked by the team who had announced to the world that they were going to be more analytical than any other team in cricket history. The 'data-driven team' had just made the least data-looking pick in the entire history of the PSL draft.

HELPS IF YOU SPEAK THE LANGUAGE

Cricketers are a resilient bunch. When it comes to spending long periods away from home, most are past masters. But this tournament was going to be especially challenging to that resilience, with stringent security protocols and players entirely confined to their hotels, whenever they were not playing or practising, for the whole duration of the tournament. It is very hard to succeed on the field if you are unhappy off it. For all the careful analysis of players' on-field effectiveness, equally important were going to be the intangible qualities that meant an overseas player could be at ease in that slightly strange environment and would be able to gel with local squads who often spoke little English.

There was a determination from Multan that however they fared on the field, they would compile a squad that could be happy and harmonious, that would enjoy each other's company and relish the challenge of the unusual circumstances that the tournament was being played in. They were delighted by the way the draft worked out, and that they were able to recruit three of their targeted overseas players (Moeen Ali, Imran Tahir and Ravi Bopara) who had strong cultural links to Pakistan and could speak some of the local language. Along with a strongly Anglo-Pakistani backroom staff, these players were able to ensure a high level of communication and mutual understanding within the whole set-up.

This value put on how comfortable players would be in the environment was to pay off in unexpected ways when the coronavirus crisis started to unfold mid-tournament in spring 2020. When the virus became a pressing concern, and most overseas players chose to leave Pakistan and fly home, those three Multan players stayed and continued to provide the backbone of the side for the remainder of the matches.

'O CAPTAIN! MY CAPTAIN!'

There is a continuum in sport in terms of the coach's relationship to the player. It runs from one end where you have strongly individualistic sports such as tennis and golf; there the player is in charge, they hire and fire the coach who is there to help and assist them. At the other extreme are strongly team-orientated sports such as rugby and soccer. In those sports, where top-down organisation and tactical planning are key, the coaches are very much in charge, and they do the hiring and firing.

Cricket has always been balanced somewhere near the middle of that continuum. It is in many ways an individual sport in a team setting. The decision-making power and responsibility are divided fairly evenly between captain and coach. And in most teams that leaves the captain largely in control when the team is in the field.

Ali and Alamgir's initial vision was that the team would essentially be run from the dugout. Bowling changes, field settings and on-field strategy would be determined by coaches and analysts using the best available live information. Their answer to the exponentially multiplying complexity of a T20 innings was to take it off the captain's shoulders and throw technology at it.

Although ground-breaking in its aspirations, it was felt in the end that such an ambitious approach would not be robust enough to survive contact with the enemy. A T20 match is a complex and fast-changing environment with multiple decisions being made in the moment in parallel on a ball-by-ball basis.

To make all these decisions in the dugout and then try to relay that information out into the middle did not seem practical. It also risked failing to capitalise on one of the best sources of information during the match, which was the live feel and instincts of the players out in the middle.

Although it is the case that all the resources and computing power available give coaches and analysts access to information that the captain and players don't have, it is also undoubtedly the case that the captain and his senior players have access to a wealth of information that the people in the dugout don't have.

In the end, it was felt quite strongly that the only person who could ultimately take the final decisions was the on-field captain. But we also felt that we could make his job much easier and allow him to carry less information in his head if we could come up with a system of signalling that allowed us to feed information out to him in real time.

For the fielding captain, a T20 innings is akin to playing a hand of bridge. (It is obviously not a perfect analogy – there are 20 overs not 13 tricks, and there is more randomness in the outcomes of each over: he might play the right card, a winning card, and still come out of the over second best. But it is a good way to think about the game he is trying to win.) He has a finite number of bowlers' overs available to him: these are his cards; some are strong, some are weak, some are best played early, some are better held back. Then there is the opposition to consider; the relative effectiveness of each of his bowlers will be different for each opposition batsman, and therefore for each partnership at the crease. Some batsmen play spin better than pace, some destroy off-spinners but are vulnerable to leg-spin. Some need pace on the ball, others pick slower balls well and score freely off them.

Likewise, each phase of the game requires different skills from the bowler. In the PowerPlay, for example, with only two fielders on the boundary, the ability to prevent boundaries with little protection is crucial. At the same time, this is when wicket-taking is at its most valuable. So a captain will favour bowlers with those two abilities.

In Brad Gilbert's *Winning Ugly* (2007), the seminal book on tactics in professional tennis, he lays out his approach as follows.

1. Give your opponent nothing.
2. What are his strengths? What are his weaknesses?
3. How do I play my strengths to his weaknesses?
4. Read No. 1 again.

This is roughly in line with what a captain is trying to do. He is looking at all the different match-ups between players and trying to find the best combinations. He wants to bowl this bowler to X and this other bowler to Y. But now X and Y are both at the crease and so it's not obvious what he should do.

Or, he would like to save some of Bowler A's overs for the death, but he is the best match-up against the batsman who is currently doing the damage in the middle overs. Does he use those valuable overs now or save them? Every over he bowls now he cannot bowl later.

You will see captains slip weaker bowlers on in the first, seventh and eighth overs because these are times when scoring tends to be lower, and the potential damage that can be done off his part-time off-spinner is less, particularly if he can line him up against the opposition's left-handed opener who doesn't go particularly well against spin.

PowerPlay	Munro	Ronchi	Malan	Hussain Talat	Ingram	Asif Ali	Shadab Khan	Fahim Ashraf
Mohammad Irfan	-0.58	-1.28	0.95	0.92	0.22	-0.40	1.39	-1.27
Mohammad Ilyas	-2.06	-1.28	-1.41	-0.95	-1.95	-0.60	-0.04	-1.86
Sohail Tanvir	-0.15	-0.80	1.27	1.20	0.62	0.02	1.60	-0.77
Shahid Afridi	0.30	1.26	-0.53	0.15	-0.75	0.26	0.21	1.94
Imran Tahir	0.89	1.33	-0.01	0.63	-0.26	0.42	0.29	2.24
M. M. Ali	-1.37	-2.82	0.39	-1.15	-0.47	-1.90	1.82	2.94
R. S. Bopara	-3.80	-0.49	-1.43	-0.13	-2.37	-0.94	-0.39	0.58

Example of a match-impact model giving information about the relative effectiveness of different match-ups between Multan bowlers and opposition batsmen.

Then there is his gun bowler. The overseas star that cost his team a fortune. He wants to use him at the top of the innings where the wickets he takes will do the most damage. But he would also like to use him to target the best opposition batsman or break a match-turning partnership. And the comfort blanket of having an over or two left from him at the death is something he is loath to give up. He can't bowl eight overs in the innings, so the relative value of all those ways of using his ace have to be weighed against each other in real time, in a rapidly changing situation with lots of other demands on his concentration and decision-making.

Much of this is thought through and planned in advance, but the game will happily throw spanners at you just when you think you have found the perfect plan. In evening matches, a heavy dew can descend during the game, turning the ball into a slippery bar of soap during the second innings, batting becomes easier, and spinners in particular then find it very difficult to be effective.

Multan's solution to this complex problem was to run their computer models live during matches and relay that information out into the middle in real time. It was then up to the captain on the field to use that information as he wished.

In Shan Masood, Multan had the perfect man for the job. Educated, intelligent and a long-time fan of cricket analytics, he seized enthusiastically on the opportunity to make use of better information and real-time feedback.

As Ali Tareen describes it, 'The best way of thinking of it is as an extra scoreboard. Every ground already has a scoreboard displaying all types of complicated information, that updates in real time so that the players don't have to keep count themselves, don't have to remember totals and targets and how many overs have gone, etc.

'The scoreboard is a resource that you can look at whenever you want to check something. It is there if and when you need it. Multan's signals work in exactly the same way. The calculations are made in real time and updated continually. The information is then displayed in a simple, easy way for the captain to see. He can see it and use it whenever he wants to, and ignore it when he doesn't.'

'IT'S NOT F***ING DRESSAGE!'

It is occasionally worth taking issue with the types of people that claim stats should not be a part of cricket. If only because it is patently obvious that they are and always have been an integral part of the game. It is how we decide who wins, for a start.

It is not like football or hockey, where you can generally keep score on your fingers and so there is no problem if the complex tactical and strategic thought remains number free.

Just take a look at a scorecard. Cricket is a complex statistical exercise disguised as a game of bat and ball. It is a game of numbers: the team with the highest number wins. If you don't understand the numbers, you don't understand the game. As one coach I used to work with puts it, 'It's not f***ing dressage!'

LEFT-ARMERS, LEFT-HANDERS AND LEGGIES

The squad that the Sultans assembled at the draft did not impress everyone. None of the big-name pundits were talking about them as potential winners of PSL 5. Indeed, before every match of the tournament, the expert commentators were made to pick which of the two teams they thought was the most likely winner. In every one of Multan's first four matches, the commentators opted for the opposition team.

But the Sultans just kept winning. By the end of the group stages, the Sultans of Multan were sitting pretty at the top of the table. After just nine games they had already qualified and assured themselves of finishing first, having lost just one match. They had led the tournament table since the third game and topped most of the team-performance metrics as well. They had the best bowling economy rate, the best net run rate, as well as the most wins and the most points. More importantly, they had dominated all the key areas of the game that had been identified by the Multan management group before the tournament started.

Ali and Alamgir had not only done it the way they wanted, but the squad they had assembled had left the rest of the franchises in their wake.

Sadly for all of us, the Multan Sultans' great experiment in analytical methods was cut short. Having qualified well clear at the top of the table, an hour before they were due to leave for their semi-final the PCB was forced to suspend the PSL due to the worldwide coronavirus pandemic.

At the time of writing, it looks unlikely that the knockout matches will ever be played.

But, hopefully, there is always next year.

Conclusion: 'History never repeats itself . . .'

'. . . but sometimes it rhymes.'

Mark Twain

In the early 1990s, 25 per cent of top-order batsmen in Test cricket were left-handed and the home team supplied both umpires.

Then the International Panel of Umpires was introduced. And steadily, over the next 25 years, the standard of umpiring in Test matches rose. First with the introduction of one neutral umpire, then with two. Then the advent of Hawk-Eye helped refine umpires' understanding of LBWs and their decision-making improved again.

Finally, the introduction of the Decision Review System and increasingly professional training of the best umpires in the world pushed standards higher still.

As the accuracy of umpiring decisions rose, simultaneously and apparently of its own accord, the proportion of left-handers started to rise too. As the umpiring improved, left-handed openers became more and more common, until they comfortably outnumbered the right-handers.

You know now, of course, that this was no coincidence. The increased success of left-handed batsmen was a direct, unforeseen consequence of better umpiring.

Left-handed openers have always had an advantage under the LBW law but, pre-1990, inconsistent umpiring was too blunt an instrument to reveal that advantage. Protection in law against the ball pitching outside your leg stump is of little use to you if the umpire gives you out anyway.

But as the accuracy of decision-making grew, the value of

that protection grew too, and so therefore did the performance of left-handers at the top of the order.

This was, of course, just one of the many ways in which improving the umpires changed the patterns and trends of Test cricket. It also pushed the finger-spinners round the wicket, changed the way batsmen defended against the turning ball, and stretched the batting averages of the best batsmen further away from those of lesser players.

We hope you have enjoyed our whistlestop tour of cricket analytics. We hope we have shown you a few things you didn't already know. And that we have changed your mind on some others.

Most of all we hope we have shown you the value of using data to investigate how cricket really works. That it can reveal things that are otherwise invisible and that, used well, it can help propel teams to glory.

We hope you agree that analysis changes our understanding of cricket, and changes it for the better.

There is one other way in which analysis has changed cricket.

Data also democratises cricket knowledge.

The world of sports expertise has traditionally run itself like a mediaeval guild. In the absence of objective facts, the dominant source of information is the revealed truth of those higher up in the guild. (If that sounds cynical or satirical, it is not meant to. It is actually a pretty good analogy of the traditional approach in most sports.)

As you rise through the ranks of experience within the game, from First Class, to international, to Test captain, quite naturally your authority to speak about it grows. And in the absence of objective truth we accept the revealed insights of the most experienced among us as fact.

For most of cricket history, if you wanted to determine the truth about a particular aspect of the game, then you assembled the most senior experts on that topic and had them debate the subject and tell you what they thought.

And in the absence of better choices that is not a bad method to use.

But it is fallible. And more crucially it is untestable. How do we know that what they say is correct? How do we tell accurate insights from mistaken beliefs?

In most cases we can trust them enough to believe that it is an honest opinion. But that doesn't mean that they aren't mistaken. How do we know that what they are saying is right?

Their experience of the game, the way they think, the things they have learned through decades of involvement at the highest level are undoubtedly important to our understanding of it. But how do we keep them honest?

Data democratises truth. It makes us all, perhaps not equal, but closer to equal in the validity of our thoughts. It allows us to tell right from wrong, insightful from mistaken.

The data is never enough on its own. But expert insight buttressed by objective fact has a far better chance of being truth than myth and story.

BEYOND OBJECTIVE HISTORIANS

So where next in cricket analytics? Ten years ago, this book was inconceivable. Even five years ago it would have been very difficult to write. If things are moving that quickly, where will they go next?

The best way to get an idea of the direction of travel is to look at the limitations of what we do now. Principal among those limitations is that, however complex and detailed our analysis currently is, we are largely operating as objective historians.

However cleverly we interrogate the data, and however much information and insight we can pull out of it, we are only revealing the past. We are looking at things that have already happened.

Currently, we identify patterns of play, strengths and weaknesses from the past and assume/hope that they will continue into the future.

We are constantly running up against Graeme Swann's principal objection to stats – 'I have never bowled at him on this particular pitch before. So how do we know what's going to happen?'

Therefore, the next step forward in cricket analysis, and more generally in sports analysis, will be to create methods and techniques that are genuinely predictive of the future.

The first steps in that direction have already been taken. As we revealed in the 'Sultans of Spin' case study, predictive modelling is already capable of adding value to captaincy decisions in real time. And that is only the first, most basic move towards a new science of sports artificial intelligence.

We are on the threshold of an explosion of what is technologically possible when it comes to performance analysis and coaching. Technologies that didn't exist 15 years ago, and are currently prohibitively expensive, will be cheap within a few years.

Smartphone-based ball-tracking is already starting to arrive. Within five years, having Hawk-Eye in your pocket will not seem unusual. It will be used for decision-making and data collection at every level of cricket.

Couple that with cheap, cloud-based artificial intelligence systems and you have the means to make talent identification and development truly scientific.

Marker-less biomechanical analysis via ordinary cameras will make automated coaching systems possible, and available to all. You can all have your own expert batting or bowling coach, sitting in an app on your phone. Fully bespoke and individually designed just for you.

The medical screening and injury prevention that currently seems so sophisticated in the international game will be vaulted past by what becomes cheaply available to the sporting public once these new capabilities are harnessed and combined.

And in professional cricket, intelligent systems that understand the game better than we do will be augmenting selection and tactics, adapting to conditions faster than we can and guiding everything from field placings to bowling changes.

If that sounds like science fiction, then take a walk behind the scenes of a Formula 1 team and you will see that it is already a reality. There are more human elements in cricket, and more things we don't yet understand. But where F1 goes today, cricket will follow tomorrow (once we've worked out how to calculate the tyre wear on a fast bowler anyway).

And at every step we will learn more about the game we love. Every new technology will reveal fresh insights into her complex heart. And yet, for all that, for all our advances in understanding, cricket will always keep her secrets, there will always be a level of mystery she won't let us penetrate. We will never know it all.

Acknowledgements

COVID changed many things. One of the least important things it changed was that it made putting this book together much slower and more difficult than would otherwise have been the case. As such we beg your understanding for any errors or inaccuracies that may have made their way into the text or accompanying diagrams. It was impossible to produce a perfect book under the circumstances.

We would also like to thank all those people who were so helpful to us at such a difficult time and without whom this book would have been impossible to research, write and produce.

The list of those who have made this a better book than it otherwise would have been is very long indeed. But, in particular, we would like to thank Eoin Morgan for his considerable help and support in putting together the World Cup chapter as well as the input he gave on the rest of the book. Caspar Berry for allowing us to write about his ideas and methods, and for the generous amount of time he gave to the project. Paul Hawkins, Jason Roy, Jonny Bairstow, Moeen Ali, Andy Flower, Ali Khan Tareen, Manoj Badale and everyone else who supplied interviews, quotes or input. And all the players, coaches and support staff of the England cricket team, the Multan Sultans and the Rajasthan Royals for their time and help in putting together those respective chapters.

Thank you to Andreas Campomar, Claire Chesser and all the lovely people at Little, Brown for their help and support, their patience and understanding of missed deadlines and shoddy first drafts, and their skill and expertise in producing a book we are all proud of despite all the restrictions on our usual way of working.

Thank you to CricViz for the opportunity to use their data

and analytical tools, without which the book would have been impossible to produce. In particular, thank you to Imran Khan for allowing us to discuss his Wicket Probability model, and for giving us access to his work at the cutting edge of this field.

Thank you too to Ed Smith, Nessa Leamon, Chris Elliott, Lottie Limb, Freddie Wilde, Nick Friend, Patrick Noone, and all the friends and colleagues who read early drafts and did so much to help us improve them.

Index

Page numbers in *italic* refer to charts, diagrams and tables.